THE AMERICAN INDIAN WARS

John Tebbel, who is one-sixteenth Indian, the descendant of an historic Michigan family, worked for major newspapers and magazines until he became chairman of the Journalism Department at New York University, where he divided his time between teaching and writing. He is the author of forty books, including historical fiction, biographies of William Randolph Hearst and other media figures, and is the editor of Francis Parkman's *The Battle for North America* (Phoenix Press). He has contributed more than four hundred articles to magazines and newspapers. Retired but still writing, he lives in Durham, North Carolina.

Keith Jennison was a Canadian, born in Winnipeg, who spent most of his life in Vermont and New York City, where he was a legendary figure in book publishing, as well as an author of books, mostly about Vermont. Starting as a book salesman for Harcourt, Brace in 1935, he held major positions in several New York houses, and at one time headed his own. With John Tebbel, he helped found the Graduate Institute of Book Publishing at NYU, the first of its kind in the country.

ALSO BY JOHN TEBBEL:

History

George Washington's America

The Battle for North America
(*editor*) (Phoenix Press)

Biography

An American Dynasty

The Marshall Fields

George Horace Lorimer and
The Saturday Evening Post

The Life and Good Times of
William Randolph Hearst

Novels

The Conqueror

Touched with Fire

A Voice in the Streets

Medical

The Magic of Balanced Living

Your Body: How to Keep It Healthy

Textbook

Makers of Modern Journalism
(with Kenneth N. Stewart)

ALSO BY KEITH JENNISON:

Novel

The Green Place

Non-fiction

Vermont Is Where You Find It

The Maine Idea

Dedication

New Hampshire

New York and the State It's In

The Half Open Road

Green Mountains and Rock Ribs

The Boys and Their Mother

THE AMERICAN INDIAN WARS

John Tebbel & Keith Jennison

PHOENIX
PRESS

5 UPPER SAINT MARTIN'S LANE
LONDON
WC2H 9EA

A PHOENIX PRESS PAPERBACK

First published by Harper & Brothers Publishers,
New York, in 1960
This paperback edition published in 2001
by Phoenix Press,
a division of The Orion Publishing Group Ltd,
Orion House, 5 Upper St Martin's Lane,
London WC2H 9EA

A CIP catalogue record for this book
is available from the British Library.

Printed and bound in Great Britain by
Butler & Tanner Ltd, Frome and London

ISBN 1 84212 294 0

CONTENTS

LOCATIONS OF PRINCIPAL INDIAN TRIBES

1

THE WHITE MAN COMES

Before the white man came, the vast, magnificent, and comparatively empty region that is now the United States was inhabited by one million Indians, organized into six hundred distinct societies and scattered from the desolate ice wastes of the Far North to the hot swamps of the South; from the great forests of the East to the plains, deserts, and mountains of the West. These Indian societies existed in balance with themselves and with nature, a balance achieved through ages of development from Neolithic or Paleolithic time, when Indians first began to populate the continent.

The impact of white conquest on this culture was immediately abrasive and ultimately disastrous. After four centuries of nearly continuous warfare—roughly 1500 to 1900—the Indians were reduced numerically to less than four hundred thousand. Their lands gone, they were confined for the most part to reservations in Western United States, the victims of discriminatory laws enacted by white bigots and of governmental neglect and mismanagement of their affairs—not to mention the cupidity of land-hungry business interests deriving their support from the United States Senate.

Yet what the Indians gave up, slowly and bitterly, was only material. As one of their best historians, John Collier, points out, they were never successfully enslaved by their conquerors, "and even, to the end, [there was] no yielding by the Indians to anything but the sheer fact of being physically overwhelmed. . . . Indian social individuality held its own, and even deepened its consciousness of itself. Is it to be wondered at that the Indians north of the Rio Grande have always awakened a strange yet intimate excitement in the white man's soul? They speak to us from out of our long foregone home, and what hears them is the changeless, eternal part of us, imprisoned and immured by our social epoch even as the Indian societies were imprisoned and immured by us in the century behind. . . ."

Thus the Indian lost his substance but saved his soul. The permanent damage was done by his conquerors to themselves. In the four-century Great War of their conquest, they wrote a page in their history so black it can never be expunged. The conquest itself may be explained by the inexorable march of history, but the manner of its accomplishment cannot be excused. From the first atrocities of the Spanish, French, and English explorers and colonizers to the final, frightful massacre of Indian women and children at Wounded Knee in 1890, the white man's war against the red man is a record to match in savagery, if not in scope, anything the refinements of twentieth-century civilized warfare have produced.

One of the objects of those who first came to explore the continent that would stand forth to the world as a symbol of liberty was to take Indian slaves—either as curiosities, evidences of successful exploration, or as recruits for the mines of Europe.

Such was the result of one of the first recorded meetings between European explorer and Indian. Gaspar Corte Real (or Cortereal), a Portuguese from the Azores, came to the bleak northern reaches of North America in 1500 and again in 1501. On one of these expeditions he abducted fifty-seven (or sixty, depending on the source) Indians whom he intended to sell into slavery. This high purpose was largely frustrated on the voyage home when his vessel sank in a storm, carrying to horrible death all but seven of the Indian captives, who had been chained in the hold. These seven reached Portugal safely in another ship, and their surviving captors reported themselves so pleased with the hospitality the unsuspecting

2

savages had shown them that they named the Indians' native land Labrador, meaning "the place with an abundance of labor material."

Equally instructive is the narrative left to us by Giovanni da Verrazano (or Verrazzano), a Florentine navigator sent out from Dieppe near the end of 1523 by Francis I, King of France, to find a westward passage to Cathay. Driven back to Brittany by storms, he set out again with only one of his original four caravels, the *Dauphine*, and on March 7, 1524, hove to in the vicinity of what is now Wilmington, North Carolina.

The Indians who watched one of Verrazano's small boats come ashore fled in terror at their first sight of white men, but soon returned in wonder and admiration to help them land, offering their friendship by signs.

A few days later, needing water as he cruised northward along the coast, Verrazano sent another boat ashore, but the surf was too high for a landing. Again a small party of wondering Indians had come down to the beach. Taking some beads and trinkets for them, a daring young sailor jumped over and began to swim ashore. Fear overtook him as he neared land. He flung his gifts at the waiting savages and tried to swim back to the boat, but the heavy surf picked him up and tossed him on the beach into the arms of his prospective hosts.

The more the young sailor cried out in terror, the more the Indians yelled back at him to assure him of their friendship. But as he watched them make a leaping fire on the beach, he shrieked anew, convinced they were going to eat him. When he realized they were only trying to warm him and dry his clothes, he recovered his wits enough to make it known he wanted to swim back to his boat. The Indians led him down to the water, so the narrative goes, "with great love, clapping him fast about, with many embracings." They watched until he was safely aboard the *Dauphine*.

Such kindness, apparently, was lost on Verrazano and his men. Going ashore again somewhere in Virginia or Maryland, they discovered a somewhat less confident reception committee—an old woman, a young girl, and a few children, huddled together terrified in the tall grass near the beach. With calculated brutality, they

3

first won the confidence of these innocents, then abducted one of the children as a trophy of the chase. They would have taken the good-looking young squaw, too, for their later pleasure, but she screamed loudly enough to frighten them away.

After exploring the Bay of New York, Verrazano went on up the Long Island coast, past Block Island, and into what was probably Newport Harbor. There he was well received by two ornately clad chiefs, surrounded by their warriors—so much like a European court that Verrazano calls them "kings" in his narrative. He refers also to the "queen" and her "maids," whom the chiefs prudently kept out of reach of the white men in a separate canoe.

At this point the hospitality of the New World ended. When he came to New England, Verrazano found the natives as forbidding as the coastline. As the historian Francis Parkman puts it, in his dryly ironic fashion: "Perhaps some plundering straggler from the fishing-banks, some man-stealer like the Portuguese Cortereal, or some kidnapper of children and ravisher of squaws like themselves, had warned the denizens of the woods to beware of the worshippers of Christ." These Indians would do no more than let down furs on a hook from the forbidding cliffs over the water, hauling up fish-hooks, knives, and steel in return, after which they saluted their visitors with indelicate gestures and noises. When the Frenchmen tried to go ashore, they gave them a sterner salute with arrows.

That was the last Verrazano's men and the Indians saw of each other. The *Dauphine* went as far north as Newfoundland, and then returned home. Of the several reports concerning the Italian navigator's death, it would be poetic justice if one could accept the story that he went on another voyage and was killed and eaten by Indians while his own men looked on; but history authenticates that he was hanged as a pirate in 1527.

These early meetings between white men and red, as the first explorers nibbled at the fringes of the new continent, were only mild foretastes of what was to come. The Indians had welcomed the newcomers, with few exceptions, and they had been repaid with rapine and abduction. But these incidents had been so widely scattered up and down the far reaches of the coast that there was

4

The Town of Pomeiock, now in Hyde County, N.C. *From a watercolor by John White painted circa 1587.*

yet no organized hostility on the part of the natives. That was inspired first by those notorious masters of deceit and cruelty, the Spanish adventurers, whose bloody history below the Rio Grande is familiar to everyone today but in the early 1500s had not yet reached the ears of the unsuspecting savages in Florida, Georgia, and farther inland along the Gulf Coast, where the Spaniards began to penetrate in their feverish search for gold. With these sanguinary episodes, the Four Hundred Years' War truly began.

As a prelude to the exploits of Hernando de Soto, the deeds of an obscure commander named Lucas Vásquez de Ayllon served well enough to foreshadow the future. In the very year that Verrazano was swinging from his gibbet, De Ayllon swooped down on the shores of Georgia and South Carolina, fresh from decimating the population of Haiti, and seized more than a hundred Indians as slaves destined to work in the mines. He lost a shipload of them at sea on the way to Haiti; the others died in the mine shafts.

This raid led indirectly to the death of a far more famous man, old Ponce de León, who had come to Florida nine years earlier in search of the fountain of youth. On that expedition his relations with the Indians had been cordial; but when he returned, intending to plant a colony, the natives had meanwhile learned about the white man from De Ayllon and others. They warned the youth-seeker not to land, but he could not believe they intended him any harm and disregarded the warning. The Indians attacked, killed most of his followers, and gave him a mortal wound. Soon after, in Cuba, Ponce de León came to the inglorious end of his superstitious search.

Hernando de Soto was described by a later historian as a man "who was much given to the sport of slaying Indians." It was no exaggeration. In the two years, 1540–42, that he marched from Florida to Tennessee and onward to the Mississippi, his acts of murder, kidnaping, and looting became an indelible part of Indian tradition, generating fierce hatreds that were not extinguished for many generations. It was De Soto, as one of Pizarro's companions in the conquest of Peru, who is credited with trying to stay the murderous hand of his leader before it slew Atahualpa, the Inca emperor. No further evidence of honor appears on his otherwise crimson record.

De Soto landed at what is now Tampa Bay with 620 picked men and the declaration that everything he was about to do was undertaken for the glory of God. "These devout marauders," says Parkman, "could not neglect the spiritual welfare of the Indians whom they had come to plunder; and besides fetters to bind, and blood-hounds to hunt them, they brought priests and monks for the saving of their souls." Before 311 survivors reached a Spanish settlement on the Gulf Coast, after three years of wandering, having left their leader in a midnight grave beneath the rolling waters of the Mississippi, De Soto's expedition had done precious little soul-saving; but it had cruelly abused the generous hospitality of the Indians.

One night, in what is now Arkansas, De Soto determined to make a show of force against the Nilco Indians, whose sole crime had been to feed and shelter the Spaniards. His men fell upon their sleeping village and slaughtered a hundred warriors before they had a chance to draw a bow. Some of the badly wounded were permitted to escape so that they might carry the word of Spanish terror to other villages and thus engender a proper respect. There were those among the Spaniards, the narrative reports, who were so enthusiastic about their work that they killed men, women, and children indiscriminately.

In Georgia, where the Creeks lived, a lovely "princess" of the tribe, as the narrative describes her, welcomed the Spaniards with much hospitality, which they repaid at once by seizing her as a hostage. This was the customary pattern as the expedition advanced: to come into a village, accept the hospitality of the chiefs, and, once inside, to seize them for barter, then burn the village and its surrounding cornfields. Other Indians were taken along as manacled slaves; still others were tortured until they provided needed information. Before De Soto's infamous career ended, he had discovered the Mississippi; and, as John Collier remarks, "Indians from the Georgia coast to beyond the Mississippi had discovered the white man."

Not all the Spanish conquistadores were so ruthless. Coronado, on his long journey through the Southwest, exhibited a good deal more moderation, although he was not above hanging the Indian guide who led him into Kansas in search of a mythical golden city which did not exist. Nevertheless, he left behind him a general atmosphere of good will which persisted so long that it influenced profoundly for many years the relations between white men and red in that corner of the continent.

We think of these Spanish adventurers today as ruthless gold-hunters, which indeed they were; but it must not be supposed that they held a monopoly on cruelty and deceit toward the Indians. More than twenty years before the first white settlement at Jamestown, Sir Richard Grenville appeared off the shores of Virginia, in 1585, with a fleet of seven ships. Landing his men, this noble Eng-

From a watercolor by John White.

lish sea dog penetrated inland as far as the Roanoke River, received everywhere with the simple, openhanded welcome which the Indians extended almost invariably to white men when they beheld them for the first time. But when an Indian at one village appropriated one of Sir Richard's silver cups, the Englishman burned and plundered the town without the slightest mercy.

(Grenville is embalmed as a hero in English history for a single act of foolhardy courage, in which his small ship, the *Revenge*, took on the entire Spanish fleet off the coast of the Azores and fought until it went down in the traditional glorious defeat.)

These first meetings between Indians and white men in the Southeast and along the Atlantic Coast were not important historically in themselves, but they kindled the flames that blazed savagely for four centuries. The Indian nations, living in peace and prosperity for the most part, in spite of an intermittent but limited intertribal warfare, learned that the white invaders could not be trusted, and that their object was not the peaceful intercourse of trade which the Indians offered them, but naked conquest.

Still it was not yet war. Two further developments were needed to draw the lines and set the bitter, seemingly endless struggle in motion. One was the establishment of a frontier, in itself a crude battle line. The founding of permanent colonies at Jamestown and Plymouth marked the beginning of frontier conflict, when the Indians realized that these white men had come not to explore but to stay, and not only to remain in their initial villages but to push out boldly and ruthlessly into the territories held by Indians for centuries.

The other ingredient was provided by the white men of various nationalities who soon began contending with each other for possession of the continent. This became a gigantic battle for North America between France and England. The prime strategy of these contenders, as far as the Indians were concerned, was appallingly simple. Too few in number to fight each other with any effectiveness for nearly a century, and much less able to fight the Indian nations, who greatly outnumbered them, the French and English wooed the tribes as allies and used them to fight their battles.

It was a strategy that proved to be eminently successful, despite the fact that it was pursued at times with excruciating stupidity. Caught up first in the protracted skirmishes which led to the French and Indian War, then in the seven years during which that war endured, next in the American Revolution, and finally in the War of 1812, the Indian nations found themselves at last not only deprived of any rewards accruing to the victors, but in the meantime they had lost the vital battle of the frontier. The great push westward was in full swing. Everything east of the Mississippi had been lost. There remained only the valiant last stands in the West, which could be no more than rear-guard actions, although there were Indian leaders who dreamed large dreams of rolling back the white invaders to their Eastern cities.

In the four centuries it took to accomplish the red man's final defeat, splendid leaders rose on both sides. It must not be supposed that all the white commanders were villains, nor the Indian chieftains entirely a band of heroes. Both sides learned a new kind of warfare from the other. There was overwhelming tragedy in the conquest, but there was sentiment and even wry humor as well. More than anything else, there was pathos and nobility in the spectacle of a people vanquished. The story of their physical defeat and spiritual victory is told in the pages that follow.

Life in Secota, Virginia. *DeBry engraving from a watercolor by John White.*

2

JAMESTOWN AND PLYMOUTH: THE FRONTIER BEGINS

The English settlers who came to Jamestown in 1607 were not like the rapacious Spaniards or the wily French who had preceded them in the previous century. Because they were not hungry for gold or slaves and settled down to the hard business of surviving in the wilderness, which was the Indians' own preoccupation, the new invaders at first won the confidence of the natives. There was much talk of friendship, and in fact it is doubtful whether the colony could have survived without the help of the Indians.

It ought to be made clear that the popular conception of life on the early frontier as a day-by-day combat with the Indians, in which the scalping knife, the tomahawk, and the musket were as much in use as the knife and fork, is far from the truth. Especially at the beginning there was much fraternization. Both sides were intent on providing food, shelter, and the other necessaries for survival, and discovered that there was much they could do to help each other. How, then, was this primitive peace shattered?

The answer lies in the kind of human frailty that is universal. Living so closely together, these neighbors experienced the same small incidents that led to the intermittent warfare characteristic among the Indians themselves. An Indian would be offended by a white man and murder would follow; or, as often as not, the white man would be the aggressor in the wake of some insult, real or imaginary. These actions sometimes led to the mob violence that the uninformed imagine was an everyday occurrence. The Indians are customarily pictured as swooping down in a frightful whirlwind of slaughter, pillage, and burning; but quite as often the white mobs were guilty of the same barbarisms, usually self-justified by the contention that it would deter the Indians from further crimes.

As the settlements grew, these isolated incidents became more numerous because there were more people and more opportunities for friction. With this growth, too, hunting rights and territories were soon in dispute, and the Indian began to feel the pressures of an invading, growing, pushing population. The result was the sporadic, violent frontier war with which the long battle began. It was warfare marked by frequent peace negotiations, and the signing of treaties which were promptly violated by one side or the other.

As the frontier began to move westward, there was organized resistance wherever the pressures were greatest, and whenever a great Indian leader rose to rally his people. In time these resistance forces became large enough and dangerous enough to demand the use of regular army troops, and there followed the series of major engagements which have provided endless material for fiction and motion pictures.

Such was the course of frontier warfare that had its origin in the Virginia and New England settlements. At Jamestown, the colony was begun in the very teeth of a powerful and able chief, Powhatan, whose Confederacy could have extinguished it easily at any time in the first fifteen years or so of its existence. His failure to do so is still unexplained, notwithstanding the popularity of the Pocahontas legend.

It was the marauding Spaniards who were indirectly responsible for Powhatan's grip on tidewater Virginia. His father had fled northward from them—whether from Florida or the West Indies is not definitely known—and, when he reached Virginia, began a confederacy by first conquering five tribes of the region and then uniting them. Powhatan, whose Indian name was Wa-hun-sen-a-cawh, inherited this empire and strengthened it from time to time by the addition of more tribes.

Captain John Smith, the colony's leader, described him as "a tall, well proportioned man, with a sower looke; his head somewhat gray, his beard so thinne that it seemeth none at al. His age neare 60, of a very able and hardy body." Powhatan's "sower looke" reflected his forbidding personality. He was a grim, suspicious man with a reputation for cruelty to prisoners and to those who crossed him. He understood the long-range implications of the Jamestown colony, and he watched the oncoming waves of settlers with rage and dismay. Yet he did nothing. The confederacy and the colony lived in comparative peace while Powhatan reigned, although the settlers were occasionally disturbed by the ambush of a small hunting party or a plowman murdered in his field. Sometimes, perversely, the chief would not sell his corn to the colonists when their supply was short.

Still, there was peace. The English made what they considered a diplomatic effort to perpetuate it by crowning Powhatan king of the territory, in 1609, with considerable pomp and ceremony. It was not an entirely successful maneuver. At the ritual, as Smith complained, Powhatan was much more interested in the gifts which accompanied his coronation than in the crown itself—"he neither knowing," as Smith put it, "the majesty nor meaning of a Crowne." There was some difficulty in getting the proud old man to bend his head so that Smith could place the crown on it.

Perhaps the romanticists are right, and Powhatan withheld the stroke wisdom told him he should make because of the dramatic act of his daughter, Pocahontas, who legend says threw herself over the body of captured John Smith, and by her pleading not only saved him from execution but in doing so preserved the peace between colonists and Indians. Providing, of course, the incident ever took place. Certainly her marriage to John Rolfe in 1613 led Powhatan to make a firm peace with the colony, which he kept faithfully until his death in 1618.

With that event, however, the era of comparative good feeling

15

ARGOSY GALLERIES

Pocahontas Saving Life of Captain John Smith. *From the painting by Chappel.*

came to an end. Powhatan's successor was his brother, whose name is variously rendered but is commonly spelled Opechancanough. He was already an old man when he came to power, but he had been waiting a long time, with a slow-burning hatred, for his opportunity. No one knows why Opechancanough so hated the English. He was a man of formidable pride and dignity, and presumably he had been deeply offended, conceivably not once but many times. He had no accomplished daughter married to an Englishman, nor was he as conservative as his brother. His life was dedicated to extinguishing the settlement and driving the hated English back into the ocean. With his ascension to power, he began to plot the means to do it.

Opechancanough was nothing if not thorough in his preparations. While presenting a carefully maintained façade of friendship to the colonists, he spent four years in perfecting his plans, which seems an unnecessarily long time considering their lack of any special ingenuity. He plotted in the utmost secrecy; not even neighboring tribes, who might be friendly to the English, were permitted an inkling of what impended.

With all his thoroughness, however, Opechancanough made a single fundamental and fatal error. He did not perceive that in the years while Powhatan had hesitated, the constant flow of new settlers had tipped the balance of power fatefully against him. He had waited too long. The grand opportunity had slipped through his fingers.

Nevertheless, the old chief carried out his bloody intentions. On the cool March morning in 1622 that he chose for his descent on the colonists, his squaws were up early about their morning tasks. While they prepared the morning meal, the warriors were daubing their faces and readying their weapons. Only a few miles away, the settlers in their cabins looked out on a peaceful Virginia, burgeoning in the first spring flush, and many of them saw it for the last time. Their women, too, were busy with breakfast for the men, who were readying the weapons of peace to attack their fields. Indians and whites alike were about to join hostilities, the real beginning of the long war, yet both were the pitiful victims of his-

17

tory, of immense stirrings and movements which would remake a continent.

But Opechancanough and his friends thought only of revenge for injustice and the invasion of their country. Sweeping down on the settlers in their tobacco fields, they laid about with knife and tomahawk. In a single hour they massacred 347 men, women, and children. Up and down the James River they raged, destroying the plantations, reducing the number of these farms from eighty to six. The half dozen were spared by the timely warning of a friendly Indian.

The colony reeled from this blow; but it was not wiped out, as Opechancanough had intended. While an uneasy, armed quiet prevailed during the spring and summer, the colonists prepared for a counteratrocity. Filled now with a full measure of Opechancanough's hatred, they even neglected their crop planting to ready a deadly revenge.

Their strategy was borrowed straight from Opechancanough himself, with a treacherous twist of their own devising. As the Indian chief had done, they made a pretense of peacemaking until the warriors and chiefs were convinced that the settlers had been utterly intimidated by the March massacre and desired only safety. Then the Indians were invited to a council for the ostensible purpose of drawing up a treaty. But when they were gathered, the white men sprang on them and killed many on the spot, although they had assured the Indians that their lives would be considered sacred if they came to the council.

Thus treachery and massacre were repaid in kind. The instigator of the whole bloody episode escaped, however; old Opechancanough was not among the slain, as he was at first believed to be. Not only had he escaped, but with formidable patience he waited twenty-two years until he was able to strike again. By that time he was reputed to be a hundred years old (he was certainly no less than ten years younger) and had to be carried to the battle on a litter at the head of his war party.

Again the chief had planned well. This time every Indian for six hundred miles around was in on the plot, whose strategy called for a concerted, simultaneous attack up and down the length of the Virginia frontier, with the object of pushing the English into the ocean, as Opechancanough had intended for more than a quarter-century.

The attack opened on schedule in April, 1644, and for two days had the appearance of success. Losses inflicted on the whites were even greater than in the first attempt; nearly five hundred settlers died, particularly along the York and Pamunkey rivers, where the ancient chief himself was in command. But again Opechancanough had grossly underestimated his enemy's strength. Governor William Berkeley mustered a strong armed force of militia, whose fire-power far exceeded the numerically stronger Indian forces, and the result was inevitable, although the fighting was savage and desperate for a time. In the end, Opechancanough was captured and borne in triumph on his litter to Jamestown.

As Berkeley's soldiers carried him through the curious crowds in the little town, the feeble centenarian, cruelly emaciated and near death, did not open his eyes to return the gazes of horror, hatred, and morbid fascination that were directed at him. Some historians believe he was too weak to lift his eyelids, and that may well have been true.

How much is true and how much is legend in the dramatic episode that followed the chief's capture is impossible to determine. But there is little doubt that he was taken inside a building and put under guard, while the mob outside, torn between curiosity and hatred, struggled to get a look at him through doors which stood wide open. One of his guards, brooding no doubt on the bloodshed the old man had caused—possibly family or friends had been among the massacred victims—deliberately turned his gun on Opechancanough and put a bullet in the sachem's wretched frame.

It was a blow that hastened the inevitable end, but the iron patriarch survived it momentarily. The shot had stirred the crowd outside anew, and now with bustle and clamor they surged at every opening of the building, trying to get a glimpse of the chief's death throes. Opechancanough heard the mob's unruly stirrings and asked an attendant to lift his eyelids. Turning his head on the litter, his somber eyes glared out with unquenched hatred at the crowd, and then with a magnificent effort of will, he pulled himself from the litter and stood erect. He swayed with his wound and his great age, but his majestic air of command awed the white guards around him. When he demanded that the governor be brought to him, one of the guards hurried without argument to summon Berkeley.

The governor, too, must have been impressed by the terrible, almost supernatural figure that rose before him as though from the dead. Opechancanough raised a trembling, wrathful arm and cried out to him: "If it had been my fortune to take Sir William Berkeley prisoner, I would not have meanly exposed him as a show to my people."

What Governor Berkeley replied is not recorded; it would be fascinating to know. All we do know is that Opechancanough, having made this final statement with awesome dignity, lay down and died. With his passing, Virginia and the Southern colonies knew peace again, and enjoyed it for a long time.

In the North, meanwhile, the English settlers at Plymouth and Salem were having an easier time, thanks to a pair of unexpected allies. One was a mysterious illness which had decimated the New England Indians from Rhode Island to Maine; "the woods," Cotton Mather observed with characteristic self-righteousness, "were almost cleared of those pernicious creatures, to make room for a better growth." The epidemic had raged for three years before the *Mayflower* landed, and the Indians were in no position to oppose the precarious planting and growth of the struggling colony. If they had been, it could not have survived.

The other ally was more powerful and long-lasting. He was Massasoit, variously spelled and freely translated as "great chief," whose proper Indian name was Ousamequin, meaning "yellow feather." Massasoit was the undoubted ruler of the New England tribes at the time the Pilgrims arrived. His territory, subject to change without notice, comprised all of Massachusetts, including Cape Cod, and Rhode Island as far south as Narragansett Bay. His rule extended westward until distance enabled recalcitrant chiefs to be bold.

Massasoit himself was chief of the Wampanoags and lived at Pokanoket, known today as Mount Hope, in the vicinity of Bristol, Rhode Island. When he was born has never been determined, but at the time the *Mayflower* arrived he must have been in his prime because a member of the colony described him the following year as a "very lusty man, in his best years, an able body, grave of countenance, and spare of speech."

The white man was not a stranger to Massasoit. John Smith may have met him during his exploration of the New England coast before he settled down in Virginia. Only a year before the Pilgrims came, the chief had negotiated successfully with a British sea captain for the return of two castaway sailors. Whatever the circumstances of his meetings with the white men, he had evidently formed a permanently good impression of them, for he remained their friend and ally as long as he lived.

Legend says that the first encounter between the Plymouth colonists and Massasoit's empire came a few months after the Pilgrims had landed, when the colonists were struggling through their first cold, wet New England spring. The story is that Samoset, one of Massasoit's chiefs, came walking out of the forest and greeted the colonists with some English he had acquired from white fishermen encountered off the coast of Maine: "Welcome, Englishmen!"

While this may well be doubted, it is a matter of record that on March 22, 1621, Massasoit came with ceremony to the colony, accompanied by his brother, Quadequina, and by the chiefs Samoset and Squanto, along with sixty warriors. When the interminable speechmaking of which the Indians were so fond was over, and after Massasoit had taken a ceremonial drink of whiskey which "made him sweat all the while after," as the old chronicle tells us, a treaty of peace was concluded.

For the first time land was given freely to the white man by the terms of this treaty. "Englishmen, take that land," Massasoit observed sadly, "for none is left to occupy it. The Great Spirit . . .

21

has swept its people from the face of the earth." The land he meant was Massachusetts and Rhode Island land, for the most part, and while Massasoit kept faith with the treaty, including its land provisions, during a half-century of vicissitudes, neither his generosity nor his loyal friendship could stem the inevitable frictions that arose.

The peace was kept by Massasoit's Wampanoags and their allies, but the Pequots of the Connecticut River Valley were in a different posture. From the north and east they were beset by the Massachusetts settlers, pressing westward as the first settlements grew and expanded. From the south and west, the land-hungry Dutch, already the proprietors of Manhattan Island and of rich estates up the Hudson River, were moving into Connecticut. The Pequots were caught between them.

The incident that touched off what came to be known in history as the Pequot War was, strangely enough, a naval engagement, if an action between two fishing boats can merit that distinction. In the summer of 1636 a Boston gentleman named John Gallup was fishing at sea in his small craft off Block Island, accompanied by a friend and two boys, when he saw another boat nearby behaving peculiarly. It was drifting idly, sails flapping, apparently without crew or passengers. But looking more closely, Gallup saw the movement of figures lying flat on the deck; simultaneously he recognized the boat as one belonging to a neighbor.

"There's something wrong here," he said to his companions, and headed his own craft toward the other boat. While he was still a distance away, he saw a canoe lowered hurriedly into the water and several men in it began paddling for shore. A closer look confirmed what he had already concluded, that Indians had seized the ship, killed or captured those on board, and taken possession.

Gallup assessed his position. He had a man and two boys in his naval force. Among them they possessed two guns, two pistols, and enough ammunition to carry on a prolonged fight. He himself was a noted frontier marksman; he was confident no bullet of his would be wasted. Ordering his crew to steer toward the other vessel, Gallup stationed himself in the prow and opened fire. His self-

Meeting of Governor Carver and Massasoit. *Drawn by H. L. Stevens.*

confidence was justified. He accounted for an Indian with every pull of the trigger. The others joined in the barrage, and meanwhile Gallup's boat bore down swiftly on the Indians.

Realizing the white man meant to run them down, a half-dozen Indians leaped overboard before the two boats collided. Gallup's craft recoiled from the shock, then came on and struck again. With that, all the Indians aboard leaped into the sea except four. Calling on his crew to follow him, Gallup jumped over the prow like any pirate and boarded the vessel. Two of the four Indians remaining fled below; the other two fell to their knees and asked quarter. Magnanimously, Gallup took them prisoner.

The Indians on the boat proved to be Pequots. It is not clear what led to their act of piracy, but of its consequences there remains no doubt. It led to the virtual extermination of the Pequot tribe. For when Governor Vane of Massachusetts heard about the episode, he dispatched a force of ninety men to Block Island, where they fell upon the Pequots who lived there, killed every living human being in sight, burned the lodges, and went back to Boston without having lost a single man.

This ruthless assault stirred the whole Pequot nation. Already fearful of what was happening to their lands by virtue of Dutch and English pressure, they rose to defend themselves. Unfortunately, they were afflicted with Opechancanough's large resolve to kill every white man in the territory or else push them into the sea. Since they had enjoyed more contact with the whites, they were more sophisticated than Opechancanough had been at the beginning of his campaign, and understood that they would need substantial help to accomplish their purpose.

Looking about for allies, they saw near at hand the Narragansetts, old enemies but nevertheless capable of putting five thousand warriors in the field if they could be persuaded to join hands with the common enemy. Artfully, the Pequots sought an alliance. They sent messengers with rich gifts; they showered the Narragansetts with possessions, flattery, oratory, and every persuasive device they could muster.

The Narragansetts were nearly persuaded, except that living

Naval Engagement of the Pequot War. *By A. R. Waud.*

among them momentarily was a renegade from the Massachusetts clergy, an unfrocked minister named Roger Williams, who was a man of peace and besides knew what the Narragansetts had failed to comprehend—that they had a great deal to lose and little to gain by helping the Pequots. As the result of his forceful tongue, the Narragansetts declined the Pequot invitation politely, with regret.

Frustrated and desperate, the Pequots saw no other useful allies within reach and determined to go it alone. They began in the usual way, with isolated sniping on lone cabins and men working in the fields. When reprisal was not forthcoming, they increased the scope of their operations until more than a thousand Pequot warriors were on the warpath in Connecticut. The colonists of that province, less numerous and well equipped than their neighbors, were so alarmed that they pleaded with the Plymouth and Massachusetts Bay colonies to come help them.

Massachusetts responded by sending them John Mason. They could not have chosen a better man for the job. A professional soldier who had seen service in the Low Countries before coming to the New World, Mason had been one of the bold leaders who had led a party of migrants from Dorchester into Connecticut to found the town of Windsor. For at least a year before Gallup's naval engagement, he had been in the pay of the Dutch to harass the Pequots wherever possible.

In May, 1637, Mason led a strong force against the Pequots. He had in his command eighty white men and a hundred or so Indian allies under Uncas, a sachem of the Mohicans. At Saybrook Fort this small army was joined by Captain John Underhill, who brought nineteen Massachusetts men to relieve twenty of Mason's company who were needed for home defense. Pausing in Narragansett country, through which he passed to strike the enemy from an unexpected quarter, Mason persuaded the Narragansetts where the Pequots had failed, and a large party of their warriors joined the Mohican allies.

Embarking from Saybrook in three small boats, the expedition sailed along the coast and entered Narragansett Bay as night fell on May 20. Next day was Sunday and the pious executioners spent it in exhorting God to aid them in the bloody business at hand. If they had been superstitious, Mason and his men might have been alarmed by the dreadful storm that followed their praying, but once Sunday was passed, Captain Mason, a practical man, was only irritated because the bad weather kept him from landing until the twenty-third.

As the troops approached the Pequots' well-fortified stronghold, which stood on a hill overlooking the present town of Groton, Connecticut, Mason experienced for the first time that unreliability of Indian allies which so plagued both the French and English for nearly a hundred and fifty years thereafter. The Mohicans and Narragansetts professed to be terrified by the size and stoutness of the Pequot fort. They retired to a respectable distance and gave the white men the honor of opening the assault.

In war the Indians were pragmatists. They fought only where and when it seemed to their best advantage. In this instance, they were under the leadership of Uncas, a chief who was notorious all his life as an opportunist of the first water, as treacherous with his own people as he was with the white men. Sassacus, the Pequot chief, was his father-in-law, and having lived with the tribe, Uncas knew their situation better than anyone else in the expedition, and apparently concluded that there was enough doubt about the assault's success to merit waiting until he could see how the battle was going to turn out. Doubtless he meant to join the winners.

But he gravely underestimated the ingenuity of Captain Mason, who was not at all intimidated by what he saw confronting him in the May twilight of the twenty-fifth. The fort was a stockade encircling about an acre of ground, the posts about a dozen feet high and so close together they could not be penetrated by a man's body, although separated enough so arrows could be shot from the apertures. The Pequot village, row upon row of wigwams, was inside.

By the normal village noises—dogs, children, and adults making their customary clamor—Mason knew that the Pequots were unsuspecting. He sent out a patrol which reported the fort had two entrances, opposite each other; consequently Mason decided to

27

divide his force and strike from both directions. He attacked at dawn, and before the startled dogs and the drowsy sentries could give a proper alarm, his men stormed through both gates.

Caught by surprise, the Pequots nevertheless quickly demonstrated why they were feared and admired by other tribes. They fought with courage and resourcefulness, pushing back the invaders until it seemed that Uncas's doubts were about to be realized. It was then, at this critical moment, that Captain Mason picked up a firebrand, whirled it around his head to set it blazing, and threw it onto a wigwam. It burst into flames at once, and Underhill, witnessing this strategy, imitated it. Fire now added to the battle's turmoil and confused the defenders, many of whom were caught in the flames. Mason now ordered his men to withdraw outside the fort, and as the Indians fled their blazing village, the soldiers were able to pick them off with ease, without the necessity of hand-to-hand combat. Those who escaped this shooting gallery fell at once into the hands of the Mohicans and Narragansetts, who contented themselves with peripheral slaughter.

"God is over us!" Mason is supposed to have shouted during the massacre. "He laughs His enemies to scorn, making them as a fiery oven." It was a most unlikely shout, but it unquestionably expressed the captain's belief. Certainly it was the pious conviction of Cotton Mather, who wrote later that he supposed "no less than six hundred Pequot souls were brought down to hell that day."

Some historians estimate the Pequot casualties at a thousand or more, including men, women, and children, but in any case, the nation was destroyed, while Captain Mason lost only two men. From a military standpoint, it was nearly total victory for a relatively small force over a numerically much larger enemy.

By chance, as they marched back to their ships, the expedition encountered most of the Pequots who had not been in the village. This was a war party of some three hundred warriors, returning from a marauding adventure of their own. This time the white men were caught by surprise and narrowly escaped their own destruction. But they contrived to get behind the Pequots, and fighting a constant rear-guard action, were able to reach the harbor.

With fresh supplies and renewed purpose, Mason soon led his men out again, determined to exterminate what remained of the Pequots. He went about his task without mercy, scouring the country from New London to Saybrook for the remnants of the tribe. What survivors remained quickly surrendered and were sent in chains to the Bermudas, to live out their lives in slavery. Some were assigned to the same fate in Massachusetts and Connecticut. A few stragglers found refuge with other tribes.

Thus, within a few weeks, a strong and brave tribe of Indians, whose culture was not inconsiderable, simply disappeared from human affairs. That was the price New England paid, willingly and without compunction, for the era of peace and prosperity that now came to its colonies. By ironic chance, it was not the seed of these or any other enemies that caused the next threat to the white frontier, but the son of Massasoit, the chief who had been their only consistent friend. When Metacomet, or Philip as he was known in English, succeeded his father in 1660, in company with his brother Alexander, or Wamsutta, New England was confronted with an Indian leader of determination, resourcefulness, and intelligence. The war he began was the worst such conflict of the seventeenth century, a struggle in which nothing less than the survival of the New England colonies was at stake.

3

KING PHILIP AND HIS WAR

For decades in the nineteenth century there existed a polite fiction that the real causes of King Philip's war were unknown. Modern scholarship, however, has established quite clearly the reasons for this first major clash between red men and white which decided the fate of both the New England colonists and the New England Indians.

There were about 20,000 of these Indians in the southern part of that territory in the years just before the war, and of these the 4000 Narragansetts comprised the strongest tribe. Their chief rivals (peaceful, for the most part) were the 3000 Nipmucks and (constantly warlike) the Wampanoags, who numbered little more than a thousand. The other 12,000 were scattered among at least a half-dozen tribes, none of which was strong enough to contest the others seriously.

The white neighbors of these tribes were the Puritan colonists of Massachusetts (about 17,000) and Connecticut (10,000); Plymouth Colony in southeastern Massachusetts, with a population of 5000; and that black sheep of the New England confederation, Rhode Island, with three or four thousand highly contentious inhabitants.

Like all wars, the struggle that resulted between these opposing populations was complex in its origins. There were several broad reasons for conflict. Basic among these was the quarreling over possession of land, fired among the whites by grants and speculation, among the Indians by the realization that their territories were shrinking and, with them, the way of life they and their forefathers had always known.

The New England settlers did not simply seize the land, as is sometimes supposed. They paid for it, in most cases, although there were a good many cases of fraud. The trouble arose because the Indians could not fully grasp the white man's legal procedures. They seemed to believe that a land transaction did not include their immemorial hunting and fishing rights, and that there was nothing really exclusive in the occupation rights they conferred when they made their mark on a deed.

When the Indians violated a civil contract, the English naturally haled them into a colonial court and tried them under the English law that had been their bulwark for generations. To the Indians, English law was for the English; they had never known any need of it for themselves. Its application to them, in both civil and criminal cases, appeared to them as humiliation, not justice. Their resentment accumulated year by year, decision by decision.

Another cause of conflict lay in the gradual economic subjection of the Indian population by the English traders, who were slowly making the native villages more and more dependent on the goods brought over from England, and were saddling the inhabitants with an increasing load of debt. Attracted by the white man's comparatively abundant life, some Indians hired themselves out as servants or laborers in the colonies, and thus incurred the small indignities that their employers visited upon those whom they regarded as little more than slaves.

The Indian way of life was also threatened by the zealous activities of the colonial missionaries, who worked night and day at conversion. The great contest between them and the French Jesuit missionaries for possession of the Indian soul had only begun, but already it was proving to be a divisive influence in Indian society, resented particularly by the chiefs and medicine men, whom Christianity endangered most.

ARGOSY GALLERIES

King Philip.

Still another source of conflict was the pressure of geography. As the Pequots had been caught between powerful white populations surrounding them, the New England Indians in general were trapped between the aggressive, growing colonies on the seaboard and the hostile might of the Iroquois Confederacy to the west. If they wanted to retain their ancient lands, they would have to make a stand and fight for them.

Thus the two antagonists confronted each other, with the fundamental issue clearly drawn, as it would be for centuries afterward. The white men considered the Indians an inferior race which must give way before a superior culture. God had ordained that white Englishmen should occupy and develop this land, to which the Indians had no right that could be found in English common law. As for the red men, they regarded the colonists as intruders whose laws, church, ideas, and very presence threatened everything that had been theirs from time immemorial.

Upon this scene Metacomet, the son of Massasoit, appeared like an angel of vengeance, a liberator of the enslaved. But he was no firebrand. This thoughtful, meditative sachem apparently understood from the beginning what was happening to his people, yet he was in no hurry to precipitate a war he must have known was inevitable. When Massasoit died, the English even made a bid for his friendship, misguided though it was, by giving him his English name of Philip, as they similarly conferred the name of Alexander on his older brother, Wamsutta.

The passing of Massasoit, however, had changed the mood of the Wampanoag nation. It was like a present-day change from Republican to Democratic government. The middle-of-the-road conservatism of old Massasoit and his counselors had given way around the council fires to the youthful boldness of the two brothers.

This change, so pronounced, could not fail to attract the attention of the colonists, who suspected incorrectly that a war plot was brewing. In 1662 they called Alexander to Duxbury for questioning, as though he were a suspect in a murder trial. Alexander came and submitted gravely to the probing and prodding of the authorities. After it was over, he went to visit his friend Josiah Winslow, in Marshfield, where he came down with a violent fever and died a few days later as he was being taken home to Mount Hope.

Alexander's widow was certain the English had poisoned him. Other Indians thought he had been abused by the authorities until the illness came upon him. No proof of either theory exists. Probably Alexander succumbed to one of the viruses all too common and lethal in those days long before antibiotics.

In any case, Philip now came into sole possession of the Wampanoag throne. But instead of seeking to avenge his brother's death, he reaffirmed his father's treaty with the colonists and appeared intent on keeping the peace that had so long prevailed. However, Philip had no illusions about the future. He well understood that it was a question either of total submission to the whites or eventual war to the death for possession of the land.

Meanwhile, an uneasy peace prevailed. There were war scares in 1667 and 1669, and again in the spring of 1671. Philip was apparently not behind these ominous maneuverings which so alarmed the colonists; more probably the Narragansetts were at fault. But because he was the most prominent of the Indian chiefs, and the most likely candidate to lead an uprising, it was Philip whom the authorities called to Taunton in 1671 and virtually demanded peace of him.

These Plymouth authorities were arrogant and peremptory in their approach. Among other things, they insisted that the Indians surrender their guns. Philip, a proud and sensitive man, was affronted and deeply angered by the way the hard-faced white officials treated him and the councilors who had accompanied him, but he knew that he did not possess the military strength to resist. The time was not yet. He signed a treaty and agreed to give up the guns.

Of course only a few weapons were confiscated, and those largely the ones Philip and his retinue had brought to Taunton. Most of the other Indians refused to give up their weapons. Again the Plymouth officials threatened and demanded, placing Philip virtually on trial in his next appearance before them, but again the Wampanoag chieftain swallowed his pride and signed a treaty that represented nothing less than the most abject surrender. It was a humiliation he would not soon forget.

During the next four years Philip, like Achilles, sulked in his tent. He must have spent endless hours discussing with his chiefs the accumulation of wrongs visited upon them by the white man, and he must have spent melancholy hours by himself, reflecting on the degradation of his tribe and considering what was to be done.

Like other Indian leaders before him, Philip concluded that he could not fight the colonists alone. He would need the help of every available ally. Patiently—and again, as the others had done—he sent out his messengers in every direction and lighted the fires of his secret councils. This was a war to the death, he told the other tribes, between the great family of the Algonkians, to whom they all belonged, and the white man who would destroy them. They must forget the old quarrels between the nations and unite with common purpose, or they would themselves be destroyed. He worked at his plans with deadly purpose, month after month, and soon the stage was set for the war that would avenge fifty years of humiliations.

A murder trial was the prelude to war. On January 29, 1675, a converted Christian Indian named John Sassamon was found dead beneath the ice of Assawompsett Pond, fifteen miles southwest of Plymouth. He was pulled out and buried on the spot by the Indians who found him, but a tip-off came to the authorities a few days later that Sassamon had been murdered. He was exhumed and an examination offered persuasive though not conclusive proof that he had indeed been struck and killed by assailants unknown before he was thrown into the water.

The victim was no ordinary Indian. John Sassamon had been raised as a Christian, been given the rare privilege of studying at Harvard, and seemed on his way to becoming a "white Indian," when he suddenly deserted his colonial benefactors and his new faith and returned to the Wampanoags, where he was employed as Philip's secretary—not, of course, in the exact sense of the word as we understand it today. He spoke English well, and was described as a "cunning and plausible Indian." He was also, it developed, a spy. Repenting of his retreat to the wilderness, he went back to the white men, re-entered the church, became a native preacher, and ostensibly settled into a life of extreme respectability, moving freely in both the white and Indian communities. But his loyalty was to the whites. A few days before he was murdered, he told the Plymouth authorities about Philip's conspiracy, a piece of treachery canceled out by their disbelief in his story.

An Indian witness appeared who declared he had seen the murder of Sassamon, and named three Wampanoags as the killers. They were Tobias, one of Philip's counselors; Tobias's son, Wampapaquan; and a warrior called Mattashunnamo. All three denied their guilt, but they were duly tried, convicted, and sentenced to be hanged. At the hanging, Wampapaquan's rope slipped or broke and he fell to the ground. Apparently hoping for clemency as the result of this miraculous reprieve, the convicted man gasped out a complete confession, although insisting that the other two had done the actual killing. The government was satisfied that justice had been done. They rewarded Wampapaquan by hanging him again, and this time they made certain there would be no reprieve.

The executions stirred the Wampanoags to a fury. Philip undoubtedly knew the suspects were guilty; it was probable Sassamon's deception had been discovered, and he had been given the treatment either side would have given a spy—possibly at Philip's instigation. But the executed men had been the chief's friends, and there was also the consideration that the white authorities now believed Sassamon's story and the conspiracy was no longer a secret.

There is evidence to show that even at this critical juncture Philip was not certain the time had arrived, and would have refrained from violence if he could, but the young braves were highly excited. They were on the point of boiling up out of Mount Hope peninsula and precipitating the war that had been brewing for so long.

The first object of attack was inevitable—the village of Swansea, which stood at the peninsula's entrance and would have to be overcome before the Wampanoags could swarm into Massachusetts and Rhode Island. Indian patrols were seen in the vicinity of Swansea, 37 and the whole colony was alarmed. Governor Winslow sent an emissary to Philip, asking him why he intended to make war on the English. Philip replied, with hauteur: "Your governor is but a subject of King Charles of England. I shall not treat with a subject. I shall treat of peace only with the king, my brother. When he comes, I am ready."

Not even Charles could have prevented what was about to occur. Winslow appointed June 24 as a day of fasting and prayer that war might be avoided, and it was on that day the war began, at Swansea. A party of Wampanoag braves fired on some worshipers returning home from services, killing one and wounding two others. Two survivors were running for a doctor when they, too, were shot down. Six other men near the garrison itself were shot and mutilated, after the Indian manner. The braves took time to burn a few buildings before they fled.

There is some reason to believe this attack took place against Philip's wishes, but whatever the truth might have been, it was lost in the storm of bloodshed that followed. The Indians, now unrestrained, swept down on the white communities. Swansea's inhabitants had fled after the first blow, but the Indians burned the town anyway. Then they attacked Taunton, Middleborough, and Dartmouth, destroying parts of all of them. From every village, runners went flying to Boston and Plymouth, beseeching help.

When the news got to Boston, the government's drummers stood in the Commons and beat for volunteers. In three hours, 110 men were mustered and put under the command of Captain Samuel Mosely. This force moved out of Boston on June 26, and two days later were in what was left of Swansea. It was nearly nightfall when they arrived, but Mosely foolishly sent out a patrol of a dozen men in the direction of Mount Hope. They encountered an equal party of Indians, and in the brief skirmish that followed, one man was killed and another wounded. Two Indians lost their lives.

Next morning a much larger force of Wampanoags appeared outside Swansea and dared Mosely to come out and fight. The captain, a brave man, accepted the challenge and charged at the head of his troops. Apparently the Indians thought the dare would not be taken up. They turned and fled, with Mosely and his men in pursuit. The white men killed a half-dozen of them before they could reach the protective cover of a swamp; only one colonist was lost.

Next day Mosely marched forthrightly to Philip's own village, but found it deserted except for the grisly heads of eight white men staring down at him from poles. Mosely ordered them buried and returned to establish headquarters at Swansea.

The first scalps taken in the war were, for a change, lifted by white men. A detachment commanded by a young lieutenant named Oakes was on its way from Rehoboth to Swansea on the morning of July 1, when it came suddenly upon a party of Indians, several of whom were killed in the resulting skirmish. Oakes took the scalps and sent them up to Boston as a token of victory.

A new commander came into the field to aid the embattled colonists. He was Benjamin Church, a Plymouth soldier who had recently brought his wife of three years to live on the frontier at Little Compton, Rhode Island. Church had been genuinely fond of the Indians around his home, and had gotten on well with them, but he took the field against Philip with vigor and a deal of good advice which his superiors ignored.

With thirty-six men, Captain Church marched down into Pocasset Neck on July 8 and, taking stock of the situation, urged the officers over him to pursue Philip down the Neck because he was convinced there were no Indians at all on the Mount Hope peninsula. Dismissing this wise counsel, the colonial officers led their force to Mount Hope, whereupon Philip emerged from Pocasset and began to burn the towns toward Plymouth.

Church divided his small army, taking nineteen men for himself, and made his way down to the southern point of Tiverton, a finger of land jutting into Narragansett Bay, covering his advance by stationing three boats on the Rhode Island side of the Bay. He believed he would find Indians there, and he did—three hundred of them.

Against these frightful odds, Church's men fought well for a time, but it seemed they would be massacred nonetheless. The captain ordered a retreat before they were completely surrounded, and coolly cheered his men on when they showed signs of panic, urging them into making temporary fortifications out of the stones lying about. Glancing for help toward the Rhode Island shore, Church saw that his boats were aground, although the crews were struggling to free them. One did swing free eventually and came to the rescue, but as it approached the Tiverton side, the Indians directed so hot a fire the crew dared not land. Church shouted at them to go back and send a canoe, which could slip in more easily. The crew yelled back that they would not desert him, whereupon the captain lost his temper.

"If you don't leave at once, I'll fire on you!" he bellowed; and the crew, knowing him, departed in haste.

That left the tiny force in a plight which could only be described as desperate, although in spite of the battle's fury, there had not been a single white man wounded. At this moment, however, a sloop appeared and drew in to shore, and her captain dispatched a small canoe to take off the besieged men. The canoe could take only two at a time. A kind of Dunkirk began, in which the little craft plied back and forth from the sloop under heavy fire, taking a pair of soldiers to safety with each trip.

Captain Church was the last to leave. As he stepped into the canoe, a bullet creased his hair, two others struck the canoe, and a third ricocheted off a stake in the water directly in front of the redoubtable captain. The sloop's men cheered. Church's entire expedition had been saved. Incredibly, they had been besieged for six hours and not a man had been killed. Church must have thought that if this was a fair sample of Wampanoag marksmanship, there was little doubt about the outcome of the war.

Meanwhile, the other detachment of Church's original army, under Captain Matthew Fuller, had gone through a similar experience. They had encountered another large Indian force and been driven into an old house at the water's edge, farther down the shore, from which they were rescued by boats.

In all these initial skirmishes, the object had been to smoke out the main body of Indian warriors, under Philip, but the colonial leaders had succeeded only in blundering into bypaths. Near the

Attack on Brookfield.

end of July, however, the sachem was run to earth in a swamp near the Taunton River, and the settlers closed in for the kill. They were exultant, thinking they had Philip hopelessly trapped, and the chief took immediate advantage of their gullibility.

Observing that he was surrounded, the resourceful chief put out a few braves as decoys and the colonists charged after them, believing the Indians were trying to escape. The braves withdrew into the swamp, leading the white men on in pursuit, until the early evening air was filled with arrows from Philip's men, who struck at them from a cleverly planned ambush. In the twilight gloom of the swamp, the white men shot each other with more effect than the Indians could achieve. A hasty order to retreat was given, and somehow the Englishmen contrived to extricate themselves before they were annihilated.

Still, the colonists were convinced that Philip could not possibly escape from the swamp. They withdrew most of their troops and left a small force to starve him out. These besiegers promptly did what the settlers always did instinctively: they built a fort. This action annoyed an astute officer like Captain Church, who was constantly urging his superiors to pursue the enemy instead of waiting for them behind a palisade. He thought the fort outside the swamp was a monument to absurdity. "You are building a fort for nothing to cover the people from nobody," he declared.

He was right. After thirteen days, during which Philip gathered a flotilla of canoes for the purpose, he floated his men out of the swamp and into the Connecticut River country, leaving the besiegers secure in their fort. On his way, however, he was attacked by a band of Indians friendly to the whites, who did more damage than all the forays of the colonists, costing him several of his best men.

In his new position, Philip was able to strike almost at will in the back settlements of Massachusetts, which he began to do with devastating effect. He expected help momentarily from the Nipmucks, who lived along the northern tributaries of the Thames, and the colonists, anticipating this development, sent a peace mission to meet with the Nipmuck chiefs at a rendezvous three miles from Brookfield. The mission consisted of twenty mounted men, under Captains Edward Hutchinson and Thomas Wheeler; and three Christian Indians who were to be guides and interpreters.

When these trusting people reached the appointed place, they found no Indians. After a consultation, they decided to push on to a place where they thought the Nipmucks might be, although the Christian Indians counseled return. On the way they were ambushed by a large party of Nipmucks, who were waiting for them with their Wampanoag allies. Eight men were killed on the spot and three others were mortally wounded. Captain Hutchinson was carried from the scene and died a few days later. Captain Wheeler was rescued by his son when his horse fell dead, and he himself toppled to the ground with a bullet wound. Young Wheeler jumped down, lifted his wounded father to the saddle in front of him, and galloped away safely. The survivors fought a cool rear-guard action and managed to reach Brookfield without further losses, primarily because two of the Christian Indians knew of a back route to the village. The third Indian ally had been captured.

The two who had in fact rescued the party by showing them a safe route were subsequently treated so badly by their white friends that they had to seek Philip's protection. One of them was later killed in battle while fighting for the Indians; the other was captured by the whites and sent as a slave to Jamaica, from which he was eventually rescued by John Eliot, the "Indian apostle." The Indian taken prisoner at Brookfield escaped and returned to the doubtful protection of the settlers.

Although they had reached Brookfield safely, the survivors of the peace mission were far from secure. Shouting the alarm as they entered, they hurried into the garrison house with the eighty other inhabitants of the village, who scarcely had time to gather up their guns and their children and secure the doors. The Nipmucks were at their heels, and at once burned every house in Brookfield except the one where the settlers had taken refuge.

Not all the settlers reached the garrison's safety. One fell in the first volley. Another was captured, decapitated, and his head kicked

43

about like a football until the Indians tired of this sport and stuck it on a pole in front of the unfortunate man's own house.

The Indians tried to fire the garrison house, but they could not get a man near enough with a torch. Inside, the defenders concluded that they were doomed unless they could get help, and twice sent out a messenger, but both of these runners were discovered at once and barely had time to scurry back to safety. Eventually the Indians resorted to a well-tested method of firing a house. They tied burning tow to their arrows and sent them in flaming arcs against the sides and the roof, but this time the method failed. The torches died before they could ignite.

By now it was nearly midnight, and a full moon had risen to illuminate what the Nipmucks confidently believed would be the final stage of the siege. Under cover of earlier darkness, they had heaped a pile of combustible material against the corner of the garrison house, and now they lit it. Again they were frustrated. A few brave men, covered by the fire of the best marksmen in the building, dashed outside and scattered the blazing stuff. The Indians tried the maneuver again, and this time one of the men who came out to scatter succeeded in slipping off unobserved into the forest and began to run for help, but the defenders had no certain hope he could bring aid in time to save them.

As the second day of the siege dawned, the Indians were still hard at work trying to ignite the fortress, and when evening came, the Nipmucks, still unsuccessful, did not sleep. All day and through the night they heated the air with a shower of flaming arrows whose bright parabolas lit the sky. Some of the arrows ignited fires, but the defenders cut holes in the roof from below and dashed water on the flames. Meanwhile their exhausted, terrified children slept as the wives helped load guns, passed ammunition, and did what they could for the comfort of their men.

On the third day, it seemed impossible that the garrison could hold out any longer. The Indians loaded a wagon with hemp, flax, hay, and dry wood, set it on fire, and ran the flaming vehicle hard against the building. There was no hope of scattering it or pushing it away in time; the defenders were certain they would either be

General Goffe Repulsing the Indians at Hadley. *By E. H. Corbauld.*

incinerated or massacred. They fell to their knees and prayed, and their prayers were answered. A hard shower of rain came down, put out the fire, and soaked the wagon so thoroughly it could not be rekindled immediately.

The garrison did not know it, but help was on the way. The messenger had been lucky enough, as he neared Lancaster, to come upon a body of fifty men commanded by Major Simon Willard, a seventy-year-old veteran of warfare in and out of the wilderness. Fortunately, the major's men were mounted, and they rode to Brookfield as fast as they could push their horses, sweeping into the village as the United States cavalry would later ride through a thousand motion pictures. The Nipmucks were cut down without mercy. Those who escaped left eighty dead behind them.

The siege of Brookfield was only a dramatic episode in what now became a spreading, furious warfare that illuminated New England with the sullen red glow of burning towns and cabins. It had spread far beyond Philip's control or command, and today it is clear that the man in whose name the war was fought was himself not a great

45

leader, although to the colonists he was the fearsome symbol of all Indian resistance. Certainly he was often persuasive. He even cajoled the model Christian Indians of the Connecticut Valley to join him. Soon no town was safe, and the attack might as easily come during church services as at any other time.

It was such an attack on a day of devotion, a fast day, that created one of the war's most melodramatic legends, which unfortunately appears not to have a word of truth in it. Hadley meeting house, so the story goes, was besieged by a fierce war party of Wampanoags (or, variously, another tribe) and seemed in danger of being fired, when the terrified townsmen, who had locked themselves up in it, were awed by the sudden appearance of a mysterious stranger among them. He was tall and soldierly looking, with a long gray beard, and carried in his hand a sword he evidently knew well how to use. His manner was that of an aristocrat and a leader. Placing himself at the head of the defenders, he rallied their spirits and led them in a counterattack of such skill that the Indians were dispersed. Then he disappeared as abruptly as he had come.

For years this manifestation was regarded with superstitious awe, but in time the legend grew—and persisted for at least two centuries —that the stranger was no other than William Goffe, who had fought with Cromwell, had presided as one of the regicide judges in the trial of Charles I, and had been forced to flee when Charles II came to power. It is true that Goffe fled to the colonies, but whether he was hiding in Hadley and emerged to deliver its inhabitants is not confirmed by any historical evidence.

On the same day Hadley was attacked, the Indians burned several dwellings and barns at Deerfield, and a few weeks later they besieged the Northfield blockhouse, killing a dozen men. A relief party hurrying to Northfield was ambushed, with the loss of twenty more victims. Deerfield was attacked a second time, while its inhabitants were on the way to church. Farmers in the fields about the village fled in such fright that they left a considerable quantity of grain only partly threshed.

After the Indians were gone, eighty men came from Ipswich with eighteen wagons to save this valuable grain crop, if possible. They

BROWN BROTHERS

Burning of Deerfield.

had completed the threshing and were on their way home with
loaded wagons the following morning when they stopped in a pleasant grove to rest, drink from a brook meandering through the
trees, and gather the grapes which grew abundantly there. While
they were engaged in these pastoral pleasures, a band of seven hundred Indians who had followed their trail during the night fell
upon them and killed all but seven of the men.

47

Captain Mosely, the hero of Swansea, heard the firing in nearby Deerfield and hurried to the rescue with a small force under his command. He was badly outnumbered, but he attacked with resolution, surprising the Indians while they were scalping the dead, and harried them until nightfall, when enough reinforcements arrived to drive the red men away. The brook in this grove, from which the Ipswich men drank before they died, is still called Bloody Brook.

The war had consisted of such sanguinary but isolated skirmishes as these, and although the damage had been heavy in lives and property, the colonists did not unite for a decisive campaign until the Narragansetts finally abandoned their neutrality and decided to ally themselves with Philip. Against this powerful foe, Massachusetts mustered 520 men, Plymouth 159, and Connecticut 300. About 150 Mohicans were persuaded to join as allies, and the whole force was put under the personal command of Governor Josiah Winslow, of Plymouth. It was a respectable army for the times, but hardly more than was needed. The Indians were numerically much stronger; the Narragansetts alone had 3500 men under arms in their fort at Kingston, Rhode Island. The fort itself was a model of wilderness engineering. Its several acres, protected by deeply entrenched palisades on every side, stood on high ground in the midst of a swamp. Its only entrance was a log bridge.

Against this fort, a prime stronghold of Indian revolt, Winslow's little army moved through the snowy forests on December 19, 1675. Undismayed by the obvious strength of the fortification, the men were split into two divisions and attacked forthrightly from front and rear. Those at the main entrance, all Massachusetts men, were hurled back under a deadly fire that accounted for many of them. The doughty Benjamin Church, attacking from the rear with a contingent of Plymouth and Connecticut men, was more successful. Shot three times, he nevertheless strode at the head of his troops through the entrance he had forced and stood inside the fort.

With rare humanity, Church opposed burning the wigwams, where the village's corn was stored, but others convinced him the

Indians could not be defeated in any other way. The torches were brought and soon the six hundred wigwams of the Narragansetts were fused in a giant torch. Faced with the choice of burning alive or flight, the Indians swarmed over the palisades and began the struggle anew outside. Disorganized though they were, the Narragansetts fought with valor, and for a time the battle was in doubt, but eventually they were driven through the swamp and out into open country.

It was the severest and probably the climactic battle of the war. Eighty white men were killed and twice that number wounded. The Narragansetts lost more than six hundred men, including at least twenty chiefs of the tribe. Both sides suffered from the arctic cold that dogged the survivors, and more of Winslow's men perished before they could get home again. Presumably the Indians had similar casualties.

A victory so decisive and of such scope might well have ended the war if Philip had not still been alive. It could never end while he lived, and the colonists knew it. His Wampanoags and their remaining allies were not only active, but appeared sometimes to believe it was they who had the white men on the run. Nothing else would explain the cool confidence with which they planted the deserted fields at Deerfield with their own crops.

Captain Turner, of Boston, was sent with a hundred men to displace these squatters. He attacked at dawn on May 10, 1676, with such dispatch that some of the Indians ran for their canoes without taking their paddles, and found themselves helpless in a swift river which carried them over the falls a little way downstream. In the assault and pursuit, Turner accounted for three hundred or so Indians with the loss of only a single soldier.

Still flushed with his victory, the captain made the mistake of relaxing his guard. A large Indian war party in the vicinity had heard the shots, and in turn they surprised the white men. Someone shouted that Philip himself was among the attackers, and this so disconcerted the colonists that they lost a third of their men, including their captain, before they could save themselves.

Philip was now the flaming leader in the field, striking lightning

49

blows everywhere, although with infrequent success. Twice he attacked Hadley and was repulsed. But he was facing a growing colonial determination to stop him, expressed in the passage of laws impressing soldiers and forbidding all trade with the Indians.

The scene of war gradually shifted southward, and the settlements of Connecticut and Rhode Island learned what Massachusetts had suffered. Captain Church, recovered from the wounds he had suffered at Kingston, went into the field again to become Philip's nemesis. On August 1, he made a direct and headlong assault on the chief's headquarters, killed or captured 130 of his men, and narrowly missed seizing Philip himself, who was compelled to leave all his wampum behind. He soon lost possessions far more valuable to him when Church captured his wife and son.

Deprived of his best chiefs, his family, and most of his personal possessions, Philip was now little better than a fugitive. He cut off his long hair to avoid recognition, which saved him when his uncle was shot standing by his side, with a bullet that would surely have been aimed at him if his identity had been known. His followers deserted him one by one until he was virtually alone, moving constantly from place to place, hunted like a slave, his only hope to save his life. Yet he remained as proud and implacable as ever. When a warrior who had endured his misfortunes advised him to surrender, Philip clubbed him to death without pity.

It was the blackest deed of his life, perhaps the act of a man driven to near insanity by his misfortunes, and it led to his death. The victim's brother, outraged and fearful that the same fate might well overtake him, went directly to Captain Church, told him where Philip was hiding, and offered to guide him there.

The end came on the morning of August 12, 1676. Church quietly surrounded the swamp camp where Philip lay with the few of his faithful followers who remained, and sent in a few men under Captain Roger Goulding to seize the chief. But Philip heard the Englishmen approach. He leaped to his feet and ran out of the swamp by a trail he believed was the only one left unguarded.

As he emerged, the figures of two men rose before him, one an Englishman and the other an Indian named Alderman. The Englishman raised his gun and pulled the trigger, but it missed fire. Alderman had two balls in his musket. He sent one of them through Philip's heart, and the second about two inches from it. The King of the Wampanoags fell upon his face in a pool of mud and water, his gun beneath him.

When his body was dragged before the jubilant Captain Church, that practical soldier saw nothing of the tragedy in Philip's rugged, sullen features, unrelaxed even in death. To him, Philip only looked like "a doleful, great, naked, dirty beast," as he wrote later in his self-adulatory memoirs. He ordered this relic beheaded and quartered. The job was performed by an old Indian executioner in the captain's employ.

Philip's head was sent to Plymouth, where it was exposed on a gibbet for twenty years as a reminder to other chiefs of the white man's superiority. One of his hands was sent to Boston, where it was on exhibition for years, for the delectation of the morbidly curious. And there was a final indignity. The Plymouth officials would not permit the mangled remains to be buried. All that was mortal of Philip was left to rot in a field.

King Philip's War was over, although it flared in New Hampshire for nearly a year afterward and Captain Church had to be dispatched to the rescue again. But in southern New England the Indian had been conquered forever. It was an expensive victory for the New Englanders—twelve towns destroyed, several thousand settlers killed, and a debt for the whole affair amounting to a hundred thousand pounds. The loss to the Indians was beyond a simple accounting of lives and property. They lost the most precious possession of all men—their freedom.

4

THE SEVEN YEARS' WAR

Only a year before Philip came to his inglorious death and ended forever the threat of organized Indian resistance in New England, the curtain fell a little farther westward on a savage drama that had taken more than forty years to play out to its bitter climax.

It was a drama of the utmost significance, and one of consummate irony. For it was the Iroquois Confederacy, that powerful league representing the best hope of the Indians to stem, or at least delay, the westward march of the white man, which blasted that hope with an internecine war of extermination against their potential allies. At its conclusion in 1675, the victorious Iroquois had nearly destroyed their Huron neighbors, weakened themselves seriously, and doomed the prospect of successful Indian resistance from the Great Lakes to the Hudson.

"It was a strange and miserable spectacle," says Francis Parkman, "to behold the savages of this continent at the time when the knell of their common ruin had already sounded. Civilization had gained a foothold on their borders. The long and gloomy reign of barbarism was drawing near its close and their united efforts could scarcely have availed to sustain it. Yet in this crisis of their destiny these doomed tribes were tearing each other's throats in a wolfish fury, joined to an intelligence that served little purpose but mutual destruction."

53

That the Iroquois should have been the agents of this destruction remains one of the riddles of Indian history. The Five Nations—Mohawk, Oneida, Cayuga, Seneca, Onondaga, and later the Tuscarora—inhabited the broad, fertile valley of the Mohawk River from Albany to the Lakes. Their numerous tribes and tribal groups comprised the linguistic group known as the Iroquoian family, and collectively the nations were called the Iroquois.

The Iroquois possessed the most highly organized political and social life of any Indians on the continent—far in advance even of the white settlements in some respects. Their women could vote and inherit property; their government was a rude democracy; their military organization was well devised.

Stretching from the Hudson to the Genesee, the Iroquois Confederacy lay like a great island in a sea of enemies. These enemies were the tribes that spoke the numerous Algonquin languages and dialects. They occupied a vast territory encompassing part of Virginia and Pennsylvania, New Jersey, southeastern New York, New England, New Brunswick, Nova Scotia, then in a broad sweep across lower Canada to the upper Great Lakes and the wastes beyond, westward through Wisconsin, Michigan, Illinois, and Indiana. Sometimes their hunting parties ranged as far southward as Kentucky.

Yet all these tribes, collectively, were hardly a threat to the security of the Iroquois even though they surrounded the Confederacy and greatly outnumbered its three thousand warriors. If it had been possible to unite so far-flung and disparate a collection of tribes, in itself an impossibility, the Algonquins would have mustered about eight thousand warriors at the peak of their strength.

Why Indians as intelligent as the Iroquois should have elected a war of annihilation against these neighbors, who were their only possible allies in the face of the encroaching white settlements, is hard to understand. The Algonquin tribes did not threaten them except in the customary local skirmishes over hunting grounds or insults to honor, real or imaginary. But the Iroquois, it seems, were in a period of their history when pride, self-confidence, and sheer vitality led them to a frenzied lust for conquest.

They soon became the victorious tyrants of the eastern territories. Their neighbors to the south, the Andastes, who lived on or near the Susquehanna, gave them determined opposition for a time until smallpox completed what knife and tomahawk could not accomplish. The Eries and the Neutral Nation, inhabitants of the southern and northern shores of Lake Erie, were not strong enough to be troublesome. The Mohicans, Pequots, Narragansetts, Wampanoags, Massachusetts, and Penacooks, who were such terrors to the Puritan settlements, were themselves in mortal fear of the Mohawks, who exacted yearly tribute from some of these tribes.

There remained only the Huron nation. These people, who lived in western Ontario and along the eastern shores of Lake Huron, were not so advanced as their formidable neighbors, but they represented the best of the Algonquin tribes.

The Hurons were no more a threat to the Iroquois than the Confederacy's other neighbors, but it was against them that the Five Nations launched, shortly after 1630, a ferocious and concerted harassment that went on for forty-five years until a prosperous tribe of some 22,000 people had been reduced to a few hundred scattered, starved fugitives. Meanwhile, the Iroquois went about subduing the Algonquin allies of the Hurons with such success that the tribes remaining existed only because, like the New England nations, they were willing to pay a yearly tribute.

The Iroquois paid an enormous price for this rise to absolute supremacy—far more than they dreamed of at the time. They could measure the cost only in warriors. By 1675 they had scarcely more than 2200 left, and 800 of these were adopted Hurons, Eries, and other Algonquins. Beyond that, however, by destroying the strength of their possible allies they had ended whatever chance there might have been of a great Indian coalition that would prevent, at least for a time, the spread westward of the young colonies.

More immediately, the Iroquois found themselves alone, caught between the opposing forces of the French and English colonists who now were beginning to decide, in truth, the fate of the continent—whether it would be French Catholic or English Protestant. The Confederacy was like a wedge driven between the two camps.

55

Both sides wooed it, and the Confederacy responded typically at first by lending its support to whichever seemed at the moment most likely to win. Later the allegiance of the various nations was hopelessly divided.

The Iroquois were not a decisive factor in the Seven Years' War (or the French and Indian War, as we have been taught to call its American phase); they were at best desultory auxiliaries of either the French or British. But they became for nearly the whole of the eighteenth century, through the Seven Years' War and the American Revolution that followed it, a symbol of the white man's victimization of the Indian. In these wars they were no more than pawns in two great power struggles, first between Great Britain and France and then between Britain and her revolting colonies.

This was a role, of course, that they shared with all the other Indians of eastern America who happened to be drawn into the conflict. But because of their geographical position and their awesome reputation, the Iroquois were always the object of more attention than any of the others, either to persuade them as allies or to secure their neutrality.

Long before the armies of England and France appeared on North American soil, there was constant border warfare between the colonies of the two powers, from which the Iroquois and other Indians might have been able to gather some foreknowledge of the role they were to play if they had been able to understand what was occurring. They could, for example, have seen a splendid instance of how the white man would conquer by dividing them when Count Frontenac, the French governor of Canada, sent out a war party from Montreal in the winter of 1689 to attack the English in Albany. There were 96 Christian Iroquois among the 210 men of this expedition, members of the Confederacy whom the French priests had persuaded to leave their homes in upper New York State and settle in Canada. When these expatriates were called on to fight their friends and relatives from home, they exhibited an understandable reluctance. On the other hand, they were willing enough to join the French against the English, whom they had no reason to love.

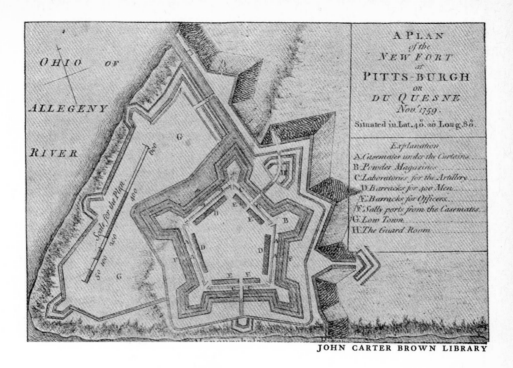

A PLAN
of the
NEW FORT
at
PITTS-BURGH
or
DU QUESNE
Nov. 1759.
Situated in Lat. 40. 20 Long. 80.

Explanation
A. Casemates under the Curtains.
B. Powder Magazines.
C. Laboratories for the Artillery.
D. Barracks for 400 Men.
E. Barracks for Officers.
F. Sally ports from the Casemates.
G. Low Town.
H. The Guard Room.

OHIO OF
ALLEGENY
RIVER

But if there were those among the Iroquois, like these Christians, who had been disillusioned enough with the Dutch and English settlers of New York to go away to Canada and join the French, most of those who stayed behind remained at least ostensibly loyal to the English for a long time. It was not that they had any deep attachment; many of them had been robbed and cheated as much as the Christian expatriates. It was rather that the Confederacy had been suspicious of the French from their first appearance on the continent, had fought with them intermittently, and liked them even less than they liked the English.

But when the Iroquois had asked for help in their private wars with the French, the English had offered them little or none. Occasionally they would be invited to Albany, given some presents, and told to fight harder for the righteous English cause. Only a few sensitive, perceptive white men kept the contemptuous chiefs from choking the pompous magistrates with their own bead strings.

The English arrogantly declared that they considered the Iroquois as British subjects. "British slaves," taunted the French, who

57

once spread a rumor that the governor of New York, on direct orders from his king, intended to poison the Indians, a story that plunged the Five Nations into a state of terror. Jesuit agents were constantly busy among them with such tales, while the English in reply sent only a few missionaries to the Iroquois capital of Onondaga.

It was easy to see why, then, that the Iroquois hoped to remain neutral as the contest between the great powers deepened in the early 1700s. Always sharp traders and politicians, they planned to be the middlemen between the beaver-trapping "Far Indians," the tribes in and around the Great Lakes, and the merchants in Albany.

For a time their ambition coincided with the desires of both French and English. The English traders had no difficulty in seeing the advantage to them in this arrangement, and there were influential merchants in both the American colonies and Canada who desired the status quo. As for the French authorities, they were not eager to start new harassments on the New York frontier because they were afraid the Iroquois, in their present profitable situation, would come to the aid of the English.

Thus there was momentary peace from the Hudson to the Lakes, as the French and English confined their skirmishes to the provinces of Massachusetts, Maine, and New Hampshire, where the French missionaries had seduced the Abenakis and other Atlantic Coast tribes away from neutrality. The colonists had their homes and towns burned by these Indians and by the French expeditions sent down, from time to time, from Montreal and Quebec.

On the eve of the Seven Years' War, which would not begin officially until 1756, the two great colonial powers confronted each other in North America on a vast stage reaching from Quebec to the Ohio Valley. At its eastern end, the New England settlers were involved in almost constant small-scale warfare with the French and their Indian allies. Across the broad tier of upper New York State and adjacent Canada, the Iroquois kept their uneasy commercial truce. Farther west lay the Ohio Valley, a strategic jewel in the crown of avaricious colonialism.

For it was the Ohio Valley that was the pivot point in the French frontier, stretching in an incredible arc three thousand miles from Quebec at one end to Louisiana at the other, with a chain of military posts like beads on a string linking the terminal points. Halfway between was the Ohio Valley. If the English traders, pushing westward, should seize it, they would cut France's American empire in two. If, on the other hand, the French were able to consolidate their positions, they could bottle up the English between the Alleghenies and the Atlantic, and moreover, by controlling the Indians of the Valley, they would hold in their hands the most terrible of frontier weapons to be used in event of war.

These Ohio Valley Indians were a formidable if mixed population. In the upper or eastern part were Delawares, Shawnees, Wyandots, and some Iroquois who had migrated from the Mohawk Valley and whom the English called Mingoes. Mixed in with these tribesmen were a few Abenakis, strayed far from New England, and a scattering of Nipissings and Ottawas. Westward, along the Miami River and its tributaries, as well as the Wabash, lived the Miamis, their numerous tribes loosely bound together in a confederacy. Still farther west were what remained of the Illinois nation.

Of all these Indians, the French could be certain of the loyalty of only a few. In spite of seventy years of colonizing and ardent missionary work by the Jesuits, the Christian Indians numbered mostly the remnants of the Hurons and a scattering of Wyandots. The others appeared to feel no special ties to France, and indeed, to the dismay of the French, welcomed the English traders. The English believed they could count on the Miami confederacy as allies, and perhaps the Shawnees as well. On the other hand, the Delawares nursed grievances against the English, who had driven them from their old home east of the Alleghenies, and the emigrant Iroquois were inclined to listen to the French agents.

In the contest for Indian allies, the French could count on the eternal dissension among the English settlers. When Governor Clinton of New York appealed to his assembly for whatever was needed to help Pennsylvania in buying the loyalty of the Indians in the Ohio Valley, the Albany dignitaries told him: "We will take

59

care of our Indians, they may take care of theirs." But the New Yorkers had scarcely "taken care" of their Indians, the Iroquois, as the presence of so many emigrant members of the Confederacy along the Ohio amply testified. They had moved west in such numbers that by 1750 the center of Indian population had shifted from the Mohawk Valley to the Ohio.

As the fateful 1750s began, the Ohio Valley boiled with intrigue. The English traders were working hard to win the Indians by whatever means it took, whether it meant selling them goods at ruinously low figures, giving them gifts of unexampled generosity, or presenting them with gunpowder whenever they asked for it. The commandant of the French fort on the Maumee wrote gloomily home to Quebec:

"My people are leaving me for Detroit. Nobody wants to stay here and have his throat cut. All the tribes who go to the English at Pickawillany come back loaded with gifts. I am too weak to meet the danger. Instead of twenty men, I need five hundred. . . . We have made peace with the English, yet they try continually to make war on us by means of the Indians; they intend to be masters of all this upper country. The tribes here are leaguing together to kill all the French, that they may have nobody on their lands but their English brothers. This I am told by Coldfoot, a great Miami chief, whom I think an honest man, if there is any such thing among Indians. . . . If the English stay in this country we are lost. We must attack and drive them out."

Similar reports came from the other French posts. All agreed that the center of intrigue was Pickawillany, near the present site of Piqua, Ohio, the home of a chief known as Old Britain, or the Demoiselle. There the English traders, as many as fifty or more, gathered to plot new conquests.

Naturally, the French yearned to wipe out Pickawillany, but they did not possess the strength to do it until June of 1752, when a young French trader and adventurer, Charles Langlade, who had married an Indian squaw and settled down in Green Bay, appeared on the Detroit River at the head of a canoe fleet which carried 250 Ottawa and Ojibwa warriors. This force moved up the Maumee from Detroit, stopped at the portage near the French fort, and deployed through the woods toward Pickawillany.

They fell upon Old Britain's fortress town at nine in the morning. Most of the warriors were away on a summer hunt, but the Demoiselle himself had remained behind with a small force. There were eight English traders with him. Langlade's Indian warriors killed fourteen Miamis, including the Demoiselle, captured three of the five traders, and stabbed to death one who was wounded. Then, as though to prove that the French missionaries had worked among them in vain, they boiled and ate the Demoiselle.

Encouraged by this success, the French now prepared to move in force upon the upper waters of the Ohio and block the western progress of the Virginia and Pennsylvania traders. To accomplish this the new governor, the Marquis Duquesne, sent an impressive expedition of some fifteen hundred men down the St. Lawrence to the Lakes, terrifying all the Indians who observed it en route.

The expedition's main body landed at Presqu'Isle, where Erie, Pennsylvania, stands today, and built a fort, after which they cut a road through the woods to what is now French Creek, and there built another fort they named Le Boeuf. That gave them access to the Ohio by way of French Creek and the Allegheny River.

At first the Indians of the Ohio Valley confronted this penetration boldly. A Seneca chief, called by the English the Half-King, went to Fort Le Boeuf and peremptorily ordered the French to leave. Choleric old Marin, the French commander, who lay dying of dysentery, treated the Half-King with such haughty contempt that the chief went home in tears of rage, humiliated.

When they heard of this incident, the Indians saw that the French were not going to be intimidated or bluffed out of their move. As always, the tribes were impressed by a show of military strength, and the forthright building of a fort in their territory appeared to convince them that the French were strong men who meant business. They wavered, then began to ally themselves with the side they considered would be ultimately victorious. The Miamis, who had been the Englishmen's best friends, offered themselves to the French. The Sacs, Potawatomies, and Ojibwas followed

George Washington at Battle of Monongahela.

them. The proud Iroquois, Delawares, and Shawanoes who lived on the Allegheny even offered to help the French carry their baggage. Duquesne's move had paid off.

Legardeur de Saint-Pierre, a veteran French officer and explorer, succeeded Marin at Le Boeuf, and it was he who received the tall young man, Major George Washington, adjutant general of the Virginia militia, who came striding out of the forest at sunset on December 11, 1753, bearing a message from Governor Dinwiddie of Virginia instructing the French, in effect, to withdraw because they were there illegally.

Of that terrible wilderness journey to the fort and back, much has been written by Washington's biographers and others. Somewhat less has been said of young George's skill as an Indian negotiator. He had made a friend of the Half-King, and although he was scarcely twenty-two and inexperienced at wilderness fighting, he knew instinctively the value of his red allies. Sent by Dinwiddie in the spring of 1754 to drive out the French, he enlisted the help of the Seneca chief as an adjunct to the Virginia militia he commanded.

But it was the French, reaping the benefits of their country's bold enterprise in establishing Fort Le Boeuf, who had much better Indian help at their command than young George could summon. When they assembled an expedition at Fort Duquesne, where Pittsburgh now stands, to take the field against Washington, there was magic in the names by which the fort's commandant, Contrecoeur, addressed his newly mustered followers: "The English have murdered my children; my heart is sick; tomorrow I shall send my French soldiers to take revenge. And now, men of the Saut St. Louis, men of the Lake of Two Mountains, Hurons, Abenakis, Iroquois of La Présentation, Nipissings, Algonquins and Ottawas—I invite you all by this belt of wampum to join your French father and help him to crush the assassins. Take this hatchet, and with it two barrels of wine for a feast."

To the Delawares, who were also present, he added, "By these four strings of wampum I invite you, if you are true children of Onontio [the governor of Canada] to follow the example of your brethren."

The murder of Contrecoeur's "children" which had sickened his heart was actually a skirmish between Washington and a French patrol (they asserted it was a peace mission) near Great Meadows, in the vicinity of present-day Uniontown, Pennsylvania. Jumonville, its leader, had been killed and the French were incensed. It was, in fact, this trivial military incident that, as Parkman says, "set the world on fire," putting into motion a sequence of events that led to the outbreak two years later of the Seven Years' War.

The immediate result of Washington's small but significant victory was a French sally from their Ohio Valley forts to punish him, and thus to contest the English directly. They captured the Ohio Company's fort at the junction of the Monongahela and Allegheny rivers (Pittsburgh), renaming it Fort Duquesne, and it was from this strong point that Contrecoeur had launched his retaliatory expedition, under Jumonville's brother, the Sieur de Villiers.

Neither the impressive collection of French Indian allies nor Washington's alliance with the Half-King proved to be decisive in the battle that followed. After his success at Great Meadows, the young militia colonel had retired a little way and built a hasty shelter he named, appropriately, Fort Necessity. The Half-King, who had been with him at Great Meadows and then gone back to his own village, rejoined him with an Indian queen of some prominence, Alequippa, thirty other families, and forty Indians from the Ohio, who proved to be spies. They were besieged, along with the militia, by Villiers' force, and might have prevailed against these superior numbers if Dinwiddie had been able to supply them and if a sodden rain at the climactic moment of the siege had not left them virtually defenseless by soaking all their powder and muskets. Washington had to surrender on July 4th, 1754.

The incident sent a thrill of alarm through the British colonies. They saw the French in apparently firm control of the Ohio Valley and beginning to move eastward. The Iroquois consequently assumed a new importance because the Confederacy's geographical position made them a buffer between the colonies of the seaboard and the Ohio Valley, as well as a shield against whatever new expeditions the French might be expected to launch from Canada and the Lakes.

Yet, in this developing crisis, the English authorities displayed their customary lack of understanding in dealing with the Indians. They wrung their hands helplessly while the Senecas and Onondagas, at the western end of the Confederacy, were drawn more and more into the camp of the French mission called La Présentation, on the bank of the Oswegatchie River where it enters the St. Lawrence not far from Lake Ontario. They were equally unable to do anything about the intransigent Dutch landowners of the Hudson River Valley, who were forever encroaching northward on the lands of the Mohawks, the eastern anchor of the Confederacy.

When Hendrick, the great Mohawk chief, came down to New York with a delegation to complain about these and other wrongs, he was shrugged off, and he went away angry, declaring the chain of the covenant with the English had been broken.

Matters might have been a great deal worse if the English had not possessed a diplomat of superior quality in the tall, redheaded person of William Johnson, the nephew of Admiral Sir Peter Warren of New York. Sir Peter had sent his nephew, fresh from Ireland, to the Mohawk Valley several years before to manage his lands. There William had built himself a fortress house at Amsterdam, learned the Mohawk tongue, acquired first a Dutch wife, then an Indian mistress (Hendrick's daughter), and finally took the beautiful seventeen-year-old daughter of another noted chief, Joseph Brant, as his wife.

The agitated New York authorities turned to Johnson and besought him to repair the damage they themselves had done. Johnson first soothed his old friend Hendrick and then went on westward to Onondaga, where he found the chiefs in a state of irritation and bewilderment. One of them cried out to him:

"We don't know what you Christians, English and French, intend. We are so hemmed in by you both that we have hardly a hunting place left. In a little while, if we find a bear in a tree, there will immediately appear an owner of the land to claim the property and hinder us from killing it, by which we live. We are so perplexed between you that we hardly know what to say or think."

Johnson took the complaints seriously. He lived at home like a baronet, which indeed he was soon to become, but he was equally capable of living with the Iroquois like one of them, and did so frequently. They loved and trusted him as they did no other white man, and he understood them better than any other. Returning from Onondaga, he was convinced that the whole Confederacy would slip into the hands of the French if something of a major nature were not done immediately.

What he proposed was a commission set up by the provincial governors, on the authority of the Lords of Trade and Plantations, which would meet with the Iroquois leaders at Albany, establish a solid treaty with them, and secure them for the English cause. New York, Pennsylvania, Maryland, and the four New England colonies agreed to this plan, and soon the commissioners assembled

65

in Albany—a distinguished body of men, including Benjamin Franklin, but armed with insufficient power from their assemblies.

Sitting down with the Iroquois chiefs in the Albany courthouse, the commissioners produced a chain belt of wampum, showing the king embracing the colonies and the Five Nations, and presented it to the chiefs, along with a speech designed to elevate the British and paint the French in as black an aspect as possible.

Hendrick rose to reply for the Iroquois. He was already an exceptional leader of men in both war and peace. Probably a Mohican by birth, he had been adopted by the Mohawks and became a sachem when he was still a young man. In 1710 he had journeyed to England with Colonel Peter Schuyler and been presented at court to Queen Anne. Always a friend of the English, he had done his loyal best to hold the Mohawks in their interest, but at the same time, he had never hesitated to charge the white men with responsibility for their fraudulent land deals and their deliberate debauchery of the Indians with alcohol.

The speech Hendrick now gave to the commissioners made him a famous man. As he rose and began to speak, some of them may have remembered the secondhand impression of Hendrick reported early in his career by the English traveler, Timothy Dwight: that "his figure and countenance were singularly impressive and commanding; that his eloquence was of the same superior order; that he appeared as if born to control other men, and possessed an air of majesty unrivaled. . . ."

"We do now solemnly renew and brighten the covenant chain," Hendrick said. "We shall take the chain belt to Onondaga, where our council fire always burns, and keep it so safe that neither thunder nor lightning shall break it."

But then he addressed himself to the English complaints that the Iroquois were drifting away to the French: "It is true that we live disunited. We have tried to bring back our brethren, but in vain; for the governor of Canada is like a wicked, deluding spirit. You ask why we are so dispersed. The reason is that you have neglected us for these three years past." At this point he took out a stick and threw it behind him. "You have thus thrown us behind your back;

66

whereas the French are a subtle and vigilant people, always using their utmost endeavors to seduce and bring us over to them. . . .

"The governor of Virginia and the governor of Canada are quarreling about lands which belong to us, and their quarrel may end in our destruction. . . ." Then, in a final burst of sarcasm, he forecast the same possible fate for the English. "Look about your country and see: you have no fortifications; no, not even in this city. It is but a step from Canada here, and the French may come and turn you out of doors. You desire us to speak from the bottom of our hearts and we shall do it. Look at the French: they are men; they are fortifying everywhere. But you are all like women, bare and open, without fortifications."

Printed in the provincial newspapers and later reprinted in a leading English periodical, *The Gentleman's Magazine*, the speech further enhanced Hendrick's reputation. It also led the commissioners, in their subsequent deliberations, to agree that the tribes must be treated wisely and justly, that the French peril was very great and could be dealt with only if the colonies united in their mutual interest; whereupon Franklin laid before the congress his famous plan of union. But the colonies and the Crown were equally suspicious of the proposal when they came to consider it, each believing that it gave the other too much power, and the colonies fearful that they would lose some of their precious individual sovereignty.

There was one positive result from the Albany Congress. The commissioners were well agreed on their mutual danger, and the provincial governors, particularly Dinwiddie, began to plead with the home government in England for defense against the French. Their pleas were answered. The preposterous, lisping George II sent them Major General Edward Braddock, with two regiments of 500 men each and orders for the enlistment of 200 more in Virginia, where the expedition was to land.

Of the veteran Braddock, who had been in service since he entered the Coldstream Guards as an ensign in 1710, Franklin has given us the fairest estimate. "This general was, I think, a brave man, and might probably have made a good figure in some European war. But he had too much self-confidence; too high an opinion of

67

the validity of regular troops; too mean a one of both Americans and Indians."

But at least Braddock brought with him a plan to discourage the French, which he unfolded before a council of the provincial governors and other dignitaries when he arrived at Alexandria. It was a plan devised by the Duke of Cumberland, who commanded the king's armies, and like the king himself, it was far more ambitious than practical.

As it was unfolded to the eager governors, it envisioned a four-pronged attack designed to push the French back into Canada on the north and to their farthest western forts. Braddock was to lead his two British regiments and the Virginia recruits against Fort Duquesne. Governor Shirley, the indefatigable governor of Massachusetts, would lead two provincial regiments just raised against Fort Niagara, the vital point in the French chain, without which neither the Lakes nor the Ohio Valley could be held. William Johnson was to lead another army, drawn from New England, New York, and New Jersey, against the French stronghold of Crown Point, just above Fort Ticonderoga on Lake George. Finally, a regular officer, Lieutenant Colonel Monckton, was to command still another body of New Englanders in an assault on Fort Beauséjour, at the head of the Bay of Fundy, and then bring Acadia (Nova Scotia) into subjection.

Braddock set out first, in the late spring of 1755. He is remembered by most Americans today as a blundering Britisher who was stupidly trapped in an ambush and would never have come to grief if he had only listened to Washington's good advice. The truth is that Braddock, whatever his personal defects, was an extremely able soldier who marched a grumbling collection of disaffected regulars and green militia over indescribable terrain, beset by every conceivable problem of logistics, until at last he encountered an Indian enemy superbly equipped to fight the kind of battle that confronted them.

He was not ambushed. When his army reached the ford over the Monongahela, eight miles from Fort Duquesne, the decision to cross, which was later criticized, was in fact taken to avoid a more direct but more perilous route. Having crossed, and recrossed farther up, he did everything a prudent commander could do to protect his advance, and made rather elaborate dispositions so that he would not be surprised.

The army that met him was overwhelmingly Indian. Fort Duquesne had only a few companies of regular troops stationed there permanently. To them had been added 146 Canadians and 800 Indian warriors collected from every quarter of the compass by the assiduous French. Here were Caughnawagas from Saut St. Louis, Abenakis from St. Francis, and Hurons from Lorette, under Chief Anastase. These were mission Indians. The others were heathens: Potawatomies and Ojibwas from the northern Lakes, commanded by the redoubtable Langlade; Shawnees and Mingoes from the Ohio; and Ottawas from Detroit, probably including a young chief named Pontiac, whose name in a few years would be mightiest among the tribes.

It was an impressive array of savages, but nevertheless, Contrecoeur and his fellow officers, Captains Beaujeu, Dumas, and Ligonier, were in a state of alarm when the news reached them that Braddock's army was approaching. Beaujeu was in favor of adopting a bold and resolute course. Rather than sit in Fort Duquesne and await the enemy, he meant to attack them on the march and ambush them, if possible, preferably at the Monongahela crossing.

But when he announced this plan to the Indians and presented the war hatchet to them, he found them less than enthusiastic. "Do you want to die, my father, and sacrifice us besides?" they asked him. They met in council on the night of July 8, and next morning refused flatly to make an advance.

Beaujeu was a brave and resolute man. "I am determined to meet the English," he told them. "What! Will you let your father go alone?"

He understood his allies very well. It was exactly the kind of talk that usually inspired the warriors, and most of them hurried away to daub on their war paint. As for Beaujeu, he took communion from the priest and prepared to lead them. By eight o'clock the little army had marched off into the forest: 637 Indians, 36 French officers and cadets, 72 regulars, and 146 Canadians.

Oddly enough, they did not march as rapidly as Braddock's men. By one o'clock they had come only seven miles toward the British, who by that hour had crossed the Monongahela for the second time and thus frustrated Beaujeu's plans for an ambuscade. Braddock's path now led through dense forest, parallel to the river, along the base of steep hills.

His advance column had gone only a little way and just passed through a shallow ravine when it encountered the van of Beaujeu's Indians, who were deployed among the trees and underbrush. Perhaps if Braddock's advance guard had been operating a little farther ahead of the main body, it would have been able to reduce the element of surprise, but in any case the battle was immediately one between red men fighting in their native element and regular troops who had had no experience in this sort of warfare.

Nevertheless, it was the regulars, battling with superb courage, who had the best of it for a time. Most of the Canadians fled at the first volley. Beaujeu fell dead at the third volley. Then Lieutenant Colonel Gage, in command of the advance party, brought up his cannon, and at this the Indians fell back, bewildered. But they did not leave the field.

Dumas, who now commanded in Beaujeu's place, tried to rally his force. "I advanced with the assurance that comes from despair," he wrote later, and his fellow officers followed his example. Their steadfast bravery inspired the men, white and red alike. Dumas and Ligonier held the center with the regulars and what Canadians remained, while the Indians flanked Braddock's army on both sides and began pouring in a murderous enfilading fire, using the hilly ground to shoot directly into the milling, helpless mass of British regulars below them.

As Gage's advance guard fell back in dismay, they encountered Braddock and the main body moving up. Within a few minutes the two were hopelessly confused, huddled together in bewildered clumps of helplessness, not knowing in which direction to face as the deadly fire showered them from every side. Valiant as they were, inevitably a fatal panic gripped them. One of Braddock's officers wrote three weeks afterward: "I cannot describe the horrors of that scene. No pen could do it. The yell of the Indians is fresh on my ear, and the terrific sound will haunt me till the hour of my dissolution."

After the panic became a rout, and the dying Braddock escaped with the remnants of his army, it could be seen, although doubtless not acknowledged, that it was an Indian triumph. Never again during the French and Indian War would they play so prominent a part in the conflict erroneously named for them.

Thus the first stroke of the Duke of Cumberland's grand plan to beat back the French in North America had failed miserably. While Braddock was marching to his disaster, the other commanders in the enterprise were carrying out their assignments.

To strengthen Johnson's position, he had been made Indian superintendent and a general as well, much to the delight of the Iroquois. When he called them to a conference at his house on the Mohawk to discuss the march on Crown Point, 1100 of them turned out for the occasion.

Johnson knew the Indians so well that he displayed no impatience as the characteristic interminable speechmaking went on for three days and into the fourth. But then, seizing his moment, he threw down the war belt, an Oneida chief picked it up, and the war dance began. Johnson brought in a tub of punch, and the Indians drank the king's health and renewed their frenzy.

When the moment came to take the warpath, however, only 300 of the 1100 appeared. Hendrick did not have to explain the discrepancy to his friend Johnson; both knew the Iroquois had no heart for fighting their relatives who had gone to Canada and would undoubtedly be fighting on the French side.

It was, indeed, an ill-fated expedition, of which Hendrick took a doubtful view from the first. He was not impressed with the green army of provincials who had gathered under Johnson's command, and these rude farmers returned the compliment. In truth, he was old and fat by this time, well past seventy years old, and sometimes had difficulty staying on his horse. But his mind was as

71

keen as ever. When Johnson would have split his army as they approached the French, Hendrick disagreed. Picking up a stick, he broke it in two, after which he held several sticks in his hand and showed how it was impossible to break them when they were held together. Johnson took the hint and countermanded his order for division. Hendrick was still not satisfied; he shook his head. "If they are to be killed, they are too many; if they are to fight, they are too few."

It was a shrewd and accurate analysis, which Johnson would have done well to heed, but he was too far committed. Seeing that William would not be dissuaded, Hendrick announced that he was determined to follow his brother, and, pulling himself up laboriously on a gun carriage, harangued his wavering Mohawk followers with all his old, powerful eloquence so that the New England officers who listened were lost in admiration, although they understood nothing of what he said. Two hundred of the Indians responded; the others were not convinced even by Hendrick.

If Johnson was having trouble with his Indian allies, the commander who faced him believed himself in a worse condition. The German army veteran, Baron Dieskau, who led the French forces, had never commanded Indians in his long military career, and it was a new experience he did not care to repeat. "They drive us crazy," he wrote bluntly, "from morning till night. There is no end to their demands. They have already eaten five oxen and as many hogs, without counting the kegs of brandy they have drunk. In short, one needs the patience of an angel to get on with these devils; and yet one must always force himself to seem pleased with them."

It was the Indians of both sides who first confronted each other in the ensuing Battle of Lake George, where Johnson's army was stayed in its advance toward Crown Point by Dieskau's forces. As Hendrick and Johnson had surmised, the French commander's Indians were also Iroquois, from the western end of the Confederacy.

Some historians have surmised that Dieskau's Iroquois, lying with the other troops in a carefully prepared ambush, nearly gave away

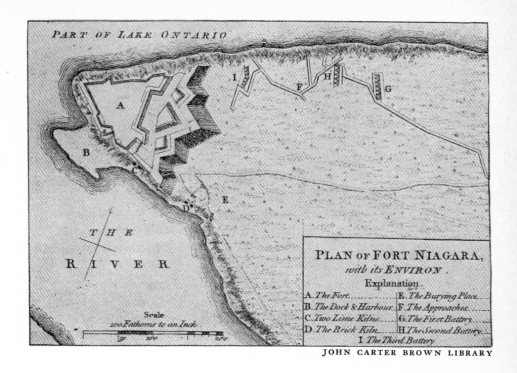

the trap by firing prematurely to warn their kinsmen. Certainly old Hendrick scented the danger, but before he could give warning, the thickets around him burst out in flame. His horse collapsed beneath him, and as he tried to rise from the ground, a French bayonet pierced his body, ending his noble life.

Johnson's men executed a notable retreat, with some loss, and thus ended the first phase of the battle, which came to be known as the "bloody morning scout." The Iroquois on both sides were sullen and disgruntled, finding that they were expected to fight, brother against brother. Legardeur de Saint-Pierre, their commander, had been killed, and without a leader they were unmanageable. There was no enthusiasm for the fight among Johnson's Mohawks, although most of them had behaved well in battle.

In the main engagement that soon followed, the Iroquois fought as they pleased and sometimes not at all, but after it was over, with Johnson in possession of the field, the Mohawks still roamed about, determined to avenge the dead Hendrick. Several of them came into Johnson's tent, where Dieskau, wounded and captured, was

73

lying. The Baron heard the Mohawks and Johnson in a furious argument. After the Indians had stalked out angrily, he inquired what the red men had wanted.

"What do they want?" Johnson retorted. "To burn you, by God, eat you and smoke you in their pipes, in revenge for three or four of their chiefs that were killed. But never fear. You shall be safe with me, or else they shall kill us both."

The Mohawks came back for further argument, but apparently went away appeased. Next morning a lone Indian tricked himself into the tent in which Dieskau lay and would have stabbed him with a sword if a colonel whose tent it was had not disarmed the intruder.

Johnson had a victory of sorts, which somewhat made up for Braddock's defeat, but he was unable to hold his army together to go on toward Crown Point. The second element of the grand plan had also failed.

Meanwhile, Monckton had redeemed these losses by capturing Beauséjour with little difficulty, but then he wrote a new chapter in infamy by carrying out Governor Shirley's determined plan to rid Acadia of the Acadians, whom the province regarded as a hostile force that could not be permitted to live in such dangerous proximity to the main settlements in Massachusetts. Consequently, there occurred that mass deportation which Longfellow made reasonably immortal in his "Evangeline." Those Acadians who did not escape were gathered up and distributed among the colonies all the way from Massachusetts to Georgia. Those who succeeded in escaping later and made their way to French Louisiana preserved their way of life.

As for Governor Shirley, his part of the plan ended in failure too, without so much as a single battle. He set out from Albany in July, with a smaller force than he had hoped for, and found himself soon on the southern shore of Lake Ontario, directly across the lake from the French strong point, Fort Frontenac. There he stopped for an excellent reason. The French had learned from Braddock's captured papers all about the British grand strategy, and both forts Niagara and Frontenac were ready for Shirley's arrival. With superior forces, they were prepared to move around the freshly minted Massachusetts general and cut him off.

Reluctantly, Shirley had to abandon the expedition. He spent several weeks in the autumn of 1755 strengthening the English fort at Oswego, where he had paused on Lake Ontario, left some men to garrison it, and went back to Albany, full of plans for a fresh series of campaigns the following summer. He intended to put an overpowering naval force on the waters of Lake Ontario and use it to capture all the French forts on the lake—Niagara, Frontenac, and Toronto. Then he meant to attack Ticonderoga and Crown Point on the north, and Fort Duquesne on the south. If he had the time and the men, he intended to launch an attack up the Chaudière River on the settlements around Quebec.

But the character of the conflict was now changing rapidly. The campaigns of 1755 had been part of an undeclared war, and although they had failed to dislodge the French, nothing whatever had been settled by them. This year of open hostility, during which the British had supplemented their effort in North America by attacking French maritime commerce with a free hand, could result only in declared war.

England was the first to so declare, on May 18, 1756; France followed on June 9. Immediately all of Europe was convulsed by what proved to be the eighteenth century's most terrible conflict. America was only a sideshow, along with India, the coasts of Africa, and the islands belonging to both nations scattered around the globe.

Sideshow or not, the continuing struggle for North America was serious enough for the men who fought it. There were great and tragic scenes that the people of Canada and the American colonies would never forget. But in this vast drama, the Indians were lost. As soon as the armies of Europe began to appear on the scene, their importance rapidly diminished.

Nevertheless, the two powers fought over them and used them whenever they could, particularly in the first stages of the declared war. Johnson was particularly hard at work in the early summer of 1756, hoping to make the Indians more useful in the important campaigns Shirley had projected. But the Iroquois wanted to re-

75

Landing of New England Forces at Louisbourg in 1745.

main neutral if they could, and if that were impossible, they favored the French more and more. Their chiefs complained constantly to Johnson about the politicians and merchants in Albany who repeatedly lied to them, betrayed and cheated them. Only their love for Sir William prevented them from throwing in their lot with the French. It took many councils to persuade them to let the English build forts near their towns.

Johnson did enjoy some small successes. In June, shortly after the war was officially joined, he journeyed to the Confederacy's capital, and, after condoling with the Indians for a fortnight on the loss of their chief sachem, Red Head, he succeeded in getting them to lift the hatchet in behalf of the British cause. A little later, at his home, now called Fort Johnson, he arose from a sickbed to harangue an Indian delegation he had invited to visit him, representing the Five Nations, the Mohegans from the Hudson, and the Delawares and Shawnees from the Susquehanna, all of whom were engaged in brisk, murderous warfare against the English border settlers. They agreed to cease and, in fact, took up the war belt against the French.

But Johnson was a realist about his Indian friends. He had no guarantee they would keep their word, and he was well aware that, while some of the chiefs treated with him, others were intriguing with the French. The only way to assure their firm support was to make a convincing display of military strength, climaxed by a victory against the French. That was why the summer campaigns assumed more than ordinary importance.

But unfortunately, instead of capturing the key French forts around Lake Ontario, as Shirley had dreamed, the French moved first and took Fort Oswego, a signal triumph of French arms that secured their western outposts for the time being. Moreover, the victory brought all those Indians who had been wavering into their camp, and inspired the western tribes to attack all along the English border in the Ohio Valley. Even the Cherokees and Choctaws, long noted as British partisans, seemed about to turn.

With growing despair, Johnson saw the Five Nations slipping away from him. In November they sent a large delegation to Montreal, prepared to renew the chain of friendship. Governor Vaudreuil boasted to them: "I have laid Oswego in ashes, and the English quail before me. Why do you nourish serpents in your bosom? They mean only to enslave you."

At this the delegates howled and threw their English medals to the ground. Addressing Vaudreuil as the "Devourer of Villages," they swore not to oppose him again. Delighted, the governor clothed and fed them so handsomely that he could not get rid of them. They insisted on staying to help the French celebrate New Year's, much to the annoyance of those who had to entertain them.

Of the whole Confederacy, only the Mohawks remained faithful to Johnson, and even their loyalty was constantly in doubt. No wonder the French concluded in the spring of 1757 that the time was ripe to strike at the English on Lake George and perhaps go all the way to Albany. During the winter they had been recruiting Indian allies among the western and northern tribes, until there were now more than a thousand of them gathered about the village of Montreal, eager to see and talk with the great General Montcalm, who had come from France and conquered Oswego.

When they were at last granted this privilege, the Michilimackinac orator told him: "We wanted to see this famous man who tramples the English under his feet. We thought we should find him so tall that his head would be lost in the clouds. But you are a little man, my father. It is when we look into your eyes that we see the greatness of the pine tree and the fire of the eagle."

By the time the whole French force was gathered at Ticonderoga near the end of July, there were nearly two thousand Indians in the army of eight thousand, from tribes so diverse and far-flung that the Iowas found no white interpreter who could understand their language. They were restless and unmanageable allies. While they waited for battle, they amused themselves by reducing the rattlesnake population sunning itself on the rocks beside Lake George, and when the army finally gathered before Fort William Henry at the lower end of the lake, for a siege in form, they irritated Montcalm by ignoring all the rules of warfare.

The French general called the Indian leaders to a council, gave them wampum, and remonstrated with them. They promised to obey him in future, but they complained because the general had not asked their advice about how to conduct the siege. "We know more about fighting in the woods than you; ask our advice and you will be the better for it."

Montcalm soothed them with promises in return, including the information that in the morning they would hear the artillery in action. When his eight heavy cannon and a mortar began to bellow at sunrise, the Indians were beside themselves with delight. They begged to be allowed to aim the guns, and occasionally Montcalm permitted it.

As it happened, they were called upon to do little more; the English surrendered Fort William Henry on August 8. But it was then that the Indians wrote a black page in their own history. Hungry for rum, plunder, and scalps, they broke every promise and every order from the French command, and would not be stayed by prayers, threats, or blandishments.

They followed the retreating columns of Englishmen, who had agreed by the capitulation terms that they would not serve for eighteen months, and although the defeated were supposedly protected by a French military escort, the Indians killed and scalped at least fifty of them, not counting the sick and wounded slain at the fort and at the first camp during the retreat. Six or seven hundred other men, women, and children were either carried off as prisoners to be tortured, or were stripped and beaten and left to die in the forest. Of these, Montcalm was able to retrieve more than four hundred.

The sequel was grisly. Arriving at Montreal with their remaining two hundred or so prisoners, the Indians were rebuked by the governor, who thereupon foolishly bought some of the captured men from them for two kegs of brandy each. A French witness wrote of what followed: ". . . My soul shuddered at the sights my eyes beheld. On the fifteenth, at two o'clock, in the presence of the whole town, they killed one of the prisoners, put him into the kettle, and forced his wretched countrymen to eat of him." Another witness swore that they "compelled mothers to eat the flesh of their children."

Frightened by such ferocity, the French showered their allies with guns, canoes, and other presents to get rid of them, and at the same time preserve them for future use. But the governor's laxity had made them bold. "He let them do what they pleased," another French witness wrote later; "they were seen roaming about Montreal, knife in hand, threatening everybody and often insulting those they met. When complaint was made, he [the governor] said nothing. Far from it; instead of reproaching them, he loaded them with gifts, in the belief that their cruelty would then relent." In a fortnight it did relent, and after a grand debauch at LaChine, the tribes paddled off to their western villages.

The hypocritical attitude of the French toward their Indian allies was expressed by the French commander Bougainville when Fort

Death of General Montcalm.

Niagara reported during the following winter that three thousand savages were only waiting for spring to be turned loose on the English frontier. "What a scourge!" Bougainville writes, aghast at his fortunate position. "Humanity groans at being forced to use such monsters. What can be done against an invisible enemy who strikes and vanishes, swift as lightning? It is the destroying angel."

Yet the destroying angels were no longer important in the outcome of the war. Able British generals were in the field, leading thousands of trained regulars. Lord Jeffrey Amherst took the great French fort at Louisbourg, on the north coast of Prince Edward Island, in 1758; and in the same year General John Forbes captured Fort Duquesne. The only victory of consequence the French were able to achieve that year was Montcalm's repulse of an attack on Ticonderoga led by General James Abercrombie.

In that historic battle, the three hundred Mohawks who had come there with Johnson ensconced themselves safely on the slopes

Death of General Wolfe. *Engraving by Falckeysen from a painting by Benjamin West.*

of Mount Defiance, and after a little desultory and harmless firing of their small arms, subsided and watched the white men kill each other through the long and frightful afternoon.

It was, obviously, no longer vital to the contending generals whether the Five Nations fought or not, or on which side. The Indians of other nations became inconsiderable auxiliaries whenever they fought; many of them served as scouts. Lieutenant Colonel Bradstreet scarcely needed the handful of Oneidas who fought with his 3000 men in the capture of Fort Frontenac.

The only show of strength the Indians made occurred in the final days of the war when Johnson brought 900 Iroquois to join the 1400 white soldiers assaulting Fort Niagara. This combined force succeeded in cutting to pieces a French army of 1100 troops, who had the doubtful help of 200 Indian allies. Even here Johnson's Iroquois tried to parley with the French Indians before the battle began, although without success.

The war's climax came in 1759 with the brilliant duel on the Heights of Abraham, outside the city of Quebec, between Montcalm, certainly one of the finest generals this or any war had produced, and the little genius of the British, James Wolfe. The armies left their two splendid leaders dead on the field, but the victory was Wolfe's, and Quebec, the citadel of French rule in Canada, fell to the British. It remained only to conquer Montreal in the following year, and the war ended, to be concluded officially in 1763 by the Treaty of Paris.

The end of hostilities between France and England left the Indian population east of the Mississippi in a sullen, embittered mood. They felt themselves used and unfairly rewarded for what little they had done to make the British victory possible. Those who had sided with the French—and these were in the majority—still viewed the English as their enemy, and most of the tribes waited with apprehension for what their wise men gloomily predicted would be a triumphal westward progression of English settlers and settlements, now that the whole West was opened to them.

The stage was set, in consequence, for the most notable resistance the Indians of the East would ever be able to offer in their struggle against the white men who, it was now plain, meant to conquer their lands and their persons.

5

PONTIAC'S CONSPIRACY

The moment of British victory was the time of decision for the red men. If the moment could be seized and turned to their advantage, they might at least postpone the inevitable day of total white conquest. One Indian leader was awake to the opportunity history presented to his people: the Ottawa chieftain, Pontiac, whose domain was the Great Lakes country.

Who was Pontiac? The Michigan historian, Howard Peckham, has asked the pertinent questions about him: "What manner of man was it who dared oppose himself to this fulfillment of progress and bring the whole European imperialistic broil to a stop? How could he lead four tribes to war and inspire the revolt of thrice that number? Why was he able to capture nine British forts, force the abandonment of a tenth, and besiege two more? Who was this savage that defied a general who had just won for his king a domain twelve times the size of England? What local circumstances motivated and encouraged him? And finally, why did he fail?" Peckham answers these questions in his admirable and definitive *Pontiac and the Indian Uprising*.

By Ottawa tradition, Pontiac's mother was established as a member of that nation and his father was given as a Chippewa, but like nearly all the biographical facts concerning the Indians of that early period, nearly everything that has been handed down to us concerning Pontiac's origin is a matter of doubt. All we know, and not even that much for certain, is that he was born in an Ottawa village sometime between 1720 and 1725, and grew up there. Not even the meaning of his name can be precisely determined.

Whether his initial historical appearance took place at the Braddock massacre is also in question, but we do know that the first contemporary document mentioning Pontiac by name is a copy of one of the chief's speeches, in French, made at Fort Duquesne. This document, dated 1757, is among the papers of Sir William Johnson.

Pontiac becomes a historical figure with the fall of the French in Canada. The day after Sir Jeffery Amherst accepted the capitulation of the governor in Montreal, on September 8, 1760, he sent the intrepid twenty-nine-year-old Major Robert Rogers, with two companies of his famous Rangers, to occupy the French forts on the western Great Lakes, which were still held by the French. That expedition brought the conquering English into the territory of the Ottawas.

Rogers published an entirely fanciful account, in 1765, of how he met and dealt with Pontiac. It is possible they did meet in November of 1760, at the mouth of the Detroit River, when a delegation of Ottawas, Hurons, and Potawatomies came to greet the English, although not under the circumstances Rogers writes about. The Indians welcomed Rogers, as Peckham points out, because they did not yet understand that the English regarded them "as living on *their* land. . . ."

It took only a year or so, however, for the Indians to realize that the British were not like the easygoing and generous French. There was to be no trading except at the forts. They got no presents or ammunition or provisions except enough clothing or powder to provide the bare necessities. Worst of all, the British refused to sell them any rum. Or was this the worst? Soon it appeared that Amherst meant to restrict their movements as well, and to parcel out their lands to deserving officers.

The Senecas were the first to be angered to the point of action. They sent the red wampum belt of war to the Delawares and

Shawnees, then to the Ottawas, Hurons, Chippewas, and Potawatomies of Detroit. These Senecas, displaying the intelligence of
the Iroquois Confederacy, had a definite plan. It was to assault,
simultaneously, the British forts at Detroit, Pittsburgh, Presqu'Isle,
Venango, and Niagara.

But the Detroit tribes were not yet prepared to make war and,
in fact, informed the British commander at Detroit of the Seneca
plot, which effectively ended it. In this exploded scheme, however,
lay the seed of Pontiac's conspiracy.

The origin of that conspiracy was the discovery by the Detroit
Indians in 1762 that the British policy toward them was indeed what
the Senecas had charged, and worse. It was bad enough to be without rum, but to be without powder, which the French had given so
generously, meant that it was increasingly difficult for them to get
enough game for their families. They believed the white man should
share so essential an item as powder with them, as the French had
done, but the English regarded powder as private property. It
was an old argument, destined to become older and more intense.

Apparently the conspiracy began to develop in the summer and
autumn of 1762, aided by a strange figure in the Ohio Valley, an
Indian known as the Delaware Prophet, who claimed to have visions
that told him the red man would be able to drive out the whites if
they would only return to their original ways of living. This
evangelistic psychopath preached a doctrine of self-sufficiency for
the Indians, beseeching them to make themselves independent of the
white man and all his goods, so that in the end they could make
effective war. Pontiac heard the Prophet's message, which was beginning to have a powerful effect among the tribes.

Physically, Pontiac was not handsome, at least by white standards,
but he was tall and strong, solidly built, lighter-skinned than many
of his brethren. The tough, alert mind that functioned under the
feathers tied to his short hair was evident in his confident manner.
The contemporaries who wrote of him, all white men, observed
that he had the air of command typical of great leaders. Some
thought his bearing "absolute and peremptory," while others considered it "commanding and imperious." Robert Navarre, a French

Pontiac and His Men Leaving the Fort at Detroit. *Painting by Frederic Remington.*

contemporary, wrote in his diary that Pontiac was "a proud, vindictive, war-like and easily offended man."

Such was the chieftain who in 1763 gazed across the Detroit River at the stockaded fort and meditated how and with what purpose he could strike at the power of the white men. He was certain of his own Ottawas, and the Potawatomies were easily acquired allies, but the Hurons were split into two camps. Their feeble strength was not sufficient to make a difference, however, and Pontiac concluded that the total of 460 warriors he could summon was enough for the assault. He assembled his force secretly in council on April 27.

Pontiac opened the meeting by presenting himself as a disciple of the Delaware Prophet and conveying the evangelist's message in his own splendid oratory. He was not above altering the message for his own purposes. Where the Prophet had called for expelling all white men, Pontiac cleverly twisted his words to direct them at the British alone. The French were to escape.

As the first step in his plot, he appeared before the gates of the fort on a Sunday afternoon, May Day, with forty or fifty men. Major Gladwin, the British commander, could do nothing but invite him in. Then, while the Indians distracted their hosts with a noisy ceremonial dance, ten spies slipped away to reconnoitre the fort's interior. When they returned, Pontiac told Gladwin he would come back in a few days and pay him a formal visit.

Safe in their own village again, across the river, the spies reported their observations, a summary of which went immediately to the Potawatomies and Hurons. These two tribes were invited to meet with the Ottawas in the Potawatomie village on May 5. Pontiac prudently sent all the women away and posted a ring of sentinels. Then he spoke to the seated warriors:

"It is important for us, my brothers, that we exterminate from our lands this nation which seeks only to destroy us. You see as well as I that we can no longer supply our needs, as we have done from our brothers, the French. The English sell us goods twice as dear as the French do, and their goods do not last. Scarcely have we bought a blanket or something else to cover ourselves with before we must think of getting another; and when we wish to set out for our winter camps they do not want to give us any credit as our brothers the French do.

"When I go to see the English commander and say to him that some of our comrades are dead, instead of bewailing their death, as our French brothers do, he laughs at me and at you. If I ask anything for our sick, he refuses with the reply that he has no use for us. From all this you can well see that they are seeking our ruin. Therefore, my brothers, we must all swear their destruction and wait no longer. Nothing prevents us; they are few in numbers, and we can accomplish it.

"All the nations who are our brothers attack them—why should not we strike too? Are we not men like them? Have I not shown you the wampum belts which I received from our Great Father, the Frenchman? He tells us to strike them. Why do we not listen to his words? What do we fear? It is time. Do we fear that our brothers, the French, who are here among us will prevent us? They do not know our plans, and they could not hinder anyway, if they would. You all know as well as I that when the English came upon our lands to drive out our father, Bellestre, they took away all the Frenchmen's guns and that they now have no arms to protect themselves with. Therefore, it is time for us to strike. If there are any French who side with them, let us strike them as well as the English. Remember what the Master of Life told our brother, the Delaware, to do. That concerns us all as well as others.

"I have sent wampum belts and messengers to our brothers the Chippewas of Saginaw, and to our brothers the Ottawas of Michilimackinac, and to those of the Thames River to join us. They will not be slow in coming, but while we wait let us strike anyway. There is no more time to lose. When the English are defeated we shall then see what there is left to do, and we shall stop up the ways hither so that they may never come again upon our lands."

After this speech the opening blow was planned. Pontiac was to take sixty of his men into the fort for a council, the whole party carrying tomahawks, knives, and muskets beneath their blankets. The remainder of the Ottawas, similarly armed, were to follow the warriors into the fort and distribute themselves, waiting for the signal. Meanwhile, the Hurons and Potawatomies were charged with seizing any white men working outside the fort, and with preventing any reinforcements from coming up the river.

Pontiac's mistake was in thinking he could keep the plot secret for two days, when the assault was scheduled. By the night before it was carried out, Major Gladwin had heard all about it, probably from more than one source. He pondered what he should do, and concluded that the best plan was to admit the Ottawas and confront them with a show of force, but without making an overt move. He reasoned that Pontiac would see the garrison prepared and ready, obviously aware of the plot, and that he would then retire—in disgrace, Gladwin hoped.

Peckham describes Gladwin as an example of the new kind of man appearing in British service, "a bull-headed Empire Builder. Given a post to hold, Gladwin would hold it till the last man was killed, never doubting the right of his country to claim such a place, nor the wisdom of his commander in ordering him to hold it at all costs. . . . Pontiac had encountered a block of granite."

The bullheaded Gladwin had apparently chosen the right course, although Amherst later questioned it. Pontiac and his 300 warriors found an armed and ready garrison and had to retire in frustration and fury, with presents of six suits of clothes and some bread and tobacco to console them.

Two days later he tried again, after he had made what he thought were suitably peaceful gestures, but again Gladwin was ready for him, and this time permitted the Ottawas to enter the fort only in small parties. Thwarted once more, Pontiac understood that he would have to do something immediate to retain his leadership. He snatched up a tomahawk and exhorted his followers to attack every white man outside the fort and cut off the garrison.

His angry warriors were only too ready to obey. They first killed a woman and her two sons in a farmhouse about a mile from the fort. Another party went to Isle au Cochon (now Belle Isle), seized the cattle pastured there, and disposed of a retired sergeant, his wife, and one of their children, besides two visiting soldiers. They took another soldier, a serving woman, and three other of the sergeant's children as prisoners.

Pontiac then laid siege to the fort, shrewdly manipulating the French *habitants* as go-betweens and unwilling allies, who were indeed far more helpless than the men in the fort. Meanwhile, a war party of Ottawas and Hurons fell upon Fort Sandusky in a surprise attack and captured it on May 16, leaving only one of the fifteen-man garrison alive and slaying the merchants who operated the fort's storehouse.

The Indians were much encouraged by this and a series of other small victories. Pontiac, on June 2, sent a war party of two hundred men down the river, bent on further mischief. Ironically, it was on this day that Major Gladwin got a letter by a French courier informing him that Great Britain and France had signed a treaty of peace in London on February 20, ending the Seven Years' War. The war was far from over for Gladwin. Perhaps it was equally ironic that Pontiac did not know what Gladwin knew, and therefore was unaware that he fought alone and could expect no real help from the French anywhere in North America.

At the moment, Pontiac needed no help at all; the war was spreading satisfactorily. After Sandusky, the British outpost at Fort St. Joseph (now Niles, Michigan) fell to a band of Potawatomies. Then Fort Miamis (the present Fort Wayne, Indiana) was captured by the very Indians for whom it was named. Next it was the turn of Fort Ouiatenon, on the site of Lafayette, Indiana, where Pontiac's traveling emissaries brought the local tribes—Weas, Kickapoos, and Mascoutens—into the conflict.

None of these forts had offered any problems. They were ill-manned, and for the most part unprepared; the simplest of treacheries was enough to bring about their downfall. But the next one on the list, Fort Michilimackinac, was the largest, and its capitulation was not achieved without a bloody struggle.

Captain George Etherington and his garrison of thirty-five men were lured outside the fort to watch an apparently innocent game of lacrosse being played between their neighbors, the Chippewas, and some Sauks who were visiting them. While this pleasant pastime was going on in the warm June sun, squaws strolled about and casually filtered into the fort. Then, at a signal, the ball was seemingly arched by accident over the stockade, and the players ran after it through the open gate. Once inside, they dropped their sticks and seized the guns that the squaws had concealed on their persons.

Captain Etherington and a lieutenant were captured at once. Another lieutenant was wounded and beheaded. Twenty soldiers fell dead, and only the French traders escaped. One of the noteworthy accounts of that day's massacre was written by Alexander Henry, a young English trader, who set down with horror in his *Travels and Adventures* this vivid description:

"Through an aperture which afforded me a view of the area of the fort, I beheld, in shapes the foulest and most horrible, the ferocious triumphs of barbarian conquerors. The dead were scalped and mangled; the dying were writhing and shrieking under the unsatiated knife and tomahawk; and from the bodies of some, ripped open, their butchers were drinking the blood, scooped up in the hollow of joined hands and quaffed amid shouts of rage and victory."

The fall of Michilimackinac sent a shudder of horror through the remaining British who heard of it. At Fort Edward Augustus (now Green Bay, Wisconsin) Lieutenant James Gorrell, in command, decided to abandon it when some Ottawas brought him a letter from Etherington, ordering him to L'Arbre Croche (Cross Village, Michigan). Fortunately, the neighboring Sauks, Foxes, Menominees, and Winnebagoes hated the French, and helped Gorrell persuade the Ottawas to take Etherington and the other British prisoners to Montreal, where they were promised a great reward.

With the abandonment of Fort Edward Augustus, Pontiac's victory was nearly complete. Except for besieged Detroit, there were no more British posts in the western Great Lakes territory. But his eager warriors, far from satisfied, were carrying news of the rebellion far beyond this region. Hurons took the message to the Delawares, who at last listened to the words of their own Prophet and allied themselves with Pontiac's forces, bringing the Mingoes with them. These tribes swept up the Monongahela River, fell upon the settlement which is now West Newton, Pennsylvania, and killed five persons, including two women and a child, after which they laid siege to Fort Pitt. That, however, was an even sterner proposition than Detroit presented to Pontiac. Captain Simeon Ecuyer had 250 men in his garrison, besides sixteen cannon and a well-built fort.

Balked, the Delawares ranged as far as Fort Ligonier, forty-five miles southeast of Pittsburgh, and then another forty miles eastward to Fort Bedford. Neither of these establishments was in serious danger, however; they were well prepared to defend themselves.

But now the Shawnees joined the Delawares, early in June, and almost simultaneously the Senecas accepted Pontiac's invitation to the uprising, although little urging was needed. With Detroit and Fort Pitt under siege, these Indians directed their efforts at the forts north of Pittsburgh. Senecas struck at Fort Venango, where Franklin, Pennsylvania, stands today, and left no survivors. Sir William Johnson learned with sorrow from a Mohawk chief that his beloved

Iroquois had brutally murdered the whole garrison of Venango and forced the lieutenant in command to write down the reasons why they had entered the war—the complaint about powder, and their conviction, which was true, that the English intended to take all their country for themselves. After the lieutenant had finished this document, the Senecas roasted him to death with deliberate slowness.

Then these western Iroquois moved on to Fort Le Boeuf (the site of Waterford, Pennsylvania), but here the tiny garrison of thirteen men put up a spirited battle, and all but two escaped under cover of night. Next day the Senecas moved on to Fort Presqu'Isle (Erie, Pennsylvania), where they found about two hundred Ottawas, Hurons, and Chippewas sent by Pontiac to help them. The augmented force besieged the twenty-nine-man post, which held out for two days and then offered to surrender under the promise that the men would be allowed to retire to Fort Pitt. If the white men's promises meant nothing, no more did the Indians'. As soon as the agreement was signed, the four tribes simply divided the garrison among them as prisoners for later amusements.

After this victory, the Detroit Indians turned westward, while the Delawares, Mingoes, and Shawnees directed their attention to Fort Pitt once more. They told Captain Ecuyer that all the forts between him and Niagara had fallen, and he had better make his peace with them. The wily captain, a Swiss soldier of fortune, told them he intended to hold out, but he sent the Indian delegation away with a present: two blankets and a handkerchief from the smallpox hospital. The epidemic thus begun raged among the three tribes all that summer and autumn and into the following spring, removing them from full-strength participation in the war. Captain Ecuyer believed quite sincerely that any means of killing Indians was a good one.

But even with Fort Pitt and Detroit still holding out, Pontiac and his allies momentarily had control of the west. This gloomy intelligence reached Sir Jeffrey Amherst in New York, where he was waiting impatiently for permission from London to go home from the wars and leave a country for which he had no love or admira-

Major Robert Rogers.

tion. The news of disaster came with every post, and against his will Amherst had to believe at last that he was faced with a major Indian war.

Sir Jeffrey reacted to the news with the conviction of his built-in prejudices, which sometimes interfered with his superior military talents. Ordinarily a kind and generous man, as well as an excellent general, he was contemptuous of the Indians, made no attempt to understand them, had no knowledge whatever of their grievances, and intended to suppress them without mercy. In this he was not as knowledgeable as His Majesty's ministers, who interpreted the uprising correctly when they heard about it in London and hastened to carry out a plan they had already conceived—to establish a western boundary between whites and Indians in America, along the crest of the Appalachians. They called their intention the Proclamation of 1763, announcing it on October 7. It was too late. The war had begun, and the settlers had no intention of observing any such boundary.

Already, however, the groundwork for ultimate British victory had been unwittingly laid by Pontiac himself. For he continued to besiege Detroit, and every day thus passed brought the certainty of British reinforcement nearer. If he had stormed the fort and captured it, the inevitable rescuers would have had no island of resistance to work from; they would have had to fight every foot of the way westward on a line running from Niagara to Pittsburgh. Perhaps Pontiac sensed his mistake, but he could have done nothing about it if he had. His assembled forces had overwhelming numerical strength, but Indians would never storm a fort if they knew in advance that their losses would be great, notwithstanding the fact that they might lose as many in a surprise attack—to which none of them was in the least averse. It was a matter of individualism with them. The white man's concept of sacrificing the few for the many was foreign to them.

There were also beginning to be defections among the Indian besiegers of Detroit. The Potawatomies and Hurons made a deal with Major Gladwin, giving up their English prisoners in exchange for a Potawatomie chief held by Gladwin, with the major's further promise that he would recommend them to Amherst. But when the Potawatomies brought their prisoners, Gladwin accused them of not bringing the whole lot, and furthermore spotted an Ottawa spy among them. He sent them away in confusion. At a later Indian council, where the conduct of the war was discussed, Pontiac was able by dint of his powerful oratory to win back most of these Potawatomies who had fallen away.

Meanwhile, help was coming to Detroit. Captain James Dalyell reached Niagara on July 6 with 220 men, including Robert Rogers, acquired forty more there, and set off with his bateaux across Lake Erie. He ran a daring gauntlet of the Indian villages along the shore of the lake and river and reached Detroit, safely and miraculously, on July 28. He urged an immediate offensive of some kind, and although the conservative Gladwin would have been content to sit out the siege a little longer, he considered Dalyell a representative of Amherst and thought it prudent not to deny him, particularly since the captain intended to lead the sortie.

At dawn on the morning of August 1, Dalyell led 247 officers and men quietly out of the fort and up the river road. About a mile and a half away, near a narrow timbered bridge spanning Parent's Creek, Pontiac waited with 400 Ottawas and Chippewas. His French allies had given him ample warning of the attack the night before, and his plan was to cut off and annihilate the captain's little army.

He waited until the British were on the bridge, and then his braves struck with savage force in the pre-dawn darkness, lit dimly by a waning moon. At the first volley, that old Indian fighter, Major Rogers, took a party of his Rangers into a nearby house, and using it as a fort, prevented the Indians from achieving their encirclement in that quarter, then covered the retreat that Dalyell was soon compelled to order. The young captain had to fight his way past one of Pontiac's strong points that commanded the road back, and he led the charge against it bravely—at the cost of his life. Another officer took up the command, and the retreat was accomplished. Besides Dalyell, a sergeant and eighteen men had been killed; thirty-seven other men were wounded.

Conservative Gladwin had been correct, but he could have found little joy in his judgment when he heard the news that Pontiac's men had recovered Dalyell's body, taken it back to their village, cut out his heart and wiped their prisoners' faces with it, and hacked off his head to be mounted on a pole. Small wonder that Parent's Creek was thereafter known as Bloody Run.

A story handed down from generation to generation, and no doubt true, relates that Pontiac invited several of the prominent French settlers to a feast celebrating his victory, and after it was over, said to one of his guests: "How did you like the meat? It was very good young beef, was it not? Come here, I will show you what you have eaten." Whereupon he opened a sack lying on the ground behind him and displayed the bloody head of a British soldier, which he held up by the hair and added, with a grin, "There is the young beef."

But in spite of Dalyell's gruesome defeat, Detroit nevertheless had been reinforced and the siege resumed, with Gladwin in a better position than he had been before. On August 5 the schooner *Huron* arrived and got safely up to the fort's water gate, bringing sixty more men and some much-needed provisions. Pontiac, too, had acquired 200 more men, but the Potawatomies had definitely withdrawn.

Meanwhile, another of Amherst's rescue parties, this one commanded by Colonel Henry Bouquet, was having much better success than poor Dalyell. Bouquet's two Scottish regiments, one the famed Black Watch, reinforced by a battalion of Royal Americans and a detachment of Rangers—460 men—was coming to the relief of Fort Pitt, where the Delawares and Shawnees, having failed to break Captain Ecuyer's defenses, turned to meet Bouquet's relief.

Reinforced by Mingoes and Hurons from Sandusky, they attacked Bouquet twenty-six miles east of Pittsburgh, near Bushy Run, on August 5. They surrounded his force, but the Scots were tough and stubborn. All day the battle went on, the Indians fighting cautiously in the belief that they would certainly win. Bouquet's men were drawn tightly into a circle on top of a hill, with their wounded and horses in the center.

B.West inv.   Grignion sculp

The Indians giving a Talk to Colonel Bouquet in a Conference at a Council Fire, near his Camp on the Banks of Muskingum in North America, in Oct.r 1764.

There they must certainly have perished if Bouquet had not displayed what none of the British commanders had yet exhibited a special talent for—deception. He withdrew two of his companies into the circle, making it appear that he had been weakened by the attack, and the deceived Indians charged into the gap, believing they had only to hack out the final massacre. At that moment the withdrawn companies reappeared behind the Indians and attacked their flanks. Now the red men were compelled to turn around and try to fight their way back into the forest, but the wily Bouquet had prepared another surprise for them. Two more companies, which had meanwhile moved around to their rear, poured in a devastating fire. The Indians broke and ran, utterly routed.

It was a costly victory. Bouquet had lost fifty men, with sixty others wounded. The Indians never reported their losses, but they must have been heavy, and it was known that two noted Delaware chiefs had been among the slain. Fort Pitt, however, was saved. Bouquet arrived there on August 10, and the danger to western Pennsylvania was over. For Pontiac, the end was in sight, but not without a further heavy cost in blood and savagery.

Pontiac's implacable enmity had stirred up a conflict full of deadly hatred on both sides, involving the whole western frontier. Besides the organized movements of the opposing forces, there was a constant running warfare between frontiersmen and small parties of Indians. George Croghan, the trader, wrote to the Lord of Trade in London that the Indians had "killed or captivated not less than two thousand of His Majesty's subjects and drove some thousands to beggary and the greatest distress."

In this kind of frontier warfare, the settler is depicted traditionally as the innocent victim of howling, marauding savages. But it was not always so. The settlers were fully capable of atrocities on their own account, as they proved on a December night when the so-called "Paxton Boys," seventy-five Pennsylvanians bent on revenge, descended on a band of twenty peaceful Indians in Lancaster County, killing and scalping eight of them as they lay in their cabins, utterly defenseless because they had taken no part whatever in the war. When Governor Penn, outraged, ordered the arrest of these outlaws, they promptly returned and killed the rest of the Indians, women and children alike.

As the historian Peckham points out, the frontier attracted the worst of the settlers—"the congenitally dissatisfied, the fugitives from justice, the army deserters, the debtors, the swindlers, all were churned out of seaboard society and thrown to the frontier." These were the men who squatted on Indian lands, cheated them in trading, and provoked their hatred. That hatred, in turn, led to wholesale, indiscriminate atrocities which the whites repaid by a deliberate policy of annihilation rather than simple defeat. This was to be the pattern of frontier warfare for the next century.

One immediate result of such warfare in 1763 was to horrify Amherst, who was appalled by the gross violation of European rules of warfare as well as by the massacre itself, and turned to extreme measures of revenge. He even advised Bouquet to try spreading smallpox among the Indians with infected blankets. "You will do well to try to inoculate the Indians by means of blankets, as well as to try every other method that can serve to extirpate this execrable race. I should be very glad your scheme for hunting them down by dogs could take effect. . . ."

Later, sending a new expedition westward, he instructed that the Senecas and other Indians of the Lakes were to be treated "not as a generous enemy, but as the vilest race of beings that ever infested the earth, and whose riddance from it must be esteemed a meritorious act, for the good of mankind. You will therefore take no prisoners, but put to death all that fall into your hands of the nations who have so unjustly and cruelly committed depredations." Amherst promised a reward of one hundred pounds to the man who succeeded in killing Pontiac, and when he learned of Dalyell's fate, he doubled the amount.

Pontiac, meanwhile, was beginning to encounter serious trouble. His braves had attacked the schooner *Huron*, bringing up fresh supplies to the fort, and had been repulsed with severe losses. The defection of the Potawatomies had caused the Chippewas and Ottawas to lose some faith in the cause and in Pontiac's leadership. One

Ottawa faction went so far as to disown Pontiac and appear to be seeking peace.

In this critical situation, a powerful old Missisauga chief from Toronto, Wabbicomigot, arrived with twenty-four warriors on October 1 and hastened Pontiac's ruin. Wabbicomigot was through with the war; he wanted to talk peace with Gladwin. While he was waiting to get into the fort, a hundred Miamis arrived to see how matters were going, and observing the indecision that prevailed, half of them went home again. The other half stayed to find out what would happen, casting their lot with the Hurons.

Wabbicomigot had three conferences with Gladwin. He gave the harassed major, whom Amherst had recommended to be a lieutenant colonel, some welcome news: the Chippewas and Ottawas were also ready to talk peace. Winter was approaching, and they had no stomach for the suffering cold and snow would bring them. The Chippewas did indeed come to the fort to talk peace on October 14, the day after Wabbicomigot left it, and three days later the Ottawas sent a delegation.

Any other chief but Pontiac would have been carried along by the general sentiment, for that was standard Indian procedure, but the leader of the revolt was a stubborn man. Apparently he still expected help from the French, holding their treaty with the English in no regard, and the Frenchmen to whom he talked were not unwilling to let him believe it. They wanted the English to suffer as long as possible, but realists that they were, they could see which way the war was going and began to help the eventual winners by sending badly needed wheat into the fort. Pontiac, too, was a realist about food. He well understood the time was soon coming when his people would have to be fed; there was little hunting time before winter.

Nevertheless, he made one more grand gesture at another council on October 20, but this time not even his magnificent oratory could hold his dwindling forces together. Nine days later the weather struck him an early blow; a hard frost froze the ground and four inches of snow fell on it.

100   On that same night, a worse disaster befell with the arrival of a

messenger from Major de Villiers, the French commander at Fort de Chartres, in Louisiana Territory. He had been traveling since September 27, bearing similar letters to the tribes along the Wabash, to Pontiac, Gladwin, and the French of the Lakes region. The burden of these letters was the same. In Pontiac's, he called the Indians his "French children," and told them to bury the hatchet. "What joy you will have," he wrote, "in seeing the French and English smoke with the same pipe, and eating out of the same spoon and finally living like brethren." There was more of the same soothing language. At the end De Villiers promised that the French would not abandon their children and would continue to supply them from the far side of the Mississippi, but meanwhile he bade them all farewell and instructed them to live in peace.

At that moment Pontiac must have understood his true position. He knew there was no hope of victory if help from the French was not forthcoming. In fact, De Villiers had said plainly that an enemy of the English was also to be considered an enemy of the French, so both nations now opposed him. There was only one course open to him. He must raise the siege and leave Detroit with as much grace as possible. De Villiers' messenger agreed to carry a message from him, translated into French, and give it to Gladwin. Pontiac wrote, addressing Gladwin as "My Brother":

"The word which my father has sent me to make peace I have accepted; all my young men have buried their hatchets. I think you will forget the bad things which have taken place for time past. Likewise I shall forget what you may have done to me, in order to think of nothing but good. I, the Chippewas, the Hurons, we are ready to go speak with you when you ask us. Give us an answer. I am sending this resolution to you in order that you may see it. If you are as kind as I, you will make me a reply. I wish you a good day. Pontiac."

Gladwin's reply declared that he had not started the war, and therefore he could not end it. Only Amherst had the power to negotiate for peace. He promised to send Pontiac's letter to the general, which he did, but along with it went his own hardheaded estimate of the situation. He wrote:

"They have lost between 80 and 90 of their best warriors; but if your Excellency still intends to punish them further for their barbarities, it may be easily done without any expense to the Crown by permitting a free sale of rum, which will destroy them more effectually than fire and sword. But on the contrary, if you intend to accommodate matters in the spring . . . it may be necessary to send up Sir William Johnson.

"I believe as things are circumstanced it would be for the good of His Majesty's service to accommodate matters in the spring; by that time the savages will be sufficiently reduced for want of powder, and I don't imagine there will be any danger of their breaking out again, provided some examples are made of our good subjects, the French, who set them on. No advantages can be gained by prosecuting the war, owing to the difficulty of catching them; add to this the expense of such a war which, if continued, the entire ruin of our peltry trade must follow, and the loss of a prodigious consumption of our merchandises. It will be the means of their retiring, which will reinforce other nations on the Mississippi, whom they will prejudice against us and make them our enemy forever. Consequently, they will render it extremely difficult (if not impossible) for us to possess that country, as the French have promised to supply them with everything they want."

As for Pontiac, he could not believe that what had occurred had really happened. It was simply incomprehensible to him that the Indians should suddenly find themselves without their old friends, the French, to support them in the fight for their ancient lands. Yet here were the French, allied with a mutual enemy, the English. He must have felt cruelly alone, not only because of the Indians' plight, but also because he himself was now a leader without a victory and the people of his own village had turned against him. He determined to return with De Villiers' messenger, Ensign Dequindre, to Illinois, perhaps to seek an answer to his questions from the Delaware Prophet. He departed in November with a few of his faithful followers.

He did not go at once to Illinois, but spent the winter along the Maumee River in company with enough Ottawa families to form

Sir Jeffrey Amherst. *Engraving by James Watson from a painting by Sir Joshua Reynolds.*

two large villages, and a few renegade Frenchmen who feared Gladwin's wrath. While the winter storms blew themselves out, Pontiac's hopes revived. He could still count on the Delawares, Shawnees, Miamis, and Wabash tribes, he thought, and possibly he could stir up the Illinois Confederation. With that last idea uppermost in his mind, he set out for Illinois in March, 1764.

Although the details of the journey are not entirely clear, Pontiac is known to have stopped to talk to many of the tribes en route before he reached Fort de Chartres on April 12. He found De Villiers simply marking time until the British came to take over the fort and he could return to France. Pontiac saw that the French commandant would be no help at all, but he was welcomed by the chiefs of the Illinois, who were well aware of his reputation. In two days he had convinced them to oppose the English whenever they appeared, and in the next two months it is probable he succeeded in exciting many of the Illinois villages to renewed hostility.

News of what Pontiac was doing filtered back to New York, where a new British commander, General Thomas Gage, was in charge of affairs, replacing Amherst, who had at last gone home. Gage had fought with Braddock and knew Indian warfare; he took Pontiac's continued resistance seriously, and wrote of him: "There is reason to judge of Pontiac not only as a savage possessed of the most refined cunning and treachery natural to the Indians; but as a person of extraordinary abilities." The chief, he went on, was said to keep "two secretarys, one to write for him, and the other to read the letters he receives; and he manages them so as to keep each of them ignorant of what is transacted by the other."

With all his ability, however, Pontiac could not keep the war flame burning. Returning to the Maumee on July 1, he found that the Hurons of Sandusky were asking peace, the Senecas had surrendered to Sir William Johnson (he learned this later), and the remaining hostile Ottawas were wavering. The Indians of the upper Lakes were also in Detroit, begging for the resumption of the fur trade which Pontiac's war had interrupted. There were a few more gestures from the Shawnees and Delawares, but for all practical purposes, the war was over.

Through the fall of 1764 and the winter of 1765, Pontiac continued to plot against the British wherever he could find anyone to listen to him. The Illinois Confederation for a time appeared to offer the possibility of resistance, but eventually Pontiac conceded in a conference at Fort de Chartres, in April, 1765, that he could do no more. He even helped the British subdue the remaining hostile elements, composed mainly of intransigent Illinois tribes who were constantly incited by renegade Frenchmen.

The peace negotiations Pontiac conducted with George Croghan in August revealed the basic disagreement which guaranteed that the ending of Pontiac's war would not be the end of the great conflict between white men and Indians. The Indians argued, with justice, that the land had been theirs before the French came; the French had been merely tenants, who gave the Indians tribute in the form of powder, rum, and other considerations as a kind of rent. The British argued that they were governed by international law, and the Indians were not members of the "family of nations." To them the Indians had no rights whatever, no more than the animals they both hunted. But since the red men were there, and troublesome, they could be kept pacified with gifts, if need be, or with false promises in the form of deeds and treaties that were meaningless as far as the British were concerned. Such was the spirit of the treaty that ended Pontiac's war.

In its wake, Pontiac emerged as the Indian leader admired and respected by the English, and therefore the object of a corrosive jealousy among his fellow chiefs. His continued loyal support of the British while the Revolution threatened cost him the support of many of his own people, and by 1768 had made him a virtual exile. He made another visit to the country of the Illinois, but it appears that he was now only a solitary hunter, accompanied by a few relatives and friends, to whom no one listened any more. And this was the man who had once swayed eighteen tribes ranging from Lake Ontario to the Mississippi.

In the spring of 1769 he journeyed once more to the Mississippi, but peacefully, intent only on drinking a little, talking a great deal, and trading as much as possible. For some reason his presence

105

alarmed the Illinois, who apparently did not understand that he had lost his former power. Possibly their hostility was the result of an obscure quarrel Pontiac had with them on his visit the year before.

In any event, a village of Peorias decided to assassinate Pontiac and end the argument about him. In council assembled, they delegated the job to a young nephew of their chief Makatachinga, or Black Dog, and this brave immediately sought Pontiac's company. On April 20, he and Pontiac were in the little village of Cahokia, where the chief was trading in the store of Baynton, Wharton, and Morgan. As they left the place and began to walk down the street, the Peoria assassin, who walked a little in the rear, suddenly struck Pontiac on the back of his head. The old chief fell stunned, whereupon the Peoria gave him a fatal stab wound and fled. In a moment Pontiac was dead.

When news of this foul deed was brought by courier to Fort de Chartres and then across the river to St. Louis, there was consternation. No one knew the true situation, and Pontiac was still a great and feared name. Everyone believed his death would be a signal for violent retaliation. Even the Peorias were apprehensive—especially when Pontiac's two sons and his loyal handful of Ottawas heard the news in silence, did not even ask for the body, and left immediately.

But nothing happened. Presumably some of the Ottawas were not sorry to see Pontiac dead, and in any case the tribes in general had no desire for war in his behalf. Only Minavavana, the great chief of the Chippewas, received the news with anger as well as sorrow. Always a friend and ally of Pontiac, and a hater of the English, he went to Cahokia in 1770 with two warriors and killed two servants of the trading company—who had had nothing whatever to do with the assassination.

Thus Pontiac passed from the scene of his great revolt, largely unmourned. His fame was made secure by Francis Parkman, whose classic *History of the Conspiracy of Pontiac,* published in 1851, is still in print. But aside from the seven towns and assorted lakes named for him, his name is familiar to most Americans today as an automobile. Sic transit . . .

Behind him he left the Indians, friends and foes alike, at the mercy of the British, who regarded them, Peckham says, "as an expensive nuisance," now that it was no longer necessary to court them to fight the French.

It is easy to recall the savagery with which Pontiac fought his cause, more difficult for many to remember that it was a just cause, since he wanted no more than to preserve what independence remained to the Indians, and to make the British recognize it and revise their arrogant concept of servant-and-master where the red man was concerned.

The Indians had been on the losing side in one white man's war. They were about to repeat this experience in another conflict, and at its end, the new United States of America was to show that it had learned nothing from the failures of British policy.

6

THE BRITISH AND INDIAN WAR

If it is proper to call the American phase of the Seven Years' War the French and Indian War, it is equally accurate to call the Indians' part in the War of the Revolution by the title of this chapter.

It was as natural for the Indians to side with the British as it had been for them to be allies of the French. The result of Pontiac's conspiracy was, in effect, an exchange of the French king for the British king as their father, or rather an acknowledgment on their part that the exchange had actually taken place. In spite of every injustice, they looked to the British for trade, and for help when they needed it. To them the rising storm of revolt in the colonies meant an attack on the only authority they recognized, and on which they depended; as far as they were concerned, the incipient citizens of the United States were only English settlers with whom they had contended bitterly for years.

Indians and settlers faced each other, at the opening of the Revolution, in a great frontier arc beginning in Maine, stretching across northern Vermont, through the New York borderland, across northern and western Pennsylvania, on to Ohio and Detroit, then south to the Ohio River and hence into the Kentucky country, turning south again and following the Appalachians through Virginia and the Carolinas to Georgia.

It was a cruelly exposed frontier. No settler could feel safe anywhere along its length, for there was vast dissatisfaction among the Indians as they watched the pioneers moving daily across their lands.

To advance on the colonies, the British had to go through Indian territory in any march they might make by land, whether they came from the north by way of Canada, Niagara, or Detroit, or up from the south through Georgia. Consequently it was inevitable that the Indians would be involved in the war, most of them on the British side.

Here, once more, British policy toward the Indians was short-sighted, even stupid, as it had always been. They approached the Indian problem without a strategy. If they had employed the obvious one open to them, it would have been a sorry day for American arms. But none of the British generals had sufficient imagination to visualize how devastating it would be if they combined their sea attacks on the Atlantic seaboard from Boston to Charleston with a concerted assault on the inland frontiers. The Indians could have been a decisive factor in such a strategy, provided the British had the foresight to organize them, put knowledgeable officers in command, and give them proper arms and supplies.

How easily the British might have turned the precarious fortunes of Washington's uncertain army, which trembled on the verge of defeat through a good part of the war, into a full-scale disaster! If they had coordinated their attacks on Boston, New York, and Charleston with simultaneous thrusts down Lake Champlain, at the Mohawk and Susquehanna frontiers, along the Allegheny and Monongahela rivers, as far west as Kentucky and as far south as back-country Carolina and Georgia—if this strategy had been followed, the history of our nation might well have been far different, including the history of the American Indian.

Of course, this presupposes that the Indians would have cooperated fully with such a plan. It would have taken better diplomacy than the British had ever shown themselves capable of in North America to accomplish it. As it was, a few tribes were friendly to the colonists; others remained neutral, or tried to do so.

The remainder who allied themselves with the British—and it was an overwhelming percentage—were a terror to the Americans on the frontiers, but as military allies, they were more of a distraction than a help, as might have been expected.

At the beginning there was a somewhat ridiculous debate in Parliament about whether to "use" the Indians at all. It had been one of the colonists' chief complaints against George III, as the Declaration of Independence tells us, that he had ". . . endeavored to bring on the inhabitants of our frontiers, the merciless Indian Savages whose known rule of warfare is an undistinguished destruction of all ages, sexes and conditions."

There were eminent English statesmen who agreed with our founding fathers on this matter. When the Earl of Suffolk made his famous speech in Parliament in November, 1777, urging the king's minister to use every means "that God and nature had put in our hands" to beat down the Revolution, including the use of Indians, William Pitt made an equally famous reply, joining Burke in outraged condemnation of the whole idea of Indian allies.

"From the tapestry that adorns these walls," Chatham's majestic voice rang out in Parliament, "the immortal ancestor of this noble lord frowns with indignation at the disgrace of his country. In vain he led your victorious fleet against the boasted armada of Spain, in vain he defended and established the honor, the liberties, the religion, the protestant religion of this country, against the arbitrary cruelties of popery and the inquisition, if these more than popish cruelties and inquisitorial practices are let loose among us; to turn forth into our settlements, among our ancient connections, friends and relations, the merciless cannibal, thirsting for the blood of man, woman and child! to send forth the infidel savage—against whom?—against your protestant brethren; to lay waste their country; to desolate their dwellings, and extirpate their race and name, with these horrible hell-hounds of savage warfare!"

Yet, after such high-sounding phrases from both sides of the Atlantic, each combatant showed himself more than eager to enlist the help of the "infidel savage." The Americans took the first step, a few weeks before Lexington and Concord, when the Massachusetts Provincial Congress made an address to the Stockbridge Indians, welcoming them to the newly formed "Constitutional Army," and promising "a blanket and a Red Ribbon" to every one of them who enlisted in the colony's service. Later these same legislators sought to recruit Indian soldiers from as far away as Nova Scotia.

The war was no more than begun, in July, 1775, when Lord Dartmouth, a devout man, gave official sanction to using the "horrible hell-hounds"; and the Continental Congress was not far behind, resolving a year later that "It is highly expeditious to engage the Indians in the service of the United Colonies." As an inducement, bounties were offered for every prisoner the Indians took.

Even General Washington, who had good reason to know how the Indians behaved in war, wrote to the Commissioners of Indian Affairs from his Valley Forge headquarters in 1778, enclosing a Congressional resolve empowering him to use "a body of four hundred Indians, if they can be procured upon proper terms." He added, "Divesting them of the Savage customs exercised in their Wars against each other, I think they may be made of excellent use, as scouts and light troops, mixed with our own Parties." Washington did not say how he intended to divest them of their "savage customs," and must have known that he could not do so.

At the beginning, Washington's problem with the Indians had been remarkably like the situation that confronted the British at the start of the French and Indian War. Now it was the British and Indians who threatened from Canada, and once more the Six Nations lay between the combatants, uncommitted and dangerous.

On June 25, 1775, Washington detached Major General Philip Schuyler, the handsome forty-three-year-old aristocrat, and gave him command of the New York Department, instructing him to "watch the movements of the Indian Agent," Colonel Guy Johnson, "and prevent, as far as you can, the Effect of his Influence to our Prejudice with the Indians."

That was no easy assignment. By this time Sir William Johnson was dead, having died of a heart attack one hot day the previous summer after exhorting a council of Indians at Fort Johnson to remain in the British interest. Colonel Guy Johnson was his son-in-law and successor as Superintendent of Indian Affairs. He did not have Sir William's large and generous temperament, nor his extraordinary hold on the Indians, but he was nevertheless closer to the Six Nations than any other white man, and presumably in league with the Iroquois' Canadian allies, the Seven Nations, which included the fierce and unrepentant Abenakis and the Caughnawagas, a tribe of superior intelligence.

Schuyler had no trouble finding out what Johnson was up to in the summer of 1775. He was busy enlisting the Indians to fight for the British, and he had some useful allies in this endeavor. One was Louis St. Luc de la Corne, who had been superintendent of the Canadian Indians when the French were in power; another was La Corne's son-in-law, Major Campbell, who now held that office; still another was Johnson's assistant, a bold and utterly heartless soldier, Colonel John Butler. The fourth was Joseph Brant, otherwise Thayendanegea, a brilliant Mohawk chief who had been Sir William's special friend.

These agents were using various devices to employ the Indians. La Corne was dispensing powder and brandy. (He was also able to hire a few young Caughnawagas for about $16 each, but the older men of the tribe took the money and gave it back.) His Majesty's government sent a whole cargo of inducements: ". . . hundreds of proved fowling-pieces, with blue barrels, walnut stocks, trimmings of wrought brass and silver sights . . . neat, bright Indian hatchets," along with brass kettles, gold-laced hats, ruffled shirts, pipes, greatcoats, barrels and barrels of gunpowder and of bullets, and face paints of blue, rose, yellow, and vermilion.

Still, even with these inducements, it was not clear what the Indians intended to do. The Continental Congress seized upon this indecision to secure at least a neutrality. They drafted a speech to the Six Nations, describing at length the king's oppression and declaring: "This is a family quarrel between us and Old England. You Indians are not concerned in it. We don't wish you to take up the hatchet against the King's Troops. We desire you to remain

113

Joseph Brant, Great Captain of the Six Nations. *After a portrait by Romney.*

at home and not join on either side, but keep the hatchet buried deep."

This speech was delivered at a grand council in Albany, attended by 700 Indians, which went on for more than a week. The Indians took three days to absorb the long speech and frame their answer, given by the Mohawk chief, Little Abraham, who reassured the Americans: "We have fully considered this matter. . . . This, then, is the determination of the Six Nations: Not to take any part, but, as it is a family affair, to sit still and see you fight it out."

Schuyler and the other commissioners could have taken more heart from this declaration if the Indians around the council fire had really represented the strength of the Six Nations. But they were mostly Oneidas, and a rather small part of the Mohawks. The other Mohawks, along with chiefs of the Onondagas, Cayugas, and Senecas, were plotting in Montreal with Brant and Johnson. There was one small reassurance, however. In October, the Caughnawagas promised on behalf of the Seven Nations—which they had no power to do—that they would not "in the least molest," as they put it, any of the colonists.

While diplomacy was going on in Albany, the redoubtable general from Vermont, Ethan Allen, was trying to secure allies among the Canadian Indians by offering them "money, blankets, toma-hawks, knives, paint and anything there is in the army, just like brothers." But the Indians everywhere were wary of the colonists' promises; they had heard them all before. Seventy or eighty joined Benedict Arnold's ill-fated march to Quebec, but for a while neither diplomacy nor persuasion could secure any more than a scattered few to act as messengers, scouts, or guides.

As for the British, they were more successful from the beginning, in spite of the fact that their commanders displayed the most lamentable lack of talent for dealing with Indians. One reads with dismay of "Gentleman Johnny" Burgoyne, about to embark on his ill-conceived thrust at Albany in the summer of 1777, employing his cultivated sense of the dramatic to make himself appear ridicu-lous to colonists as well as Indians. While he stood poised for the assault on St. Johns, with an army of 7213 men, of whom only 400

115

were Indians, he issued a grandiose proclamation designed to intimidate the Americans.

Among other excesses in this piece of bombast, Burgoyne warned those who persisted in the "unnatural Rebellion" that he would unleash "thousands" of his savage allies to hunt them down, and for this vengeance he would "stand acquitted in the Eyes of God and Men." And he concluded "in Consciousness of Christianity" that the Americans, if they would not repent, could expect "Devastation, famine and every concomitant horror that a reluctant but indispensable prosecution of military duty must occasion."

The Americans were far from frightened. Some were angry, others amused, and the British at home were inclined to be indignant. Walpole wondered sarcastically how Burgoyne could "reconcile the scalping knife with the gospel." Then, a few days later, the British general addressed his Indian warriors in the same remarkable terms.

"Warriors," he said, "you are free—go forth in the might and valor of your cause—strike at the common enemies of Great Britain and America—disturbers of public order, peace and happiness, destroyers of commerce, parricides of state. . . ." Having thus given them leave, he added, incredibly: "I positively forbid bloodshed, when you are not opposed in arms. Aged men, women, children and prisoners must be held sacred from the knife or hatchet, even in actual conflict."

This speech was greeted with annoyance back home. Edmund Burke rose in the House of Commons to imagine a riot in the menagerie on Tower Hill. "What would the Keeper of His Majesty's lions do?" Burke inquired sarcastically. "Would he not fling open the dens of the wild beasts and then address them thus? 'My gentle lions—my humane bears—my tender-hearted hyenas, go forth! But I exhort you, as you are Christians and members of civilized society, to take care not to hurt any man, woman or child!' "

Burke need not have worried. Burgoyne's Indians had no heart for the white man's battle. As the army advanced toward Bennington, they scattered ahead of the main body, looting and destroying,

General Burgoyne Addressing the Indians.

and killing the cows to get their bells. When Colonel John Stark checked the advance at the subsequent Battle of Bennington, the Indians and Canadians, led by their commanders, fled in headlong retreat at the first volley.

Another part of Burgoyne's grand strategy involved an expedition that would travel through Lake Ontario, Oswego, and the Mohawk Valley to meet him in Albany. It was in the Valley that the kind of Indian warfare he had promised so righteously in his proclamation actually took place, aided and abetted by the Tories of the region. Here was, perhaps, the most shameful episode in Indian history. Never, in their long struggle with the white man, were they more ruthless and cruel than on this western border. They fought with a ferociousness that cannot be excused entirely as a defense of homeland.

An advancing British force could expect to find allies in the lovely and fertile Mohawk Valley. The great council at Albany in 1775 had secured no more than the passive support of the Oneidas and Tuscaroras; the other four nations of the Confederacy were quite naturally sympathetic to the British, who not only aided them

117

from time to time in their intramural wars with the Algonquins, but had been lavish with their gifts in contrast to the Americans.

Shortly after Bunker Hill, Colonel Guy Johnson had gone with Butler, Butler's son Walter, and Joseph Brant to Oswego for a council, after which these four leaders and a delegation of Indians went on to Montreal for further conferences with Sir Guy Carleton. Sir William Johnson's son, John, meanwhile stayed at the family home, Johnson Hall, which he fortified. Schuyler sent an army of 3000 men to reduce this strong point, and John surrendered in the face of overwhelming force. Paroled on a promise not to fight again, he broke the parole within four months and took a small company of his men with him to Montreal. There he was made a colonel and enlisted a Tory regiment of two battalions, the Royal Greens. Colonel Butler had a similar corps, the Tory Rangers. It was not until August, 1777, however, that these leaders returned to the Mohawk Valley as part of Burgoyne's plan to conquer the Hudson, heading the expedition that was to sweep in on Albany from the west.

The first obstacle was decaying Fort Stanwix, once a well-fortified post, which lay between the Mohawk River and Wood Creek, the nearby connecting waterway to Lake Ontario. This was the strategic point the Indians called the Great Carrying Place.

Burgoyne appointed a veteran soldier, Barry St. Leger, to reduce Stanwix, and he marched toward it in August with about 875 men, including John Johnson's Royal Greens and John Butler's Tory Rangers. At Oswego they were joined by nearly a thousand Indians, under Brant, the largest Indian force yet to appear in the war.

When the 750 defenders of Stanwix saw those bronzed bodies in such startling numbers before the gates, it had the opposite effect St. Leger had intended by exhibiting them. Instead of being frightened, the Americans were suffused with a new resolve, realizing that they alone stood between the savages and the settlements in the Valley behind them.

While they were stoutly resisting the subsequent siege, help came from the militiamen of Tryon County—800 of them, led by a Palatinate German named Nicholas Herkimer, brigadier general of militia. St. Leger learned of their advance, and plotted a trap for them at a wide ravine six miles east of Stanwix, near Oriskany. He delegated all of Brant's Indians, with a few detachments of Royal Greens and Rangers, to do the job.

It was an admirably conceived ambush, and might have been devastating if the victims had been Europeans, unaccustomed to bush warfare. But Herkimer's men were knowledgeable as well as brave. Completely encircled, they took cover and fought back, while Herkimer, who had been wounded in the leg in the first volley, calmly directed their defense from the saddle of the horse that had been shot from beneath him. Sitting astride, as though still riding, smoking his pipe and with his back against a tree, he drew his men in a circle around him, in the classic manner of the besieged.

All about the perimeter of this great irregular circle, a grim struggle raged, much of it hand-to-hand fighting and much of it going against the Americans because of the Indian trick of waiting until an enemy fired, then rushing in on him with a tomahawk before he could reload. There was a break in the hot afternoon's work when a sudden shower momentarily cleared the sultry air and wet the flintlocks so neither side could fire. Herkimer took advantage of the lull to rearrange his men by twos so that one could fire while the other reloaded, a strategic device that ended the trickery.

Not long after the contest was resumed, the Indians began to lose heart, as they often did if there was no immediate outcome in a battle. Eventually they raised the cry of "Oonah! Oonah!" meaning retreat, and melted away into the woods. The Tories had no recourse but to follow, while the Americans also retreated with their wounded.

Meanwhile, at Fort Stanwix, the defenders took advantage of the lightly guarded besiegers' camp and the absence of the Indians to make a successful sortie, so sudden that Sir John Johnson had to depart in his shirt sleeves, leaving his valuable papers behind. The Americans then systematically looted the camps, paying particular attention to the Indians' deerskins and packs, correctly estimating that this loss would make the Indians unhappy with their allies.

Fort Stanwix was saved at last by a clever ruse conceived in the

119

imaginative brain of Major General Benedict Arnold, who on August 21 was en route with another relief force. Arnold employed the services of Hon Yost Schuyler, a Mohawk Valley German of retarded mentality, who was regarded by the Indians with the superstitious respect and fear they accorded the mentally ill. Schuyler had been condemned to death for trying to recruit Valley men in the British cause, but Arnold promised to pardon him if he would become a bearer of rumors. Hon Yost was only too ready.

The plan was simple and effective. Schuyler took off his coat and Arnold's men shot bullets through it, after which he put it on again and departed for Stanwix, trailed by an Oneida accomplice. He rushed into the Indian camp, already depleted by the sortie from the fort, and told how he had escaped from thousands of American troops who were even then not far from Stanwix. Hon Yost said he wanted to warn his red brothers, and his words were immediately confirmed by the Oneida who hurried in with the same story and the same warning.

It was enough for the Indians. In panic, they prepared to leave at once; and nothing St. Leger could do or say would stop them. They feared Arnold more than any other American officer. The news that it was Arnold on their heels provoked them to riot, until poor St. Leger declared them "more formidable than the enemy." Two hundred fled without further argument, and the chiefs of those that remained compelled St. Leger to order a general retreat. The besiegers left everything; they took only what they could carry on their backs.

Thus the Mohawk Valley was temporarily safe from invasion, and the Americans could turn their undivided attention to meeting Burgoyne at Saratoga, where the first really decisive battle of the Revolution was fought, effectively ending the British threat from Canada.

The Tory forces were far from defeated, however. Johnson and Butler recouped their strength after the disastrous affair at Stanwix, and in the spring of 1778, they had established their headquarters at Fort Niagara, on Lake Ontario. From there, near the end of June, they launched an attack on the Wyoming Valley in Pennsyl-

Colonel Benedict Arnold.

vania, a fertile and beautiful place on the north branch of the Susquehanna, lying mostly in Luzerne County. The Valley was no stranger to war. Since the Moravians had first settled it in 1742, rival claimants from Pennsylvania and Connecticut had fought over it to secure its riches for their disputing provinces. By the time the Revolution began, Connecticut had won the argument.

Colonel Butler's expedition, designed to destroy Wyoming's usefulness as a supply source, was composed of 400 white men—Rangers, Royal Greens, and other Tories—and about 500 Indians, most of them Senecas, who were the most belligerent of the Six Nations. It was this force which perpetrated what has been called "the surpassing horror of the Revolution," the Wyoming Massacre.

The towns and farms struck by the fury were nearly defenseless. Most of the men among the 2000 inhabitants had gone to fight with the Connecticut line. Those who remained had a tough but untalented defender in another Butler, Colonel Zebulon Butler, who was able to muster about 300 old men and boys, whom he foolishly deployed in the open.

Brant's Senecas fell upon these pitiful defenders with devastating ferocity; all but about 60 of the 300 were either killed or captured. John Butler boasted that the Senecas had taken 227 scalps, with the loss of only one killed and eight wounded. After the massacre, Indians and Tories swept through the Valley like a Mongol horde, bent on plunder and destruction. Houses and mills were burned, fields laid waste, livestock driven away, and any property of value carried off. The surviving inhabitants who escaped fled to the mountains or to the great swamp of the Poconos, gloomily known as "The Shades of Death" thereafter. Most of them perished of starvation or exhaustion.

Early in September, a few weeks after the Wyoming Massacre, Brant and his Senecas struck in another quarter, this time in the Mohawk Valley itself. Brant led 150 braves and 300 Tories in a dawn assault on German Flats, a pretty little village where Herkimer, New York, now stands. Fortunately, the inhabitants, who expected the attack, had enough warning to remove themselves to safety, but their homes and barns were reduced to ashes and their horses, cattle, and sheep were driven back to the Indian town of Unadilla, fifty miles away.

Such a brutal onslaught invited revenge, and the settlers took it on October 8. It was the story of German Flats in reverse. The Indians, being warned, fled hurriedly, leaving corn, dogs, cattle, and furniture. Their homes—no wigwams, but stone and frame houses—were burned, except for one unaccountably spared, along with a sawmill and a grist mill.

Now the Senecas were outraged, but autumn was drawing to a close, and they were on their way to winter quarters at Fort Niagara when they encountered Captain Walter Butler, John's son, with 200 Rangers, bent on mischief in Cherry Valley, a village about fifty miles west of Albany, near Otsego Lake. This town, whose fort had been the product of Lafayette's professional direction, was defended by the 7th Massachusetts regiment, under Colonel Ichabod Alden. Neither the Colonel nor his men knew anything of Indian warfare, which is the only way one can excuse Alden's carelessness in failing to put a guard on an old Indian trail, one of three accesses to the village.

Along that trail, in the early morning of November 11, came Butler and Brant, with their Tory and Indian contingent. There was a heavy fog to cover them, and under its protection they began to attack houses, dividing the work among them. In one house alone they massacred the owner, his mother, wife, brother, sister, three sons, a daughter, and sixteen soldiers billeted there. Before the morning's bloodshed was done, thirty innocent villagers were murdered and every house in the village burned. The fort, thanks to Lafayette's skill and care in building it, was too strong to be taken.

That was virtually the end of the year's depredations; but as soon as the weather grew warm again in the spring of 1779, Brant was on the warpath once more, burning, pillaging, and scalping. It had been said that Brant disclaimed any responsibility for the bloodshed at Cherry Valley, but no one believed him, especially when it was well known that his Senecas, in close league with the Butlers, were continuing to ravage the villages of the Mohawk Valley and of nearby Pennsylvania.

123

So thorough and widespread had these depredations become by late spring that the alarm of the whole border was communicated to General Washington himself, who saw that if the New York and Pennsylvania frontier were abandoned, the Hudson Valley itself would be once more endangered. Plainly, a counteroffensive against the Indians of the Six Nations would have to be mounted at once.

Washington planned the strategy himself, giving the execution of it to Major General John Sullivan, a mercurial Irishman who never lacked dash and daring. The supreme commander's orders were unequivocal. He called for "the total destruction and devastation of their settlements and the capture of as many prisoners of every age and sex as possible. . . ." He wanted the country of the Six Nations not to be "merely *overrun* but *destroyed*."

The campaign to accomplish this was to be three-pronged. Sullivan was to lead a column up the Susquehanna to the New York border, while General James Clinton struck across the Mohawk Valley down Otsego Lake and the Susquehanna, and Colonel Daniel Brodhead was to direct an advance from Pittsburgh up the Allegheny. Altogether there were nearly 4000 men involved in the counteroffensive, the largest frontier army to be put in the field.

It was a spectacularly successful campaign. Sullivan's and Clinton's forces met as they had planned, built a fort at Tioga, and late in August took the offensive. They had first to defeat a small army of Indians and Tories who took a stand near the present Elmira, New York. Brant's Senecas and Butler's Greens did their best, but at last they had to give in to superior numbers. When it was over, the white men demonstrated themselves to be as savage as the savages. A young New Jersey lieutenant wrote in his journal that they found the bodies of two dead Indians whom they "skinned from their hips down for boot legs; one pair for the Major and the other for myself."

Then Sullivan's army moved down the valley, through the country of the Senecas, Cayugas, and Onondagas, laying waste the country with great thoroughness. They cut down orchards and burned the grain. They burned the Indians' houses with abandon, the fine ones and the hovels alike. In one village every house was burned but one, which was left standing for the benefit of an old squaw and a crippled boy who had been left behind. Other soldiers, full of youthful spirits, fastened the door of this house from the outside and set the building afire, burning the helpless inmates to death.

By October 15, Sullivan considered his work completed and wrote home to John Jay, then President of Congress, that he had destroyed forty towns, 160,000 bushels of corn, and an unknown but vast quantity of vegetables. In all the country of the Six Nations, he reported, one town remained standing. The only part of his assignment he had failed to carry out was the collection of prisoners as hostages. There were a few he might have taken, but their mutilated bodies lay in the dead villages.

While Sullivan was carrying out his assignment, Colonel Brodhead enjoyed a remarkable success of his own in Pennsylvania. With 600 men he marched up the Allegheny Valley over terrain far more difficult than anything Sullivan had confronted, and penetrated as far as the New York border. The scattering of Mingoes, Munsees, and Senecas who tried to hinder his progress were simply brushed aside. Brodhead's men burned several hundred houses and destroyed 500 acres of corn. By the time they returned to Fort Pitt, they had marched 400 miles in 33 days without losing a single man, an unexampled feat for the times.

But the government's success against the Indians was only to be measured in the statistics of physical destruction. For one thing, Sullivan's failure to take prisoners meant that the Indians had succeeded in preserving their numbers virtually intact, as had the Tories. This offset the undeniable fact that the Iroquois had sustained a severe blow as the result of Sullivan's campaign, which had not only considerably lowered their military reputation but had discouraged them more than any other reverse they had suffered. As they contemplated their burned villages, they must have seen in the ruins the twilight of the Confederacy.

By virtue of his campaign, Sullivan had deluded himself and the   125 government into believing that the Indian troubles were over. Washington's comfortable estimate in October, 1779, that the red men were "disconcerted" and "humbled" only emphasized that even this great leader did not really understand the Indians, a failing he shared with his fellow commanders, British and American. By contrast, the Tory leaders understood them very well, neither underestimating nor overestimating their value as allies.

The evidence that Sullivan had failed in his success was the flaming border itself, from the Mohawk to Kentucky, which was in turmoil until the end of the Revolution. More immediately, Brant had needed only the winter to recover from the autumn's disaster before he was ready to fight again, although it had been a terrible season for the Indians. They huddled in Fort Niagara under British protection, utterly destitute; without the aid and comfort of their redcoat allies, they would have perished. Consequently, they emerged in the spring feeling closer than ever to the British, and filled with a raging desire to revenge themselves on the Americans who had devastated their lands.

The motives of the Tories in carrying on the fight were more obscure, especially in the case of the Butlers and the Johnsons, who were certainly not moved by undying loyalty to the king. It would have been as much in their ultimate interest to side with the Americans if all they wanted was to retain their rich lands in the valley. The conclusion is inescapable that they were much more adventurers than they were British patriots.

In Brant, however, they had an exceptional leader who not only was fighting for the cause of the Indians but loved the king as well. He had been raised as a British subject, in a manner unknown to Iroquois chiefs—or to any Indian chief, for that matter. A good deal of this he owed to Sir William Johnson, who had been a most loyal subject of His Majesty in spite of his Irish origin. Johnson had recognized early the superiority of the young Mohawk and seen to it that he was educated in English at a school in Lebanon, Connecticut. There the founder of Dartmouth College, Dr. Eleazar Wheelock, was his tutor and worked with him in the translation of religious books into Mohawk. Eventually Brant went to England, where Romney painted his portrait, James Boswell entertained him, and he was presented at court.

Nevertheless, Brant remained an Indian and went home to be a leader of his people. He could hardly help being intensely loyal to the British, however, and believed sincerely that the British interest was the Indians'. He was loyal to the Johnson family, too. Not only had he worked closely with Sir William and later served as Guy Johnson's secretary, but his beautiful sister Molly had become William's wife, at least by Indian law and probably by civil law as well, and had given him eight children.

As the real leader of the Tory-Indian border war against the Americans, Brant was fighting hard for both the British and his people. He was capable, almost in the same breath, of English civility and the most primitive savagery, but it was the savagery by which he was remembered.

In retrospect, it is sad to see so much ability wasted. Not only had Brant been unable to resist Sullivan, but when he emerged again in April of 1780, with his heart full of vengeance, he was the leader of a cause doubly lost. His British allies were no longer a threat from Canada or from the northwest. The Confederacy was a broken instrument. Tories and Indians together could still spread terror and bloodshed, but there was no hope of any significant action. It could only be a war of hatred in the Mohawk Valley.

With John Johnson, Brant continued to sweep up and down the Valley, burning and destroying, until the fall of 1781, when an American expedition under Colonel Marinus Willett, a thoroughly experienced frontier fighter, defeated a Tory and Indian force at Johnstown and pursued the survivors relentlessly all the way to Oswego. That, for all practical purposes, ended the war along the Mohawk.

Farther west, however, it was a different story. There the dominant figure was George Rogers Clark, only twenty-three and already a veteran Indian fighter when the Revolution broke out. Clark saw at an early date that Kentucky, wide open to attack by

127

Indians and British alike, could only be saved by conquering the northwest, meaning in this case Vincennes, Detroit, and Michili-mackinac.

How he did it is one of the Revolution's truly memorable tales, particularly the heroic story of his capture of Vincennes. By means of masterly strategy, bold fighting, and even bolder diplomacy among the Indians who would listen to him, Clark seized control of the Illinois country and greatly weakened the strength of the Shawnees and Delawares, his most determined red foes. Probably he would have gone on to take Detroit and complete his grand plan of conquest if the coldblooded massacre of ninety Christian Indians of the Moravian towns in Ohio had not stirred up the tribes for miles around, especially the Delawares.

This brutal episode at the little village of Gnaddenhutten was perpetrated by a band of Pennsylvanians, who were not the worst sufferers from border warfare in the west. The whites who lived below the Ohio River had been kept in a worse state of terror than the settlers of western Pennsylvania. Somehow the most violent atrocities occurred in Kentucky, where the Cherokees and Shawnees showed deep resentment over the loss of their hunting grounds. Their depredations had begun long before Concord and Lexington; the war only served to intensify their struggle to hold what belonged to them.

But their war parties had spilled over into Pennsylvania, where atrocities were already a daily affair and the settlers had organized an armed band to exact vengeance. If they had met and slaughtered an armed Indian war party, it would have been regarded as only another incident in the war, but these white men chose for their victims the peaceful inhabitants of a Moravian Christian village who had taken no part at all in the Revolution. The massacre of these innocents—men, women, and children—was senselessly brutal, and it angered the very tribes Clark had taken so much trouble to pacify. Not even the news of Yorktown could stay their vengeful hands.

Colonel William Crawford, an old friend of Washington's, was first to feel their wrath. His party of 300 men were cut to pieces on the Upper Sandusky in June of 1782, and the captured Crawford was tortured so horribly that he begged the notorious renegade, Simon Girty, who watched it all, to end his suffering with a bullet.

This small victory was only a preliminary skirmish. A month later the largest number of Indians collected in a single body during the war, 1100 of them, invaded Kentucky and moved toward Wheeling. It might have been a major move, although a hopeless one, except that the fear of Clark was so great it caused the defection of all but 300 of the Indian army. Those that remained swept on until they met a force of Kentucky frontiersmen at Blue Licks, on August 19. Colonel Daniel Boone, who was one of the little body of Americans, counseled waiting for reinforcements, but he was overridden by the hot-tempered Kentuckians, who insisted on advancing toward what proved to be a disaster.

It was an expensive victory for the Indians. Clark mounted a counteroffensive and descended on the great Shawnee town of Chillicothe, which he burned. He destroyed five other towns of the tribe, along with a quantity of corn and other provisions. As always, the loss of food was a severe blow, worse than the human loss of battle, and the Shawnees made no further warlike gestures, nor did the other tribes.

With the decisive battle of Yorktown, peace had come to the nation in fact if not officially. There were two places, however, where it was not yet a substantial reality. General Greene was still besieging the British in Charleston, and would do so for a year while the government forgot him. In the Old Northwest, there also remained a dangerous indecision. Clark had conquered the territory, for all practical purposes, but he had been unable to hold it. The British still held Detroit, and their alliances with the Indians were largely unimpaired.

But there was peace, nevertheless, and to all the combatants it meant something different. For the British regulars, it meant that they could go home and leave the troublesome colonies to the Americans. They left behind their posts in the northwest and Canada and the south an encircling ring of potential trouble for the victors.

For the frontiersmen, peace meant that they could go back to their burned cabins and ruined fields and begin the process of settle-ment all over again, resuming their inevitable westward march.

For the Indian, peace meant that he was free to go back to his devastated villages or anywhere else as long as it was not to territory the white man wanted for himself. Now he stood alone, bereft successively of his powerful French and British allies, facing the naked power of a new nation from which he had learned to expect nothing but deception, hostility, and aggression, whose ablest and wisest leaders had advocated exterminating him.

The Indian did not know it, but the era of Manifest Destiny had begun.

7

THE NEW NATION'S WAR
AGAINST THE INDIANS

The end of the Revolution settled nothing as far as the Indians were concerned. Their grievances against the colonists were as serious as ever, and the fact that General Washington had become President Washington meant little to the red inhabitants of the Ohio Valley, who had lost their faith in white fathers, whether French, British, or native born.

North of the Ohio, in 1790, there existed all the ingredients needed for an explosion. With the Six Nations at last reduced in power, the Miami and Wabash tribes had become the chief troublemakers. From the close of the Revolution until October, 1790, it was estimated that these and other tribes had killed, wounded, or taken prisoner nearly 1500 men, women, and children along the Ohio and its tributaries. They had, moreover, stolen at least two thousand horses, and taken other property in the total amount of $50,000.

There were, besides, constant irritating attacks on boats navigating the midwestern rivers. One of the worst of these occurred in April, 1790, when a Major Doughty, en route to visit the Chickasaws on government business, encountered four canoes full of Shawnees and vagabond Cherokees on the Tennessee River. The Indians waved a white flag and were welcomed aboard by the major and his fifteen men, who gave them presents and parted with them an hour later after a friendly conversation.

No sooner had they shoved their canoes off into the river than the Indians turned abruptly and poured a murderous volley into Doughty's boat. The soldiers returned the fire; but before the Indians escaped, eleven of the major's men were dead or wounded.

When he heard this news, and similar stories, Washington's patience came to an end. He moved quickly to end what he considered a potentially dangerous situation, now that England and Spain seemed about to go to war, using the Mississippi as their corridor, with all that might mean in the further stirring up of Indian tribes. The President therefore instructed Major General Arthur St. Clair, as Governor of the Northwest Territory, to outfit an expedition against the Indians. St. Clair accordingly summoned 1500 troops at Fort Washington, now Cincinnati, and put them under the command of Brevet Brigadier General Josiah Harmar, who had fought with Pennsylvania troops during the war.

While he was dispensing punishment with one hand, the new President offered friendship with the other. For the first time in the history of the new nation, a band of Indians came to New York, the temporary capital, and visited the President. Washington did not love Indians, but he treated these twenty-nine head men of the Creek nation, accompanied by the noted half-breed leader Alexander McGillivray, with interest and courtesy. Henry Knox conducted the negotiations with them, which resulted in a solemn treaty giving Georgia certain disputed lands but protecting Indian hunting rights in another territory.

While the treaty was being concluded, Washington helped entertain the Indians. He gave them a reception at his residence, ordered a formal military review for them, and went with them on a visit to the ship *America*, which had just come back from a voyage to Canton, China. Other residents of the capital appeared astonished to discover that Indians were human. Fisher Ames, of Massachusetts, wrote with surprise that McGillivray was "decent and not very black." Abigail Adams thought him "grave and solid, intelligent and much of a gentleman. . . ."

132

Major General Arthur St. Clair.

At the conclusion of the treaty, Washington signed it himself and shook each chief's hand. Once more the victim of wishful thinking, he wrote to Lafayette that the treaty "will leave us in peace from one end of our borders to the other." In dispatching Harmar to deal with the "outlaws," he did not intend the destruction of the Indians, as he had during the Revolution. Rather, he remarked to Lafayette, "the basis of our proceedings with the Indian nations has been, and shall be *justice*, during the period in which I may have anything to do in the administration of this government."

By November, the President was increasingly doubtful that Harmar had been the right man to send against the Indians. There was no word from him directly, but disquieting rumors arose at home that he was a heavy drinker. Moreover, Washington learned that St. Clair had sought to reassure the British, who still held their fort at Detroit, that the American force was not marching against them, a piece of information the President concluded correctly that the British would relay immediately to their Indian friends.

This was, in fact, true. Harmar had set out with 300 Federal troops and 1133 militia, sending a force of 600 Kentucky militiamen ahead as a reconnoitering party. These men found themselves following a trail of burned villages as the Indians withdrew slowly, drawing the white men deeper into their territory. When a scouting party of 210 men sought to catch up with them, they turned around, and although outnumbered, frightened the raw militia into precipitate retreat and nearly cut off the regulars who stayed to fight.

Near the destroyed chief village of the Miamis, the Indians turned again and this time attacked Harmar's army with overwhelming strength of their own. More than 150 of the general's men fell dead. The Indian loss was severe enough that they permitted Harmar to retreat with his dead and wounded, a circumstance which led the general in his official report to represent the affair as a victory, although it was a decisive defeat, produced by sheer incompetency.

Washington undoubtedly suspected the truth, and so did a disappointed Congress, which demanded a court of inquiry. Harmar stuck to his story, however, when he appeared before the court, which not only completely vindicated him but asserted that he deserved "high approbation" rather than censure. Perhaps it was conscience that impelled Harmar to resign little more than a year later.

Arthur St. Clair now took the field, superbly unprepared for what he was commissioned to do. Washington, knowing that St. Clair knew nothing of wilderness fighting, gave him the warning he had given to other embryonic frontier commanders: Beware of surprise. The governor listened and offered a plan of his own. He wanted to establish a post 135 miles north-by-west from Fort Washington, at a place known as the Miami Village, an act intended to serve the double purpose of impressing the Indians and warning the British.

The proposal was adopted, and St. Clair was recommissioned a major general, his wartime rank, which made him the ranking officer of the active army. He was instructed to proceed to the Miami Village with 2000 men and supporting artillery, "establish a strong and permanent military post at that place," and then to "seek the enemy" and "endeavor by all possible means to strike them with great severity."

The whole problem of Indian affairs was a matter for debate in Philadelphia, the new capital. Most people in the government believed that a final settlement with Britain would end the trouble in the Ohio Valley, where the posts still held by the English were a constant annoyance, while the Creeks in the South could be pacified if Spain stopped supplying them with powder and arms from Spanish Florida. Washington's policy was to strengthen existing ties with friendly tribes, and at the same time hammer the resisting nations into submission—the task he had entrusted to St. Clair. Jefferson favored a tougher policy. He believed that the Indians, as a whole, first had to be given a "thorough drubbing," after which "liberal and repeated presents" to them would keep the nations pacified. Washington, who neither loved nor trusted Indians, nevertheless sought a permanent solution in a firm inclusive peace, and the prevention of encroachment on lands that were indubitably the property of the red men.

But once more the President had sent the wrong man. St. Clair

135

left Fort Washington on October 3, 1791, and began building small forts on his way to the Miami Village. As he made this slow progress northward, his army began to disintegrate because of the bad planning that had gone into the expedition. Arms and supplies were inadequate, and the militia, which comprised two-thirds of the force, had not been paid its regular monthly rate of three dollars, nor had they bargained to engage in such nonmilitary duties as building forts—on short rations, at that.

The result was a steady trickle of desertions, and departures of militiamen whose terms of enlistment had run out, until only 1400 men remained a month later on the afternoon of November 3, when the army encamped on one of the upper tributaries of the Wabash, a hundred miles north of Fort Washington. By this time St. Clair's incompetence as a commander was painfully evident to the officers accompanying him who had any experience. He would not accept the advice of these officers, and plainly he had no idea of how many Indians were likely to oppose him or of their whereabouts.

If he had known the caliber of the chief who faced him, he would have had good cause to be alarmed. Little Turtle, the Miami leader, whose Indian name was Michikinikwa, was as renowned for his skill in war as he was for his oratory. There were few more important chiefs in the Old Northwest. During the Revolution he had been of considerable help to the British, and the new advance of settlers after it ended had made him all the more hostile to Americans. It was Little Turtle who had brought about Harmar's defeat, and now he confronted St. Clair with a powerful force of Miamis.

The American camp had been well chosen; no one could have criticized St. Clair on that score. It stood on commanding ground, behind a creek, with artillery in the center. The militiamen had been stationed on the other side of the creek, where they spent the afternoon flushing Indians from the underbrush.

Next morning, a half-hour before sunrise, as the troops on the near side of the stream were being dismissed from parade, firing suddenly broke out on the militia side, and in a moment these raw recruits, frightened and utterly disorganized, were storming across the water into camp, where they caused so much confusion that a fatal delay occurred before ranks could be formed.

In a few more minutes the Americans were nearly surrounded and virtually helpless, although the regulars were standing firm and the cannon had been manned. It was an old story. The soldiers stood mostly in ranks and were slaughtered; the Indians fired from cover and were extremely difficult to hit. St. Clair's men fought bravely, and counterattacked with courage when they were ordered, but it was clear that they would be killed and scalped to the last man if they fought it out.

After three hours of combat, this fact was apparent even to St. Clair, and he ordered a retreat. He himself had been ill and could not get on or off a horse without help, but he did his best to organize a proper withdrawal. St. Clair had no illusions about what happened. "It was, in fact, a flight," he wrote candidly in his report of the battle. The Indians pursued them for about four miles, then turned away and permitted the 580 survivors to reach safety.

It was a defeat of the most humiliating character. Thirty-nine officers were dead and twenty-one wounded; the total casualties were more than 900 men. The cannon were gone, and so was most of the equipment—abandoned on the field. "The most disgraceful part of the business," St. Clair lamented, "is that the greatest part of the men threw away their arms and accoutrements, even after the pursuit . . . had ceased. I found the road strewed with them for many miles. . . ." In short, this was the worst military defeat suffered by the white men at the hands of Indians since the massacre of poor Braddock's redcoats.

News of the disaster had trickled back to Philadelphia unofficially by December 8, and next day the town's newspapers carried a story that was substantially correct. St. Clair's official report reached Washington's hands that night. Legend says that when he read it he lost his temper, swore at St. Clair, and stomped up and down the floor. That would have been completely out of character for Washington, who had long ago learned to control his temper. He

137

might get red in the face and walk out of a session of Congress, as he had done in New York, but he was not given to tantrums, although the news from the West was enough to justify one.

In reality, the President had no time to give the report more than a hasty glance because guests were beginning to arrive for Martha's usual Friday night levee, and he had to play his official role until they were gone. Then, indeed, it may well be surmised that he used strong words and strode up and down in some agitation when he reopened St. Clair's dispatch and read the dire message that began, with admirable candor:

"Yesterday afternoon, the remains of the army under my command got back to this place, and I now have the painful task to give you an account of as warm and as unfortunate an action as almost any that has been fought, in which every corps was engaged and worsted, except the First Regiment. That had been detached. . . ."

Washington made no attempt to conceal the bad news from the public. With the honesty that so endeared him to them, he had St. Clair's report published, right down to the last grisly fact. Nevertheless his critics in the press, notably Benjamin Franklin Bache's *General Advertiser*, popularly known as the *Aurora*, began to question the right of Americans to invade Indian lands, especially when it was so expensive in lives and money.

Gradually the clamor over the conduct and outcome of the campaign died down. St. Clair could not be subjected to a court of inquiry, which he asked, because there were no officers of sufficient rank to pass judgment on a major general. The House of Representatives ordered an inquiry of its own, and successive hearings completely exonerated St. Clair. Nevertheless, he resigned his commission.

But now there was pressure for peace with the Indians. Most people appeared to think that would be assured by an army of adequate size, the creation of which was the President's next step. There was a political scramble for the command of this army, and the major general's plum went at last to the impetuous and hot-headed Anthony Wayne, the "Mad Anthony" whose exploit in

Standing Them Off. *From a painting by Charles Schreyvogel.*

capturing Stony Point by night in July, 1779, had made him one of the Revolution's popular heroes.

Wayne had been living much of the time at his unsuccessful rice plantation in Georgia, on which his Dutch creditors eventually foreclosed, but he had come up to Congress in 1791 as Georgia's representative. A year later his seat had been declared vacant when his election and his residence qualifications were disputed. The new command, therefore, was a welcome assignment.

While Wayne was slowly building his army in 1792 and 1793, first at Legionville, Pennsylvania, and later near Fort Washington itself, he remained contemptuous of the government's peaceful gestures toward the Indians. Wayne thought no peace was possible. He believed a decisive battle would have to be fought before the Indians of the Northwest Territory gave in, and he was right.

By April, 1793, there was widespread unrest among the tribes, not alone in the Northwest but in the South as well, where Spanish and English agents were at work stirring up trouble. There was increasing hostility among the Creeks, the Seminoles were intermittently on the warpath, and the Chickasaws divided their time between fighting the Creeks and fighting the white settlers. The President made a strong appeal to the Chickasaws for peace, because he believed their help would be needed in case the government found itself involved in a war with the Creeks and Cherokees.

As for the Northwest, the government was ready to make a final attempt at negotiation, and proffer the peace pipe once more to the Ohio tribes at a great council in Sandusky. Commissioners were sent out from Philadelphia for this purpose, and Wayne was instructed to hold himself in readiness for the outcome. Much depended, said Thomas Jefferson, on this "last effort for living in peace with the Indians."

The council was scheduled for the early part of June, but it was July 31 before the chiefs made an appearance at the camp of the commissioners. They immediately demanded that the frontier be established at the Ohio River, as it had been in the agreement at Fort Stanwix in 1768. That was the old boundary, and there was no chance whatever that the government would agree to it. The commissioners waited two weeks more in the hope that the chiefs would make some other proposal that would at least form the basis for negotiation, but the only further word from the Indians was a repetition of their demand, this time in the form of a written ultimatum. In disgust, the commissioners departed for home.

Thus the great Sandusky conference, from which Jefferson and Washington and Knox had expected so much, in the end was no more than a single brief conversation. There was no recourse now but war—a climactic effort which Washington considered the last and best effort he could make to secure the Northwest frontier.

It was too late for a fall campaign. When Wayne got the news that negotiations had collapsed, he marched his three thousand men from Fort Washington northward, along St. Clair's old route, until he reached the southwest branch of the Maumee, where he built a fort which he named Fort Greenville (or Greeneville), in honor of

his old comrade and commander in the Revolution, General

Nathanael Greene. There he passed an uneasy winter, beset by desertions, expiration of enlistments, and incipient sedition among his officers.

In spite of these difficulties, Wayne conducted his campaign with masterly skill. He employed delaying tactics which drew Little Turtle into making a strategic error, one of the few in his career. Instead of seizing his chance to isolate Wayne in the spring of 1794, Little Turtle chose to make a sudden attack on the outpost called Fort Recovery, on June 29. It was repulsed with heavy losses, and a good many discouraged Indians went home.

After this failure Little Turtle seems to have realized, with his customary shrewdness, that this time the Indian nations faced a white general of resource and talent, and he foresaw ultimate defeat. He had tried to secure substantial help from the British, but perceived they were ready with urgings and a few supplies while reluctant to commit any men. Consequently, Little Turtle began advocating peace. He used his considerable eloquence in an effort to convince the other chiefs, but they were still boasting of past successes and in no mood to listen.

It was poor repayment for the many victories and the wise leadership he had given them, but the rebuff may have been in good part the result of Little Turtle's unfortunate personality. He was not popular with the other chiefs. Six feet tall and customarily morose, he stalked about in an arrogant and arbitrary manner, treating his more naïve fellows with some contempt. Like so many other exceptional leaders, his frequent contacts with white civilization had left him halfway between the two cultures. At the massacre of St. Clair's men he was said to have worn deerskin leggins and moccasins, a blue petticoat falling halfway down his thighs, and a European waistcoat and surtout. On his head, it was reported, was an Indian cap decorated with more than two hundred silver brooches and reaching halfway down his back. Two rings were in each ear, the upper part of each made of three silver medals the size of a dollar and the lower part made of quarters. These contraptions fell twelve inches from his ears, so it was said, and in his nose he wore three jewels "of wonderful pattern."

His fellow chiefs may well have been jealous of such elegance. In any case, they took his advice on peacemaking with a chill disdain, and soon Little Turtle had lost his high place in council and his command of the warriors as well. Thus the Indians deprived themselves of the one man who might have saved them from impending defeat. His place was taken by Turkey Foot, a chief of lesser talents.

Meanwhile, Mad Anthony was making his preparations for battle with more patience and care than he usually exhibited. He made a deliberate effort to pacify the British so that they would not give the help the Indians confidently expected, and which Little Turtle alone among the chiefs had given up. He was so successful that Turkey Foot could count only a few Canadian militia and volunteers to help the 2000 tribesmen he assembled for the approaching showdown.

The two armies met near the rapids of the Maumee at a place called Fallen Timbers, so named because the ground was littered with trees thrown down in a wild confusion, probably caused by a tornado, and affording ideal cover for an army.

These were no inexperienced troops that Wayne brought to the moment of decision. Seeking to avoid the common and fatal error of other wilderness commanders, he had drilled his men skillfully in everything he knew about forest warfare against an Indian enemy, until they were virtually perfect in the art.

Arrived at Fallen Timber, he took a leaf from the Indians' book of warfare and delayed his attack. Turkey Foot, expecting the assault momentarily, held his warriors in readiness for three days. By that time a large part of them had to retire a little way to fill their empty bellies, while the others, half-starved, remained behind. Then, using the favorite Indian weapon of surprise, Wayne suddenly fell upon the momentarily disorganized savages.

The result was panic and flight. Wayne pursued the Indians to the gates of the British fort of Maumee, where the commander had promised them sanctuary in case they were defeated. What bitterness must have gripped the Indians when the commander refused to open the gates. Even as they stood outside the stockade, clamor-

General Anthony Wayne.

ing for admission, Wayne's men came up and cut them down without mercy.

It was a disaster for the Indians as bloody as, and far more decisive than, the one that befell St. Clair. Wayne had lost only 38 men, with a hundred or so wounded, while the Indian losses, never revealed as usual, were tragically great. Moreover, the humiliating defeat broke the Indian spirit as nothing else could have done. It was twenty years before the Ohio confederation of tribes recovered from it. To add a final, crushing blow, Wayne burned all of the Indian settlements, destroyed the crops, and laid waste more than five thousand acres of their lands.

Turning to diplomacy, he then convinced the beaten chiefs that their cause was absolutely hopeless, and that they might as well sign a conclusive peace treaty. He was, of course, entirely correct. Jay had concluded the treaty with Great Britain, the Indians could expect no more help of any kind from the British, and without that help, Wayne argued accurately, they could not hope to fight the new American government.

Utterly disheartened, the chiefs agreed. On August 3, 1795, eleven hundred chiefs and warriors gathered with the American peace commissioners at Fort Greenville and signed a peace which ceded a territory comprising all of the present state of Ohio and part of Indiana.

Little Turtle was one of those who signed the treaty, but he took no joy in his vindication. Nor was it the last of the treaties he signed. In time he became a peacemaking go-between for President Harrison, and ultimately a popular Indian hero among the Americans, who were quite ready to forgive his iniquities now that they had his lands. He became something of a celebrity, traveling about the country and meeting such other famous people as Volney, the French philosopher, and the Polish hero Kosciusko, who gave him gifts. Often he employed his gift of eloquence, on one memorable occasion in 1801 appearing before a committee of Friends, in Baltimore, to protest the introduction of whiskey into Indian country.

As he came closer to the white man's ways, his influence with his own people declined, yet he was able to keep the Miamis from joining Tecumseh's confederacy, which was the next chapter in the Indian wars. The chiefs who prophesied that his alliance with the whites would bring him to no good end proved to be correct. In the end, Little Turtle fell victim to a white man's disease, gout, and in spite of treatment from the army surgeon at Fort Wayne, died of it (or more likely, its complications) on July 14, 1812.

The Treaty of Greenville ended Indian resistance in the Old Northwest. The scene of conflict in the long war shifted elsewhere. But at the place where the decisive Battle of Fallen Timbers had been fought, the Indians had the last word—even though it came from the white conqueror. In August, 1885, five thousand people from Michigan, Indiana, and Ohio gathered at the battlefield, near Toledo, Ohio, to celebrate Wayne's great victory. They decided that day to erect a monument. Was it a matter of late conscience that impelled them to decree that the monument should arise on the spot where Turkey Foot fell dead? No one knows.

8

TECUMSEH AND HIS WAR

One of the braves who fought with Turkey Foot at Fallen Timbers was a Shawnee named Tecumseh—Tikamthi or Tecumtha in the Indian tongue, meaning "Crouching Tiger." Into his hands fell the leadership that had once been Joseph Brant's, now retired to Canada. Brant had never been able to persuade the Six Nations to ally themselves with their brethren in the Ohio Valley, and Tecumseh considered this failure a major reason for the ultimate defeat of his people. A mighty confederation, one that would embrace all the tribes from north to south in the Mississippi Valley—that was the Indians' last, best hope against the rising flood of white migration. So believed Tecumseh, and to that dream he devoted his splendid talents.

Tecumseh was no ordinary tribal sachem. He is sometimes called "the greatest Indian who ever lived," a title also given generously to a half-dozen other leaders, but in any case he was an admirable, even a magnificent, figure.

As usual, the circumstances of his birth, which took place about 1768, are clouded. Some authorities say he was born near Springfield, Ohio; Indian tradition says it was Old Chillicothe, now Oldtown, Ohio. It was said later that he was part white, but his mother was probably a Shawnee and there is no doubt that his father was the Shawnee chief Pucksinwa, who died at the battle of Point

147

Tecumseh Saving Prisoners.

Pleasant in 1774. Tecumseh himself, although a very young boy at the time, is said to have served with the British.

After the Revolution, Tecumseh rose quickly to prominence, not only as a warrior but also as a kind of Indian statesman. Even the settlers admired him because he refused to have any part in the torture of prisoners, and would not condone or permit, if he could prevent it, the usual cruelties. He was widely known to both whites and Indians as a man whose word could be trusted.

Tecumseh had a brother, possibly his twin, who was totally unlike him. Elkswatawa, known as the Prophet, was a mystic—a one-eyed fanatic who claimed he spoke with the Great Spirit and could perform miracles on his own account. Where Tecumseh was a man of noble appearance, of formidable dignity, and a superb orator, the Prophet was a drunken neurotic who spoke in the half-hysterical voice of revelation from a face depraved enough to belie everything

148

he said. The Shawnees, his own people, took little stock in his supernatural powers, but he was widely believed elsewhere. This Prophet was, in fact, without honor in his own country.

Something more than blood held these men together. Tecumseh saw in his brother the keeper of tradition, the man who preached the old ways that would make Indians everywhere conscious of their traditions and the necessity to preserve them. The Prophet, for his part, undoubtedly visualized a holy war in Tecumseh's idea of a great confederacy, and believed his brother to be the true leader who could make it all possible.

These two lived for a time in a Delaware village, in Indiana, but by 1808 the pressure of white settlement had driven them farther into Indian territory, among the Potawatomies and Kickapoos. With their followers, they settled in time on the Wabash, near the mouth of the Tippecanoe. There they established a town, called Tippecanoe but later to be known as Prophet's Town, in which liquor was forbidden and the traditional ways were exalted by the fiery Elkswatawa.

The white settlers began by misjudging the brothers' alliance. They considered Elkswatawa as the man to be feared and watched, perhaps remembering the Delaware Prophet's influence. They were undoubtedly impressed by the Spartan life the brothers were trying to establish at Tippecanoe, where surprising success was reported in persuading the inhabitants to abjure rum and to be hard-working farmers who lived on what they earned.

Tecumseh did not spend much time in Tippecanoe. He was on the trail, selling his idea of confederation from Wisconsin and Minnesota to the Gulf of Mexico, and at the same time arguing the cause of all Indians with leaders of both the United States and Britain.

He made an impressive appearance, and he had logic on his side. Tecumseh maintained that no land could be rightfully sold or ceded unless all the tribes agreed to it, because the land was owned in common by the Indians, rather than being the property of any one tribe. The Treaty of Greenville, he pointed out, was the best proof

149

of this, because there the government had negotiated with the assembled tribes and guaranteed to all of them, as a people, the land which had not been ceded to the whites.

The whites were already aware that they had made a mistake in this respect. William Henry Harrison, then governor of the Northwest Territory, declared frankly when he came to office at Vincennes that he was "at once determined that the community of interests in the lands amongst the Indian tribes, which seemed to be recognized by the treaty of Greenville, should be objected to." He had frequent conferences with Tecumseh on this and other subjects. Both were strong-minded men, and they recognized each other as the important figures in their part of the country.

Tecumseh's mind ranged far beyond the old argument about the ownership of land. If the Indians could be united in their common interest, he foresaw, they could establish a great state of their own, centered in the Ohio Valley and the Lakes, which would be a buffer region between English Canada on the north and the United States on the east. It was not a new idea; some white men had already thought of it. But noble as it was in conception, it was foredoomed to failure—not only by the congenital inability of the Indians to submit themselves to the discipline that union demanded, but also by the irresistible force of American nationalism, which nothing could have stayed. The most that could be said for Tecumseh's grand plan was that it represented the first attempt of the Indians to adapt to white civilization. If it could only succeed for a little while, Tecumseh believed, the Indians might save themselves from being debauched by the white men, and thus eventually escape being destroyed.

Another flaw in Tecumseh's undertaking was his profound misjudgment of the English. He thought their long friendliness with the Indians would lead them to support a new state and respect its borders. They permitted him to believe it, because it suited their interest to favor anything that might stir up the Indians against the Americans and thus contribute to their own expansion. The issues between the two countries were not yet settled; they would be

150

shortly in the War of 1812, and unwittingly, Tecumseh was playing a part in that imminent drama. The English were using him, as they had always used the Indians; they had no real faith whatever in his master plan.

Tecumseh himself had implicit faith. He had the examples of Pontiac and Joseph Brant before him, and he had something of the zeal and fury of his brother to drive him on. "It is my determination, nor will I give rest to my feet until I have united all the red men," he told Governor Harrison. Already, in Tippecanoe, he had collected a nucleus of more than a thousand Shawnees, Delawares, Wyandots, Ottawas, Ojibwas, and Kickapoos. From the village he traveled up and down the country, sounding the call of union and revolt. One white observer reported that his voice "resounded over the multitude . . . hurling out his words like a succession of thunderbolts."

Governor Harrison had concluded, by 1811, that Tecumseh, and not his brother, was the man to watch. "The implicit obedience and respect which the followers of Tecumseh pay to him," Harrison wrote, "is really astonishing and more than any other circumstance bespeaks him one of those uncommon geniuses, which spring up occasionally to produce revolutions and overturn the established order of things. If it were not for the vicinity of the United States, he would, perhaps, be the founder of an Empire that would rival in glory Mexico or Peru. No difficulties deter him."

By this time Tecumseh's unflagging zeal had brought his plans for an organized uprising close to maturity. If he could only be more certain of the British, and bring a few more wavering tribes into line, he would be ready to strike. He despaired of negotiation. Harrison had been busy undoing the spirit and the letter of the Greenville treaty, as he had promised, by making separate treaties of cession with individual tribes. By 1811 he had negotiated at least fifteen of them.

To secure British help, Tecumseh went to Canada frequently to consult, and they abetted his plans with gifts of arms, ammunition, and clothing. For such help Tecumseh was grateful. He told the 151

British in 1810: "You, Father, have nourished us, and raised us up from childhood. We are now men, and think ourselves capable of defending our country."

To the tribes he was trying to persuade to join him, he proclaimed: "Our fathers, from their tombs, reproach us as slaves and cowards. I hear them now in the wailing winds." Those who heard these words from the tall visitor must have been impressed, but still Tecumseh hesitated. He was not sure of his allies, and he was not at all certain of British armed help.

Meanwhile, however, events were moving to a climax. The genesis of the resulting outburst lay in Governor Harrison's treaty of September 30, 1809, with the Delawares, Potawatomies, Miamis, Kickapoos, Wea, and Eel River tribes. It was a masterful grab. For a mere $8200 in cash and another $2350 in annuities, Harrison secured 3,000,000 acres of choice hunting grounds along the Wabash. Both Tecumseh and his brother were indignant at this barefaced fraud, but they protested in vain. Harrison pointed out blandly that the Shawnees were not even involved in the deal. He did agree to talk with Tecumseh about it.

Their meeting occurred on August 12, 1810. Told to come alone, Tecumseh appeared instead with 300 braves, armed and ready, a display that caused great alarm in Vincennes until Harrison produced a counterdisplay of two militia companies. Still, the conference was not entirely unproductive, after this inauspicious beginning. Tecumseh delivered on the first day a speech so bitter that Harrison told him to go away and come back. Next day he appeared more tractable. The governor soothed him by promising to refer his complaints to the President, and in return Tecumseh agreed to ally himself with the Americans if Harrison gave the lands back to the Indians.

Of course the governor had no such intention, and for a time matters went on as before. In the spring of 1811, however, the restless inhabitants of Tippecanoe began to plunder a few isolated houses, steal some horses, and practice the old tactics of frontier terrorizing. Harrison warned that he would wipe out the whole town if these depredations did not cease, and Tecumseh came up to

Vincennes to smooth matters. He demanded, once more, that the governor turn over the lands.

When he departed, the settlers quickly discovered by means of Harrison's excellent intelligence service that he had gone South in an effort to bring the Creeks, Choctaws, and Chickasaws into his alliance. That knowledge alarmed the settlers still further; they begged Harrison to attack while Tecumseh was gone. It was all the encouragement the governor needed, since he had already been given authority from the Federal government to act at his own discretion.

For years it was mistakenly believed, even by some historians, that the Prophet struck at the white man in his brother's absence, thus ruining all Tecumseh's hopes, but this must be qualified by the equally certain fact that Harrison provoked the attack, and indeed would have been the first to strike if the Prophet had not anticipated him. Nothing less than aggressive intention could be attached to the expedition that set out on September 26, 1811, from Vincennes. It numbered at least 900 men: 250 regulars of the 4th United States Infantry, 60 Kentucky volunteers, 600 Indiana militia, and 270 mounted dragoons and riflemen.

As he passed down the Wabash Valley, stopping to build a fort named in honor of himself on the present site of Terre Haute, Harrison sent word ahead to the Prophet demanding the return of certain stolen property and the surrender of some Indians he accused of murder. Harrison's messengers, two friendly Miamis, did not return.

Within sight of Tippecanoe, on November 6, the army stopped and a parley took place. The Prophet talked of peace, and even suggested a camp site nearby to Harrison where the army could pitch its tents while negotiations were carried on. Harrison was not fooled. He made his camp in battle array, with the baggage and supplies at the center, the troops spread out roughly in two bent lines around it, and a proper disposition of sentinels beyond them.

They were wise precautions. Just before dawn, the Prophet's warriors attacked the lines at two places, and for two hours a sharp, bloody struggle raged, while Harrison rode about on his horse, encouraging his men to stand firm, and the Prophet sat on a

153

Battle of Tippecanoe.

rock at a safe distance, presumably making potent magic that would
assure victory.

By full daylight the battle was over. Harrison's losses were
severe enough—61 killed or dying and 127 wounded—but the loss
to the Indians was incalculable. Not in lives, although it was presumed their dead and wounded far outnumbered the Americans,
but in their utter defeat. They had been repulsed, scattered, and dispersed. The Prophet had promised at a ceremony the night before
that he would charm the white men's bullets and make them harmless, a vow so convincing, the story went, that he could not restrain
the young braves from making an attack he had never really intended. This may well be doubted; the truth is probably that the
Prophet's fanaticism carried him too far. In any event, Tecumseh's
followers suffered an abrupt loss of faith. They had also lost face,
and left many dead behind them. Now they even deserted their
village and lands, leaving everything to the mercy of Harrison's
advancing troops.

As Mad Anthony Wayne had done before him, Harrison took full advantage of the opportunity. He burned all the supplies and houses in sight, which was a double blow because the summer's drought had ruined crops and driven away game. The provisions Tecumseh had carefully husbanded against the day he would need them for his grand assault were gone overnight.

When he returned from the South, Tecumseh at first was in a rage, then in a fit of deepest despondency. He blamed his brother for the whole affair, although in public he placed it on Harrison. No living creature, he declared vehemently to a council of Indian leaders the following May, could say that "we ever advised anyone, directly or indirectly, to make war on our white brothers. . . . Governor Harrison made war on my people in my absence . . . had I been at home, there would have been no blood shed at that time."

It was useless, however, to try to repair the damage. The nucleus of his alliance, the thousand warriors of Tippecanoe, were scattered. The other potential members of the confederacy, even those who had been most friendly, would never take up arms now. The dream of a united front had vanished, and all because his brother had disregarded the specific warning Tecumseh had given him before he departed: not to let himself be drawn into a battle with Harrison on any account. Superstition and fanaticism had triumphed over statesmanship.

Gloomy and disheartened, Tecumseh made his way to Canada and his English friends. There he was when the War of 1812 broke out. The British, who had a high opinion of his military talents, immediately made him a brigadier general, and Tecumseh appeared in resplendent uniform, at last the leader of trained troops.

He fought well for the British, and led his men, both white and Indian, brilliantly. For now the Indians of the Lakes and the Ohio Valley rallied once more in large numbers to the British cause, believing that this time their friends would drive the Americans out of the ancient hunting grounds and the old days would be restored. Tecumseh must have believed it too, and clung to it, furthermore, as the only hope of salvaging his dream.

155

In the late summer of 1812, he thwarted the plan of that doughty old soldier, General William Hull, the American commander at Detroit, to capture Fort Malden, the British post directly south across the river. Commanding a force of British and Indians, Tecumseh executed a brilliant ambush of the 200 men Hull had sent out under Major Thomas Van Horne, and beat them soundly, capturing at the same time a packet full of dispatches from the general to the War Department, complaining of defections in his army. These dispatches were particularly valuable to Tecumseh's superior, General Isaac Brock, the governor of Ontario, who shortly attacked and captured Detroit, again with Tecumseh's help.

The fortunes of war in the spring of 1813 brought Tecumseh once more face to face with his old enemy, General Harrison. Confronted by disaster after disaster in the opening months of the war, the American government had turned to the hardy hero of Tippecanoe and placed him in command of all the forces in Indiana and Illinois. By coincidence he was also made a brigadier general—like Tecumseh.

On April 1, Tecumseh was at Fort Malden with Colonel Henry Proctor, an officer he was coming to dislike and distrust even on short acquaintance. Proctor had spent the winter recruiting Indian allies through Tecumseh's good offices; there were now more than 1500 of them at Malden, under the command of Tecumseh and the Prophet, whose disgrace at Tippecanoe had failed to alienate his brother completely. With the aid of these braves and the 522 British regulars and 461 Canadian militiamen in his command, Proctor was ready to strike at Fort Meigs, on the Maumee River, where Harrison lay waiting with 1100 men.

Proctor besieged the fort on May 1, but it was relieved a few days later by a force from nearby Fort Defiance that drove the British back. Tecumseh would have stayed to fight, but the faint-hearted Proctor pulled back hastily to Canada.

On the way, the Indians who had been deprived of taking prisoners inside Fort Meigs took advantage of the few strays Proctor had captured and scalped twenty of them. They would have toma-hawked the others if Tecumseh, characteristically, had not pre-

156

vented it. But the incident stirred up all over again the argument about "using" Indians. The Americans had already objected to the British doing it and now the Opposition in London took up the cry against its own army, describing the practice as "injurious to the British character." The commanders in the field, on both sides, paid little attention to these pious outcries. They did whatever necessity and their own ingenuity could devise.

When he got back again to Malden, Proctor found a welcome reinforcement awaiting him—Indians in great numbers from every part of the Northwest, raising his effectives to 5000 men. That should have been sufficient to encourage him in any design he might undertake, but the colonel was an extremely cautious man. He counseled delay. Tecumseh was impatient and somewhat contemptuous; he could not understand what Proctor was waiting for, and proposed an audacious plan to trap General Henry Clay, whom Harrison had left in command at Fort Meigs.

This time, Tecumseh proposed, the British and Indians should put on a noisy sham battle in earshot but not within sight of Fort Meigs. He reasoned that Clay, thinking the besiegers were being attacked by another American force, would sally out to help and could then be cut to pieces at leisure. Somewhat reluctantly, Proctor accepted this strategy.

It was carried out on July 20, when the British and Indian force once more appeared at the mouth of the Maumee and soon were noisily engaged in their imaginary battle. As Tecumseh had predicted, the officers in the fort were taken in by the ruse. All but Clay. While the others begged him to lead them out to fight, he insisted that the battle sounds were not authentic and refused to open the gates. After a time, Proctor and Tecumseh had to give up. The Shawnee chief was particularly baffled by the failure, because he had no way of knowing why his plan had not worked. Proctor now took over and moved the army eastward for an assault on Fort Stephenson, which was situated on the Sandusky River and considered a much weaker installation.

Fort Stephenson was commanded by Major George Croghan, only twenty-two years old, an Army regular who had no more

157

than 160 men in his garrison, as opposed to Proctor's 400 regulars and several hundred Indians, supported by 2000 Indians under Tecumseh. Proctor confidently expected Croghan to surrender in the face of such overwhelming force, but the youthful major defied him and waited for the British general to attack at the fort's weakest point, where Croghan had thoughtfully concealed a masked six-pounder.

The assault developed as he had anticipated. Crying, "Cut away the pickets, my brave boys, and show the damned Yankees no quarter," Lieutenant Colonel Short led the British assault party into horrible death and maiming from the six-pounder's grape. Two charges were enough before the attackers, disheartened, drew off.

Frustrated once more, Proctor turned to Tecumseh's force, but the chief's warriors had been terrified by the cannon fire, which was a far different thing to them than braving a barrage from rifles. Neither Proctor nor Tecumseh could persuade them to charge the fort and the British general quit the field angrily, cursing his Indian allies and preparing to return to Canada. He had lost more than a hundred men killed and wounded. Croghan listed one man killed and seven others wounded.

Proctor was convinced by this time that he could not make a successful invasion of the Ohio Valley. He returned to Fort Malden with Tecumseh and said he would wait for the Americans to come to him.

As for the Americans, they had concluded that it was futile to try to invade Canada, at least until their Navy had secured control of Lake Erie. They sat back and waited for that signal event, which Commodore Perry was soon to bring about, in September, 1813. While Perry was winning his famous victory, Tecumseh set out from Fort Malden in a canoe, and paddled far into Lake Erie, trying to get a firsthand look at the engagement, but he could see the ships only dimly in the distance and hear the firing of their guns. He was not close enough to determine the outcome, and Proctor, who heard the bad news later through his dispatches, dared not tell him. He was afraid that Tecumseh's Indian army, which now numbered about 3500 warriors, might desert him.

The British commander had need of all the troops he could get, because Harrison was taking the field again with nearly 10,000 men at his disposal, including a band of 260 Indians. This formidable army, encamped on Lake Erie between Sandusky Bay and Port Clinton, also numbered 1000 mounted riflemen under Colonel R. M. Johnson, a force that had been highly successful in subduing Indians.

As he contemplated Harrison's imminent arrival across the narrow lake that separated them, Proctor's naturally cautious nature told him it would be the better part to burn Malden and retreat eastward out of danger. But how to tell the Indians? In their disillusionment, they might massacre him and his men. He tried to explain his intentions to Tecumseh, but when that proud chief heard Proctor's words, he turned on the bumbling general who was about to seal the ruin of all his hopes and lashed at him with bitter contempt.

"You always told us," he said, "that you would never draw your foot off British ground; but now, father, we see you are drawing back. . . . We must compare our father's conduct to a fat animal, that carries its tail upon its back, but when afrighted, he drops it between his legs and runs off. . . . You have got the arms and ammunition . . . sent for his red children; if you have an idea of going away, give them to us. . . . Our lives are in the hands of the Great Spirit. We are determined to defend our lands, and if it be his will, we wish to leave our bones upon them."

But Tecumseh's braves were not possessed of his indomitable spirit. They had no intention of staying behind to meet Harrison's army without British help. Besides, Proctor appeased them by promising to make a stand somewhere else. Consequently, only three days before Harrison's force landed, the British burned Fort Malden and began their retreat.

The retreat turned into a close pursuit as soon as Harrison discovered Proctor's intentions. The British were badly hampered by the wives and children of the Indians, and it was soon apparent that they would either have to abandon their Indian allies, which might be twice as dangerous, or make a stand. The Indians had already attempted one at Chatham, but it was a halfhearted effort that was dissipated at the first exchange of volleys.

Choosing between the horns of his prickly dilemma, Proctor concluded that it would be the least disastrous to make a stand. For the last time, this unfortunate general had made the wrong decision. He compounded it by choosing an indefensible piece of ground. His army had been fleeing northeastward into Ontario along the Thames River, and he elected to form his battle lines near the missionary village of Moravian Town, on level ground that had almost no natural protection except for a little swampland.

The outcome could hardly be in doubt. Colonel Johnson, convincing the doubtful and orthodox Harrison that the rules of warfare would not be irretrievably shattered if the engagement began with a cavalry charge, loosed half his mounted riflemen in a devastating assault on Proctor's open-order ranks. With the other half, he attacked Tecumseh's Indians. The British regulars were soon overcome, but Tecumseh was a far different proposition.

The chief had taken advantage of what little protection the swamp afforded him, and Johnson's men had to dismount because the horses could not find a solid footing. The battle quickly became a hand-to-hand combat of the most desperate fury and savagery. These were Kentuckians whose families and friends had long known the torture and terror of border warfare; they were out for blood, with no quarter asked or given. As for the Indians, they fought with the desperation of men who have nowhere else to go, and no doubt they were inspired by the reckless courage of Tecumseh himself, who fought shoulder to shoulder with them.

There are those who believe that Tecumseh, sick at heart by the failure of his dreams and the perfidy of the English, and convinced that defeat was inevitable, was determined to throw his life away in the battle. If that was his intention, it was sadly fulfilled. He was struck down at the height of the combat. Seeing him fall, the Indians were seized with panic and despair, and fled in bloody confusion. Proctor, observing how the day was going, deserted it hastily in his carriage, which he soon had to abandon, and hid in the woods for his life.

Battle of the Thames and the Death of Tecumseh.

The exultant Kentuckians, prowling the deserted battlefield, found a body they thought was Tecumseh's and cut strips of skin from it as souvenirs, or as razor strops, whatever their fancy. Indian survivors later disputed this story and declared Tecumseh's body was spirited away that night and buried by his people.

Thus the last great leader of the Northwest died, as nobly as he had lived. It had cost the United States $5,000,000 and the employment of 20,000 soldiers to deal with him, in his time, which may have been some satisfaction to his restless ghost. But he could only have mourned at the desolation of everything he had worked so hard and long to achieve. The Battle of the Thames effectively ended Indian opposition in the Northwest for good. The Americans now controlled everything except for the British post on Mackinac Island.

But in another quarter Tecumseh had left behind him a heritage of unrest and hatred that brought new leaders and new armies on the stage, and wrote another inglorious chapter in the brief history of the new American government.

161

9

THE CREEK WAR

The country of the Creeks lay in northeast Alabama, at the junction of the Coosa and Tallapoosa rivers, where they unite to form the Alabama River. In President Washington's time the Creeks had been troublesome, but until Tecumseh visited them they had come to be regarded as "good Indians." They were farmers, for the most part, living under the honest and benevolent rule of an exceptional Indian agent, Colonel Benjamin Hawkins.

They could not, however, resist the eloquence of Tecumseh when he first arrived, just before the Battle of Tippecanoe. He came to them as a kinsman, he said, honestly believing that his mother had been a Creek, although later authority surmises that she may well have been of his own tribe.

One of the young chiefs who was stirred by Tecumseh's dream of an Indian confederacy stretching from the Lakes to the Gulf was a remarkable man named William Weatherford, who was only one-eighth Indian. He boasted a romantic ancestry. His great-grandfather, Captain Marchand, had brought the French flag from the Gulf to upper Alabama and established a fort there. Lonely so far from home, he had taken a Creek girl to live with him (as bride or mistress, no one knows) and she had borne him a beautiful girl named Sehoy.

Marchand was murdered by his own mutinous soldiers, and

Sehoy was thrown into a world that proved to be hospitable. She married a Creek chieftain, but her father's fort fell into the hands of the English, whose young Captain Tait appropriated the lovely half-breed as his mistress. Tait entertained one day a wandering and wealthy Scottish adventurer, Lachlan McGillivray, whose gaze fell upon Sehoy. When he departed, Sehoy went with him into a life of luxury in the house McGillivray built for her on the Coosa River, from which he conducted a highly profitable fur trade.

One day the trader tired of his rural American idyll, and even of the charming family his native mistress had borne him. He left them all abruptly and returned to Scotland, never to be seen again by any of them. Among those he left behind was an extraordinary son, Alexander McGillivray, who had been educated at Charleston in the father's fond belief that he should grow up as a white man.

But Alexander, says the historian Marquis James, "fell back upon the culture of the wigwam and a career in which French urbanity, Spanish deceit, Scotch thrift and Creek savagery saw him far—his boast being that no Yankee blood polluted his veins." His career was fantastic: a British colonel in the Revolution, a Spanish civil servant later on under Miro, and at last into the sphere of Andrew Jackson, meanwhile establishing himself as the Creeks' principal chief and the protector of the Seminoles. When he died in 1793, he was a brigadier general in the United States Army, and a rich man with a fortune of $100,000. He was given a Masonic funeral in the garden of a Spanish gentleman of Pensacola, where he was buried.

Alexander left behind him a half-sister named Tait, who married Charles Weatherford, a Scot trader. When their sons were old enough to understand their mixed-blood ancestry, the trader gave them a choice between two ways of life. One of them, John, decided to remain white and forthwith disappeared from history. The other was William, who chose to be a Creek and soon rose in their councils as Red Eagle. It was William who heard Tecumseh's words and awakened to his vision.

His time was not yet, however. He was not leader of the Creeks, although he was a proud, courageous warrior, a splendid horseman, and tall and dignified in bearing like Tecumseh himself.

Andrew Jackson. *From a painting in New York City Hall.*

The Shawnee great man returned in October, 1811, more eloquent and magnetic than ever, bringing his brother the Prophet
with him. Several thousand Creek warriors gathered to hear Tecumseh at the tribe's chief village, on the peninsula formed by the con-
fluence of the two rivers, known as the Hickory Ground. The
Indian agent, Colonel Hawkins, who had done so much for the
Creeks that he had incurred the enmity of powerful men in Washington, wisely did not try to combat Tecumseh's influence. He
withdrew quietly, while the Shawnee led a war dance and the
Prophet made himself busy with the Creek medicine men.

Most of this effort was lost on the old sachems of the tribe, who
could see little virtue in casting their lot with northern Indians
who, after all, had never done anything for them. But the young
men, whose imaginations had already been captured by the Tecumseh legend, were enchanted by his magnetic presence. The Prophet
did not hesitate to help his brother by playing on the superstitions
of his hosts. He had learned from the British that a comet was about
to appear in the sky, and he spread the word that a fiery omen
would soon convince the waverers that the Great Spirit meant them
to go to war.

Tecumseh inadvertently aided this appeal to the supernatural. In
presenting a bundle of wampum and the war hatchet to Big Warrior, a noted Creek chieftain, he could not help seeing the reluctance and timidity with which they were accepted. He blazed
in sudden anger, as he frequently did: "Your blood is white! You
have taken my talk, and the wampum and the hatchet, but you do
not mean to fight. I know the reason. You do not believe the Great
Spirit has sent me. But you *shall* know. From here I shall go straight
to Canada. When I arrive there I shall stamp the ground with my
foot and shake down every house in this village."

It was an empty threat, made in the heat of the moment, but
one may imagine the consternation of the Creeks when, soon after
his departure, an earthquake occurred in Alabama. A good many
doubters were ready to take up the hatchet at once.

166   Yet, in spite of comets and earthquakes and all of Tecumseh's

brilliant oratory, the influence of Colonel Hawkins was so strong that relatively few of the Creeks decided for war. There were not more than 4000 of them, armed so poorly with such faulty firearms that they had to resort to bows and arrows and clubs after the first volley. They were hardly formidable, but they frightened the settlers on the frontier.

The white man's alarm proved to be well-founded. Peter Mc-Queen, a Creek half-breed, was first to break the peace, leading 350 men down to Pensacola, where he got some necessary ammunition from the Spanish governor. A party of settlers attempted to intercept the Indians on their way home, but they were defeated at Burnt Cork Creek, and McQueen, encouraged, went back for more ammunition and supplies.

Weatherford now assumed command of the Creeks and immediately perpetrated a deed so atrocious, although it was not entirely of his doing, that what had been a minor bush war became an occasion for the United States government to take official action.

On the Alabama River, a little way north of the Florida border, about five hundred people had sought refuge from the Indian terror in the fortified home of Samuel Mims, a Creek half-breed. Called rather grandly Fort Mims, the place was guarded by seventy Louisiana militia commanded by another half-breed, Major Daniel Beasley. The refugees inside included rich half-breed planters, a body of white farmers, and a few Negro slaves.

Weatherford approached Fort Mims on a hot August 29, 1813. Negroes outside the stockade who caught glimpses of the savages creeping up through the tall grass reported what they had seen, but Beasley called them liars and ordered them bound to whipping posts, to be flogged next day.

The morning of the 30th dawned, excessively hot. The whole establishment at Mims was lazy and relaxed, while only 400 yards away Weatherford and 1000 Creek warriors lay in the grass. When the drum beat for the noon meal it was also a signal to the Indians. Yelling ferociously, they charged the fort. Major Beasley was struck down and clubbed to death as he tried to push the stockade

167

Massacre at Fort Mims. *From a painting by Chappel.*

door shut against the stubborn sand that had carelessly been allowed to drift against it. Captain Dixon Bailey, another half-breed, took command and rallied the garrison.

But it was too late. Weatherford's warriors swept into the first enclosure, cut down two companies of soldiers, murdered the helpless slaves as they stood tied to the whipping posts, and laid siege to the second enclosure, which Bailey was defending with every man and woman who could stand.

It was an uneven struggle, in a sense. The defenders had guns; the Creeks were reduced to arrows. Probably the Indians would have quit after three hours of fighting, and they did in fact withdraw, but Weatherford would not permit them to retire. He urged the warriors to another assault, utilizing an old Indian trick—flame-tipped arrows to set every house in the stockade on fire. Those who were too frightened to come out and face the Indians were burned alive. Bailey himself suffered a severe wound, and with that, resistance abruptly ended. The Creeks rushed in, half-crazed, determined to kill every white person in the place.

Weatherford was aghast at the madness he had unloosed, but his warriors were completely out of control. Men, women, and children were hacked to death unmercifully. It was a scene of frightful brutality in the steaming August afternoon. By sundown, 400 of those who had sought the fort's protection lay dead.

News of the massacre shocked and angered the South, and there was a demand that Weatherford and the Creeks be exterminated immediately. General Andrew Jackson was in bed at his home in Nashville when he heard of the Fort Mims tragedy; he was recovering from wounds he had suffered in an altercation with his friend, Colonel Thomas Hart Benton. Yet it was Jackson who was assigned to march out against the Creeks.

Old Hickory, as his men had recently come to call him, was too weak to sit on a horse, but he sent Colonel Coffee with 500 dragoons into Alabama at once, and he prepared to follow with a militia division. On October 7, haggard and with his arm in a sling, the indomitable Jackson set out with his infantry from Fayetteville, just above the Alabama-Tennessee line, and marched them thirty-two miles in nine hours. He established a supply post he called Fort Deposit, and taking from it only enough bread for two days and meat for six, he moved rapidly with his army toward Ten Islands, on the Coosa River. There he learned that the Creeks were nearby in Tallassahatchee, and on November 3 he prepared to attack the town.

Jackson was a confident man, as well as a bold and ambitious one. When the Cherokee chief, Pathkiller, reported to him that Weatherford had threatened to annihilate any Indians who failed to support him, the general replied succinctly: "Brother, the hostile Creeks will not attack you until they have had a brush with me; & that I think will put them out of the notion." He told one of his aides bluntly that he would die rather than retreat.

His strategy at Tallassahatchee was familiar but effective. He meant to send out an advance body to seduce the Indians into an

169

attack, and after they had been drawn into a semicircle, the ends of it would close and the Indians would be trapped. On the first trial this plan worked perfectly, and Jackson achieved an easy victory: 186 Indians killed, as against 5 Americans killed and only 41 wounded. Davy Crockett, who took part in the slaughter, boasted later, "We shot them like dogs." And Jackson reported with satisfaction: "We have retaliated for Fort Mims." Whereupon he built a fort at Ten Islands, which he named Fort Strother.

Four days later he was off again toward Talladega, thirty miles away, where a band of friendly Indians were reported beset by the main force of Creeks. Jackson hastened with the utmost speed to the relief of the besieged allies. He arrived on November 9 with 1200 infantry and 800 horsemen. Employing the same tactic of encirclement, he was less successful because some of his militia turned and ran when the Creeks tried to break out of the circle. A few Indians escaped, but they left 290 dead behind them, while Jackson got off with 15 dead and 85 wounded.

In the interval before another engagement, Jackson faced a crisis in his own camp, when the militia whose enlistments were to expire on December 10 prepared to leave, homesick and hungry and in a mood to mutiny if Jackson tried to prevent them. The camp was completely without provisions, and Jackson himself was so racked with dysentery that he could scarcely stand. When a starving soldier asked him for something to eat, the general drew a handful of acorns from his pocket. "I will divide with you what I have," he said.

Supplies came at last, but in late November the mutinous troops were ready to set off for Tennessee. Jackson, ill as he was and with his arm still useless in a sling, rested the barrel of his musket across his horse's neck and declared he would shoot the first man who made a move toward home. The soldiers stared sullenly at him, but they yielded in the face of their general and the few loyal troops who stood by him. The musket, Jackson found out later, was in such bad condition he could never have fired it.

His troubles, however, were far from over. In December, while Weatherford recovered from his successive defeats and rebuilt his forces, the general was still contending with his recalcitrant militia, whose enlistments had expired by this time and who would not listen to staying. Ill and irritable, Jackson did not help matters as his patience wore thin and his naturally abrasive temperament was abused by the recalcitrant militia. He persuaded them to stay long enough until promised replacements reached Fort Strother, but when the 1450 relief troops marched in from Tennessee—"as fine looking Troops as you ever saw"—the general learned that *their* enlistments would be up in ten days, and they had no intention of staying either. Another relief detachment, this one of cavalry, was coming on apace by forced marches, but they too were volunteers, and when they met the columns of men streaming north from Strother, they turned around and went with them. No wonder Jackson, lying ill in camp, exclaimed in despair: "Can it be true what I hear?"

Left with only 500 men, his back to the wall, and ordered to retreat by his superior, Governor Blount of Tennessee, Jackson flatly refused to budge. He wrote indignantly to Blount: "And are you my Dear friend sitting with yr. arms folded. . . . recommending me to retrograde to please the whims of the populace. . . . Let me tell you it imperiously lies upon both you and me to do our duty regardless of consequences or the opinion of these fireside patriots, those fawning sycophants or cowardly poltroons who after their boasted ardor would . . . let thousands fall victims to my retrograde."

Then, having pictured for Blount the dreadful consequences of a retreat that would release 5000 Creeks, Choctaws, and Cherokees upon a defenseless countryside, the general concluded with a withering burst of eloquence:

"Arouse from yr. lethargy—despite fawning smiles or snarling frowns—with energy exercise yr. functions—the campaign must rapidly progress or . . . yr. country ruined. Call out the full quota—execute the orders of the Secy of War, arrest the officer who omits his duty. . . . and let popularity perish for the present. . . . Save Mobile—save the Territory—save yr. frontier from becoming drenched in blood. . . . What retrograde under these cir-

171

cumstances? I will perish first."

Spurred by this letter and new instructions from the War Department, Blount hastened to obey, but before fresh troops could come, most of those who had remained with Jackson went home too, and for a few desperate, anxious hours he held Fort Strother with 130 men.

Eight hundred recruits arrived to relieve the crisis. Jackson gave them no opportunity to wish themselves back in Tennessee, but led the bewildered militiamen toward Weatherford's encampment on the Horseshoe Bend of the Tallapoosa River. The general had little confidence in these troops; he saw that they were undisciplined, men and officers alike, but he had no other choice. In three days, however, he had marched them seventy miles from Fort Strother. In the evening of January 21, they made camp at Emuckfaw Creek, three miles from the Creek stronghold.

Weatherford's scouts had warned him of Jackson's approach, and the Creek leader decided on the traditional before-dawn attack. With another white leader it might have been successful, but Jackson was far more talented than the others. He had kept his men under arms and ready all night, anticipating an attempt at surprise. When the assault began, they were instructed to fire at the flashes from the Indians' guns until daylight came, when Jackson threw in his meagre reserves—one company—and ordered a charge. The Indians retired toward their stronghold, Tohopeka.

This, too, was a feint. Weatherford hoped to delude the Americans into stretching out their lines, but when he saw that they meant to wait for him, he prepared to attack. Again Jackson outguessed him and charged first. Once more the Creeks withdrew, and on that indecisive note the battle ended. Jackson dared not stay to pursue the matter. He was seventy miles from his base, nearly surrounded by a superior force, and confronted by an Indian fortress too strong to storm.

Prudently he decided to retreat, and so he did next day, moving through the silent winter landscape with the Creeks as silently dogging his footsteps. Jackson was certain they were only waiting the proper moment to leap, and he reasoned correctly that they would do it while he was crossing a broad river, Enotachopco Creek, where he would have little protection and a steep bank to climb on the other side.

Superb tactician that he was, Jackson planned to take advantage of this seeming disadvantage by laying a trap for the Indians. The men were to cross in three columns, and if the attack came, the rear ranks were to hold off the Creeks while the front of the columns were to wheel left and right, recross the river above and below, and encircle Weatherford's warriors.

The strategy would have worked as he had planned it, except that the rear guard did not stand firm. Led by their colonels, the right and left columns retreated in precipitate haste, tumbling down the bank into the water. Only one brave officer and twenty-five men of the center column stood between the retreaters and the tomahawk.

In this crisis, Jackson was truly heroic. Above the noise of battle everyone could hear his mighty oaths and orders; a good many men preferred to turn and face the Indians rather than face Jackson later. The general put his retreating colonels under immediate arrest and took charge of the confused columns himself. One of his men wrote afterward: "In showers of balls he was seen performing the duties of subordinate officers, rallying the alarmed, . . . inspiriting them by his example. . . . Cowards forgot their panic. . . . and the brave would have formed round his body a rampart with their own."

It was a glorious retreat, if not a victory, and Jackson's two earlier skirmishes at Emuckfaw and Enotachopco were presented to the government as victories. Nevertheless, it could hardly be said in January of 1814 that the United States had made much headway against the Creeks. Other American forces in the east and south had done no better than Jackson in dispersing the rebels.

In December, Weatherford had narrowly escaped capture, which would certainly have ended the war. General Claiborne had penetrated as far as the chief's own town, Econochaca, which he burned, killing thirty Indians in the process. Sitting astride his horse on a bluff high above the river, directing the defense, Weatherford was suddenly surrounded. Setting an example for later generations of motion-picture heroes, the Creek chieftain leaped his horse from the bluff into the river and escaped uninjured.

A month later, Claiborne's army had shrunk to a mere sixty men through expired enlistments—the besetting trouble of all the American commanders—and he was made not only impotent but in actual danger of annihilation.

Up to this point the United States had sent more than 7000 troops into Indian territory, and in six months of activity had succeeded in killing 800 Creeks, but still Weatherford was at large, and the nucleus of his little army was intact. Jackson knew well enough why the white men had not been successful. Aside from the matter of green militia who went home at the first opportunity, the question of supply was all important. No one could be expected to march a large body of men into the interior of Alabama unless they were well supplied.

By February 6, however, he felt considerably more confident. Fresh troops had arrived from home, and he now had 5000 in his command, including what he prized most—600 regulars of the 39th United States Infantry. With these regulars as the hard core of his forces, Jackson was confident he could shortly end the Creek War. He wasted no time in putting the iron of professional discipline into the nonregulars, not excluding his officers. A major general and a brigadier general were sent home arrested and in disgrace. A seventeen-year-old boy who defied the Officer of the Day with his rifle was court-martialed and summarily executed; the boy had been in the army less than a month. There was no further talk of mutiny or going home, and no more lack of discipline.

Events now moved to a climax. Weatherford had taken his stand with 900 men, accompanied by 300 women and children, in his stronghold at Horseshoe Bend, which was protected on three sides by the river and on the fourth side by a high log rampart. At the break of day on March 27, 1814, Jackson appeared before this wilderness fort with a field army of 2000 men. Both leaders had obviously staked their fortunes on the outcome of this battle, but it was an uneven match. For all his considerable talents, Weatherford was no match for Jackson.

The Indian leader had provided himself with a fleet of canoes to carry his men away in case of trouble, but Jackson's first act, after he had surrounded the fort, was to send a detachment of scouts who swam the river under fire and removed the craft. Then, lining up 1000 men to attack on the land side, Jackson issued his order of the day: "Any officer or soldier who flies before the enemy without being compelled to do so by superior force . . . shall suffer death." With that, at half-past ten in the morning, the preliminary bombardment began.

Jackson held the charge until the Creek women and children were led safely across the river out of range. Then the drums burst out with the long roll signaling the charge. A major of the 39th was first to appear on the Indians' ramparts and fell dead. A step behind came a tall young man, another blue-clad regular, who waved his sword and led the charge. It was Ensign Sam Houston, who lived to fight another day.

The Creeks fought with consummate bravery, but their clubs and tomahawks could scarcely prevail against American bayonets at close quarters. They broke and ran. Those who chose the river were picked off by sharpshooters. The others formed into little bands and took advantage of the rugged terrain to fight back desperately.

What had begun as a battle was turning into a merciless blood bath. Even the squaws and children were not entirely spared in their place of assumed safety: several were killed, an incident that Jackson later passed off as an accident. Still the Indians fought on and would not give up, although the ground was littered with their bodies. It was not their traditional conduct, and Jackson could not understand it. At the midpoint of the bloody afternoon, he offered to protect all those who surrendered.

Jackson could not know that what was inspiring the Creeks to extraordinary valor was their conviction that the Great Spirit would give them victory, a belief supported by the medicine men who moved among them at the height of the battle and promised the tide would turn when a cloud appeared in the sky as a sign to

175

them. In the lull that occurred as Jackson made his surrender offer, a cloud did appear. A great cry went up from the Creeks and they renewed the battle with inspired fury. But the cloud meant no more than a brief shower. As darkness began to fall, only one small party of Indians remained in a small covered fortress buried in a deep ravine. They scorned surrender and beat off a storming party. Jackson resorted to the Indian trick of the flaming arrows and burned them alive in their stronghold. With that, the battle ended.

Of the 900 warriors who had faced the Americans in the morning, 557 lay dead on and about the peninsula, while 200 others were at the bottom of the river. Of those who remained alive, many were wounded. Jackson's losses were only 49 killed and 157 wounded of his own men, and 18 killed and 36 wounded among the friendly Cherokees who had helped him. They, of course, did not count.

But where was Weatherford? Jackson did not find him among the slain or the prisoners. Could he have escaped? The general could hardly control his exasperation when he thought that the instigator of the Fort Mims massacre might have reached the safety of Spanish Florida.

Weatherford had indeed escaped death at Horseshoe Bend, but only because he was not present on the day of battle. This was not due to any act of cowardice, but only because of sheer chance. Having prepared his fort for an expected assault, he had gone elsewhere for a brief inspection, apparently not expecting Jackson to attack as soon as he did.

The general hunted his quarry in vain, and at last retired to the Hickory Ground. There, a few days later, as Jackson was about to leave his quarters, he was confronted by a tall, light-skinned Indian who was naked to the waist and dressed below in badly worn buckskins and moccasins.

"General Jackson?" this figure inquired.

"Yes."

"I am Bill Weatherford."

Jackson's response is disputed. Some say he remarked simply, "I

Interview Between General Jackson and Weatherford.

am glad to see you, *Mr.* Weatherford." Others assert he cried out indignantly: "How dare you show yourself at my tent after having murdered the women and children at Fort Mims?"

In any case, the two men went inside. Only Jackson's aide, John Reid, was present to hear what transpired, and he wrote later: "Weatherford was the greatest of the Barbarian world. He possessed all the manliness of sentiment—all the heroism of soul, all the comprehension of intellect calculated to make an able commander. You have seen his speech to Genl Jackson . . . but you could not see his looks & gestures—the modesty & yet the firmness that were in them."

The following conversation is variously reported, but it went substantially as follows:

"I am come to give myself up," Weatherford said. "I can oppose you no longer. I have done you much injury. I should have done you more . . . [but] my warriors are killed. . . . I am in your power. Dispose of me as you please."

"You are not in my power," the general answered. "I had ordered you brought to me in chains. . . . But you have come of your own accord. . . . You see my camp—you see my army—you know my object. . . . I would gladly save you & your nation, but you do not even ask to be saved. If you think you can contend against me in battle, go and head your warriors."

"You can safely address me in such terms now," Weatherford said. "There was a time when I could have answered you; there was a time when I had a choice; I have none now. I have not even a hope. I could once animate my warriors to battle, but I cannot animate the dead. My warriors can no longer hear my voice. Their bones are at Talladega, Tallushatches, Emuckfau, and Tohopeka. I have not surrendered myself without thought. While there was a single chance of success, I never left my post nor supplicated for peace. But my people are gone and I now ask it for my nation, not for myself. General Jackson, I have nothing to request . . . [for] myself. . . . But I beg you to send for the women and children of the war party, who have been driven to the woods without an ear of corn. . . . They never did any harm. But kill me, if the white people want it done.

"I look back with deep sorrow, and wish to avert still greater calamities. If I had been left to contend with the Georgia army, I would have raised my corn on one bank of the river, and fought them on the other. But your people have destroyed my nation. You are a brave man. I rely upon your generosity. You will exact no terms of a conquered people, but such as they should accede to. Whatever they may be, it would be madness and folly to oppose them. If they are opposed, you shall find me among the sternest enforcers of obedience. Those who would still hold out can be influenced only by a mean spirit of revenge. To this they must not and shall not sacrifice the last remnant of their country. You have told our nation where we might go and be safe. This is good talk, and they ought to listen to it. They *shall* listen to it."

Jackson showed himself a magnanimous victor, on this single occasion. He poured out a cup of brandy for Weatherford and the two men exchanged promises. For his part, the general said he would help the women and children. The Creek leader said he would try to preserve the peace. Then they shook hands and Weatherford left the tent, strode past the flabbergasted soldiers outside, and vanished into the brush. If he was seen again, history does not record it.

Late in April, Jackson returned to Tennessee, confident that order had been restored in the South. The Secretary of War instructed him to dismiss all his troops except for a thousand men and take a rest. But the news from the South was not reassuring. There were reports of armed British marines inciting the fierce Seminole Indians of Florida, who had welcomed the Creeks when they fled from their defeat.

"We ought to be prepared for the worst," Jackson wrote to the Secretary of War.

The worst was soon to come.

10

THE FIRST SEMINOLE WAR

Early in July, 1814, Jackson once more stood on Creek Territory, at the same Horseshoe Bend where the Indians had met their terrible defeat. The Creeks had believed it was sacred ground, on which no enemy, white or red, would dare to tread if he hoped to live. Jackson had profaned it by seizing Weatherford's little fort, which the Indians had called Fort Toulouse, and renaming it for himself.

Now he had returned and peremptorily summoned the chiefs of his humiliated enemy to a council. He was blunt about it, as usual. "Destruction will attend a failure to comply," he told them. They came, starving and lean, yet full of dignity, so that Jackson was impelled to write home to his wife: "Could you only see the misery and the wretchedness of those creatures, perishing from want of food and Picking up the grains of corn scattered from the mouths of horses." But not once did he hear them complain.

Jackson spoke first at the council, addressing himself to the loyal Creeks, who had rejoined those of their tribesmen who had not fled to Florida. "Friends and brothers," he said, "you have fought with the Armies of the United States, many of you . . . by my side." Then, turning to the defeated: "Friends and brothers, you have followed the counsel of bad men." He went on to explain that the war had been an expensive one for the government, as of course it

181

had, and then he advanced the novel proposition that the Indians would have to pay for it in land, which would also be an indemnification against future wars. He produced the terms of the proposed peace treaty and had the document read by an interpreter.

Weatherford had expected generosity toward a conquered people. What his tribesmen got was a splendid example of the white man's avarice, and his utter contempt for justice where the Indian was concerned. The blandly arrogant robbery of the peace terms Jackson proposed set a pattern that would prevail for more than a century.

The treaty demanded 23,000,000 acres, which represented half of all the Creek territory, now three-fifths of Alabama and a fifth of Georgia. About half of this land belonged to the friendly Creeks whom Jackson had addressed as "Friends and brothers," and who had helped him in the fight to seize it.

It was a brutal proposition, and small wonder that the Creek chieftains momentarily forgot their hunger in astonishment and dismay. They sent two of their chiefs, Big Warrior and Shelokta, to see Jackson next day, hoping to win some concessions and soften the terms. Both of these Indians did their eloquent best and moved the hearts of all the white men who heard them except Jackson's. The path Tecumseh had taken must be stopped up, he said, and the treaty's terms had to be accepted or rejected that night. Those who accepted would be considered as friends of the American government; the others would be branded as enemies. He declined to make the smallest concession.

There was exquisite irony in Big Warrior's reply, which apparently escaped Jackson. The Creeks desired, he said, to give to General Jackson three square miles of the land he proposed to appropriate "as a token of gratitude," with similar gifts to three other white men, including Benjamin Hawkins. Jackson told them he would ask the President to give him an amount equivalent to the value of the land, which he would use to clothe their destitute women and children. Oh no, Big Warrior and Shelokta protested, with straight-faced politeness, "they did not give to General Jackson land to give back to them in clothing; they want him to live on it, and when he is gone his family may have it; and it may always be known what the nation gave it to him for."

That night the treaty was signed and the chiefs went silently away, in the direction of Pensacola.

While he was concluding this disgraceful treaty, Jackson had dispatched a messenger to the Spanish commandant at Pensacola, demanding the return of two refugee Creek chiefs who had taken shelter there. Don Matteo Gonzalez Manriqué properly labeled the demand as "impertinent." Meanwhile, the messenger learned that the British were constructing a strong military base in Florida, and that units of the Spanish and British fleets were maneuvering off the coast.

Jackson did not know it, but these disturbances were only ripples emanating from far larger events, which were about to bring the War of 1812 to a rousing climax. Wellington's army, having defeated Bonaparte, had brought peace to Europe, and ten thousand veterans of the campaign were on their way to Quebec, where they expected shortly to demolish the new American nation by an invasion of the East. This was to be done in conjunction with a naval diversion off the Atlantic coast, and a major military and naval assault on the South, emanating from the rendezvous point of Jamaica.

When he learned of this ambitious plan, Jackson quite naturally forgot about the pathetic Creeks for a time. With the British Navy soon in control from Maine to the Chesapeake, Washington captured and the Capitol burned, and the cities of the East frantically fortifying, the new nation was perilously close to extinction. It was saved in the North by Commodore John McDonough's spectacular victory on Lake Champlain, which sent Wellington's veterans reeling back to Quebec, complaining that Trafalgar "was a flea bite compared to this," and causing a British officer to exclaim: "This is a proud day for America—the proudest day she ever saw."

McDonough's decisive victory was duplicated in the South by Jackson, whose equally spectacular defeat of the British at the Battle of New Orleans in January, 1815, two weeks after the Treaty   183 of Ghent had officially ended the War of 1812, saved James Madison's tottering administration.

With the British threat removed at last and forever, there remained only the problem of Florida to prevent consolidation of the nation's eastern half. But in Spanish Florida the Seminoles flitted through the swamplands, elusive and recalcitrant, allied with the remnants of the Creeks, and refusing to have any part of the government's land grab.

Negotiations for the purpose of purchasing Florida from Spain limped along from year to year. By 1817 they seemed little nearer to success than they had ever been, but the restiveness of the Seminoles once more made the Indians pawns in an international game between larger powers, as the American government sought to use the cause of pacifying the tribes as an excuse to enter the Spanish domain.

They did it with considerable circumspection, however. When Brevet Major General Gaines attacked some Seminoles a short distance north of the Florida border in the early summer of 1817, he was instructed to pursue the retreating savages into Spanish territory, if it should prove necessary, but not to be so rude as to attack a Spanish fort.

By this time there was a new Secretary of War who was more to Jackson's liking. On December 26, 1817, Secretary John C. Calhoun issued orders to Jackson to go into Georgia and there "adopt the necessary measures" to end the Indian troubles. Jackson had not approved of the instructions to Gaines. In a letter to Monroe, he proposed with his usual candor that the government should simply seize Florida while it was subduing Indians, and promised that if he were given permission, he would do the job in sixty days. Monroe gave him permission that was neither explicit nor authorized, but clear enough: "The mov'ment . . . against the Seminoles . . . will bring you on a theatre where you may possibly have other services to perform. . . . Great interests are at issue. . . ."

Jackson set out in February of 1818 to pursue those interests—and, of course, the Seminoles. On March 9 he was at Fort Scott, not far from the Florida border, and next day he took command of his army, which included 800 regulars and 900 Georgia militia, who were like most of the militia Jackson had seen before—hungry and not inclined to remain with him. The general gave them his usual treatment—short rations and hard marches. Six days later he was well into Florida and better able to assess the situation there.

The Seminoles unquestionably were in an irritated frame of mind, and Jackson was aware of the human agents who were causing it. They were refugee Creek leaders like Peter McQueen, and another chief named Francis, who had been taken to England by the British after the Battle of New Orleans, and sent home again in splendor in a brigadier general's uniform. There was also Captain George Woodbine, a British officer who would be able to retain his valuable Florida lands if he could keep the Americans out, and Alexander Arbuthnot, a Scot trader lately of Nassau, who was distinguished by his honest though profitable business with the Indians. Arbuthnot, white-haired and more than seventy years old, was the Indians' best friend and a power among them, sharing their secret councils and acting for them in their negotiations with the whites. "The Indians," he declared forthrightly and accurately, "have been ill treated by the English, and robbed by the Americans." Of the two, he thought the Americans were worst.

Jackson marched first on St. Marks, a fort near the west coast of Florida, and found it deserted by the Indians. He took one prisoner: Arbuthnot, who submitted quietly to arrest. Francis was captured trying to escape by water, along with another Creek chieftain, and both these Indians were hanged by Jackson the next day with little formality. Arbuthnot was held for trial.

Off again into the dense jungle of the Florida interior, Jackson's next destination was the village of Chief Boleck, more familiarly known as Bowlegs, 107 miles away on the Suwanee River. But again he found the Indians vanished when he reached there eight days later. The total bag was two white men: Lieutenant Robert C. Ambrister, of the Royal Colonial Marines; and Peter B. Cook, his British friend. A letter from Arbuthnot, found on one of the servants in the Englishmen's party, warned Bowlegs and the other

Billy Bowlegs, Seminole War Chief.

friends that Jackson's force was too powerful to resist. Obviously the Indians were well warned and had no intention of meeting him in battle, Jackson concluded.

Returning to St. Marks, he ordered Arbuthnot and Ambrister tried at once. The trial was a travesty. Only witnesses personally hostile to Arbuthnot for various reasons were permitted to testify, including a rival trader and Peter Cook, who had a personal grudge. On the other hand, there was no doubt—and documentary evidence was introduced to prove it—that Arbuthnot had written many letters for the Indian leaders, addressed to the British Governor in

186

Nassau, seeking arms and ammunition to fight the Americans. Arbuthnot believed sincerely that the Indians had just cause to fight, as indeed they did.

As for Ambrister, he was no more than an adventurer, a soldier of fortune who had fought and tried his luck in several parts of the world. He understood his position and promptly pleaded "guilty, and justification."

Arbuthnot made a dignified, eloquent defense in his own behalf, resting his case ". . . fully persuaded that should there be cause for censure my judges will . . . lean on the side of mercy." His judges sentenced this kind old man, whose only crime was that he had loved the Indians and tried to help them, to be hanged. Ambrister was sentenced to be shot on the first vote of the court-martial's members, but on reconsideration the sentence was changed to fifty lashes and a year's imprisonment. Jackson, however, rectified this act of mercy by restoring the original death penalty. Both sentences were carried out, and as the somber drum rolls signaled the time of execution, Ambrister sighed, no doubt thinking of the girl he had intended to marry in London when his Florida venture was over: "There, a sound I have heard in every quarter of the globe, and now for the last time."

These salutary events occurred on April 29. By May 7, Jackson was on the march again toward Pensacola, which he captured on the 28th, after only three days of siege. He ran up the flag, appointed one of his colonels as governor, and in effect annexed that part of Florida to the United States.

It was a strictly illegal act, and after Jackson had returned to Tennessee, for which he departed on May 30, the American diplomats had an extremely sticky time in accounting for his actions to the Spanish government. The irate Spaniards demanded restoration of all their forts, from Pensacola northward, as well as indemnity for their losses, and Jackson's prompt punishment.

President Monroe and his Cabinet, perspiring in Washington's July humidity, debated the matter for anxious days. Monroe was ready to disavow Jackson, and most of the others agreed with him, but John Quincy Adams argued stubbornly that what Jackson had   187 done was justified by necessity. In the end, Adams prevailed. The American government prepared a note to Spain saying that Jackson had acted for himself alone, but there was no intention of censuring him for it. The forts, however, would be returned.

Jackson was not the only one left unsatisfied by this decision. The Spanish Minister for Foreign Affairs demanded that restoration of the forts must be accompanied by public disavowal of everything Jackson had done and a suitable punishment of the general. If these things were not done, the Minister suggested, American hopes of purchasing Florida could be dismissed.

Secretary of State Adams drafted a long and powerful reply to the Spanish note, reviewing the history of Spain's rule there, which Adams termed a "narrative of dark and complicated depravity," a "creeping and insidious war." He closed boldly by threatening that the United States would not give up any forts it might take in Florida if it were ever necessary to capture them again.

Jackson himself came to Washington in January, 1819, to defend his actions in the face of what he termed "hellish machinations." These machinations were the result of political ambitions, primarily those of Henry Clay, who feared that his fellow Westerner would overshadow him.

Washington was in a turmoil while the House, suspending all other business, debated the whole Florida affair. Clay made a sensational speech attacking Jackson, but the general, sitting in Strater's Hotel and directing his campaign, marshaled a succession of friendly witnesses who defended him. In the end it was Jackson who won. By a series of votes, the House refused to condemn the arbitrary and essentially unjust executions of Arbuthnot and Ambrister; refused to sanction the preparation of a bill which would forbid executing captives in Indian warfare unless the President approved; refused to condemn the seizure of Pensacola as unconstitutional; and would not even consider preparing a bill to prohibit invasion of foreign soil without Congressional authorization unless it was necessary to pursue an enemy.

The verdict was a popular success; to the public, Jackson was a hero who could do no wrong. Not even the action of a Senate

General Jackson and Troops in Florida.

committee that issued a report highly critical of Jackson's conduct in Florida could dim the result. Monroe simply instructed his lieutenants in the Senate to delay any action on the report until the current Congress went out of existence, which occurred only a few days later.

Jackson's own defense of his actions is a fascinating example of honest if utterly mistaken logic. ". . . On the immutable principle of self-defense, authorized by the law of nature and of nations, have I bottomed all my operations," he wrote. "On the fact that the Spanish officers had aided and abetted the Indians, and thereby become a party in hostility against us, do I justify my occupying the Spanish fortresses. Spain has disregarded the treaties existing with the American government, or had not power to enforce them. The Indian tribes within her territory, and which she was bound to keep at peace, visited our citizens with all the horrors of savage war. Negro brigades were establishing themselves when and where they pleased, and foreign agents were openly and knowingly practicing

189

their intrigues in this neutral territory. The immutable principles of self-defense justified, therefore, the occupancy of the Floridas. . . ."

Thus the first manifestation of Manifest Destiny, hardly disguised as the immutable principle of self-defense.

But what, one may well ask, became of the Indians who were the ostensible reason for Jackson's invasion of Florida?

They were considered subdued, and after the cession of Florida to the United States in 1821, were no longer useful as pawns. They had escaped the burning of villages and crops, the conscienceless land grabs, and the summary executions that the Creeks had suffered in Alabama. Unfortunately, they still occupied Florida, whose previous occupants, Spanish and English, the Seminoles had considered only as tenants.

These lands could be secured to the American government by negotiation and purchase, or they could be conquered. By the time this question had to be decided, Jackson was in the White House and there was no question what the government's course would be. No question, either, that the proud Seminoles would not give in without a war.

Before that war began, however, the shape of events was clear—to all, that is, but a few Indian leaders. The Indians east of the Mississippi were to be assimilated if possible; if not, they were to be removed to the other side of the great river, unless they chose to leave their ancient homes and go peaceably. The war for the Eastern half of America was nearly over.

Two Indian leaders challenged the inevitable. One was Osceola, whose time was not yet. The other was Black Hawk.

11

BLACK HAWK'S WAR

He was born in 1767, in the great village of the Sauks, often called Sacs, which lay on the banks of the Rock River in Illinois, two miles from where it empties into the Mississippi. The city of Rock Island is there today. His mother named the boy Ma-ka-tai-me-she-kia-kiak, meaning Black Sparrow Hawk. To Americans, from President Jackson on down, he came to be known as Black Hawk.

The war that he fought could scarcely be dignified by that name. Able man that he was, Black Hawk could not hope to succeed where Pontiac and Tecumseh had failed in times much more propitious for success. But he compelled the American government to put an army in the field, an army filled with names of distinction—Abraham Lincoln, Jefferson Davis, Zachary Taylor, the sons of Alexander Hamilton and Daniel Boone, Albert Sidney Johnston, Winfield Scott. Not one of these men particularly distinguished himself in the field.

From boyhood Black Hawk hated the white man, no matter what his name might be. Growing up in the rich prairie valley of the Rock River, shadowed by the bluffs of northwestern Illinois where the Sauks had hunted and fished for centuries, he had known first the Spaniards who ruled the Mississippi from 1769 to 1804. Black Hawk recognized them as cruel men but brave. With the Sauks, Foxes, and other tribes, he depended on their bounty in the fur trade when he came down to the Spanish post at St. Louis. In that little river town he first heard of the Americans, learned how they had overthrown the Spanish, and began to hate them before he had ever laid his fierce eyes on them.

The Americans took over the fort at St. Louis in 1804, and to it that year came the doughty Indian fighter, William Henry Harrison, Tecumseh's scourge, who was now in the guise of a government agent. The treaty he negotiated there with three chiefs of the Sauk and Fox nations gave the white man all the land these people possessed east of the Mississippi—mostly in northwestern Illinois, where the Sauks had at least 700 acres under cultivation. In return the Indians got an inadequate financial consideration and a promise in writing that they could keep on hunting in Illinois, and planting their corn there, until the land was opened up to settlement. Limited as the promise was, Harrison did not believe for a minute it would ever be kept.

For the remainder of his life, the Treaty of 1804 obsessed Black Hawk. In the first place, he declared, the chiefs had not gone to St. Louis for negotiation at all. Harrison had taken it on himself to designate them as representatives of the Sauk and Fox nations, and dealt with them while they were drunk. That was a serious charge which might be attributed easily to Black Hawk's deep resentment, but modern scholarship has tended to prove it true.

But he also had a far more fundamental reason for opposing the treaty. When he wrote his autobiography several years later, he put into compelling words what all the great Indian leaders before him had been trying to say to the white man. "My reason teaches me that land cannot be sold," he wrote. "The Great Spirit gave it to his children to live upon. So long as they occupy and cultivate it they have the right to the soil. Nothing can be sold but such things as can be carried away."

His own people did not wholly agree with him; some thought him a radical. They were already imitating the white men's ways, and after the treaty was signed, they journeyed peacefully across the Mississippi River with their women and children into Iowa.

192   Black Hawk went with them, but he would not stay. He was

Black Hawk. *From a portrait by George Catlin.*

thirty-seven years old by then, and he had been a respected war
chief for ten years. He knew war because he had spent his life at it.
As a boy in the tepee of his father, he had heard over and over the
legend of Pontiac. When he was only fifteen, he had killed and
scalped an enemy, and to prove it he had painted on his ceremonial   193

blanket a blood-red hand, a sign the tribes recognized. He had become a war leader by working at it, helping his own people and the others around them to resist the tide of white settlers.

When the War of 1812 inflamed the Western lands, it was almost inevitable that Black Hawk should join Tecumseh and become one of his most faithful followers. He was at Frenchtown, Fort Meigs, and Fort Stephenson, and he may have been at the Battle of the Thames.

The victory of the Americans must have inflamed his resentment still more. When the war was over, he remained in Canada for a time, trying to achieve the impossible task of persuading the British to help him nullify the Treaty of 1804. Frustrated there, he began to travel among the tribes of the Northwest, as Pontiac and Tecumseh had done before him, hoping to form a confederacy. He, too, had a dream: a great coalition of Indians from the Rock River to Mexico, forming a hostile barrier to the further advance of the white man.

He found few allies at first. Many of the tribes were utterly disheartened, ready to make peace and carry on the profitable fur trade. Most of the Sauks, under the leadership of Black Hawk's rival, Keokuk, were settling themselves in their new country across the Mississippi and trying to adjust to a white world.

Only Black Hawk remained on the ancient lands of the Rock River valley, which he loved and did not mean to give up. Some of the Sauks stayed with him, and came to be known as the British Band, perhaps because they frequently traveled the familiar trail to the British post at Fort Malden, in Ontario, where they traded with the English and got presents from them.

So matters went until the spring of 1830, when the British Band returned from its winter hunt to the Rock River sites, where they and their people before them had always come home to build their lodges for as long as any man could remember. They found white squatters occupying the land, although it had not yet been included in any governmental survey, which was a direct violation of the Treaty of 1804. These whites had appropriated the Indian cornfields and plowed new fields among the graves of the dead.

194

Black Hawk was angry beyond measure, but he felt the need of advice. Traveling quickly to Fort Malden, he asked the military agent there what he should do. The white men's families had taken possession of his wigwams, he said, while the wives and children of his own people had to huddle on the banks of the river without shelter. While this was not a wholly accurate picture, it was true in substance, and something of Black Hawk's indignation appeared to communicate itself to the agent. The treaty had indeed been violated, he assured his Indian friend, and if Black Hawk resisted, the American government would surely see that he was fairly treated. It was the advice the British had always given to their Indian friends: Go and fight; we will encourage you.

The Indians returned, and the squatters suggested that they share the village. An uneasy summer passed, full of quarrels and small indignities visited upon the Sauk women and children, as well as more serious offenses which kept both sides on the alert. Then the Indians went away again on their winter hunt.

Returning in the spring of 1831, they found more whites than before, and Black Hawk came to the end of his scanty patience. He ordered the squatters off peremptorily, and assured them they would all be killed if they failed to obey. As a sample of what he meant, he sent his young men up and down the valley, burning an isolated cabin here and there and threatening the inhabitants.

In fright and alarm, the settlers appealed to Governor John Reynolds, of Illinois, who ordered General Edmund P. Gaines, military commander of the Western Department, to the scene and placed 700 militia at his disposal. Gaines made his report on June 20, 1831:

"I have visited the Rock River villages, with a view to ascertain the localities, and, as far as possible, the disposition of the Indians. They confirm me in the opinion I had previously formed, that, whatever may be their feelings of hostility, they are resolved to abstain from the use of the tomahawk and firearms, except in self-defense. But few of the warriors were to be seen; their women and children and their old men appeared anxious, and at first somewhat confused, but none attempted to run off.

195

"Having previously notified their chiefs that I would have nothing more to say to them, unless they should desire to inform me of their intention to move forthwith, as I had directed them, I did not speak to them, though within fifty yards of many of them. I had with me on board the steamboat some artillery and two companies of infantry. Their village is immediately on Rock River, and so situated that I could from the steamboat destroy all their bark houses (the only kind of houses they have), in a few minutes, with the force now with me, probably without the loss of a man. But I am resolved to abstain from firing a shot without some bloodshed, or some manifest purpose to shed blood, on the part of the Indians. I have already induced nearly one-third of them to cross the Mississippi to their own land. The residue, however, say, as the friendly chiefs report, that they will never move; and what is very uncommon, their women urge their hostile husbands to fight rather than to move and thus to abandon their homes."

Black Hawk and Gaines met in council a week later, but they had nothing to say to each other that had not been said before. Both were adamant. Gaines simply waited for his militia to arrive, and when they did on June 25, the Indians fled across the river, leaving the army to take possession of the village without the firing of a shot. Two days later Black Hawk appeared, under the protection of a white flag, and an agreement—it could not be called a treaty—was made. Among other things, the white settlers promised to give the Sauks a supply of corn, but as soon as the soldiers had gone, the amount they consented to part with proved so small that, as Black Hawk said later, the Sauks were compelled to cross the river and "steal corn from their own fields."

That was the prelude to a difficult winter. For two years now the Sauks had not been able to raise their own crops, and their suffering was severe. Black Hawk spent the late winter making a supreme attempt to form the confederacy of which he had dreamed. His chief supporter, so he thought, was the famed Winnebago prophet Waubeshik, or White Cloud, who readily agreed to help him. He also got promises of help from the Winnebagoes, Potawatomies, Mascoutens, Foxes, Sioux, and Kickapoos.

196

Going to Washington — Returning to His Home. *From a portrait by George Catlin.*

Encouraged to believe that his vision was on the point of fulfillment, and inspired by what he truly believed was an order direct from the Great Spirit Man-ee-do, he came back across the river in April, 1832, with five or six hundred warriors, most of them Sauks, prepared to reoccupy the old lands and drive the whites out.

The whole frontier was in terror. Hundreds of refugees fled to Chicago, and there was talk of abandoning that muddy frontier town. In their fright, the settlers imagined that what Black Hawk had hoped for was true, and a grand alliance of Indians was about to desolate the frontier.

Once more the militia were called out, and from Washington came the regulars under General Henry Atkinson to restore peace —an army illuminated by the presence of the soon-to-be famous. The hostile forces approached each other, Atkinson pausing to wait for reinforcements and Black Hawk hoping in vain for the promised help from his nearly imaginary confederacy. Only the Foxes came. "I discovered that the Winnebagoes and Potawatomi were not disposed to render us any assistance," Black Hawk observed drily, writing of his failure.

The Indians were determined not to begin the hostilities. Black Hawk sent a series of messages to Atkinson, declaring that his only intention was to make corn, and if the white men wanted to fight, they would have to attack him. That was precisely what occurred. About the middle of May, a Major Stillman, at the head of 270 men, advanced toward the Sauk camp, and as he approached, Black Hawk sent out three warriors with a truce flag. The response was brutal. Stillman took the three braves prisoners, and when Black Hawk sent out five others to look for them, the regulars set upon them and killed two. Now there was no retreat. The war was on.

Carl Sandburg has described it with the poet's eye: "And now over the rolling prairie and the slopes of timber bottoms along the Rock River, with a measureless blue sky arching over them, the red man and the white man hunted each other, trying to hand crimson death to each other. As they hunted they measured small and were hard to see, each trying to hide from the other till the instant of clash, combat, and death—bipeds stalking each other; only keen eyes could spot the pieces of the action and put together the collective human movement that swerved, struck, faded, came again, and struck, in the reaches of rolling prairie and slopes of timber bottom where the green, rain-washed bushes and trees stood so far, so deep under the arch of a measureless, blue sky."

Abraham Lincoln was one of the combatants, or at least a would-be Indian fighter, having enlisted because he was going to lose his clerk's job and intended to run for the legislature, where a war record would certainly help him. But "Captain Abraham Lincoln's Company of the First Regiment of the Brigade of Mounted Volunteers," which in the beginning had no horses to mount, never came to combat. It marched and countermarched across Illinois, part of an army of 1600 men under Colonel Zachary Taylor, but it never caught up with the war except to bury five men killed in a skirmish the day before. That was real enough, and most of the men no doubt thought it was close enough. Each of the dead, Lincoln remarked, "had a round spot on the top of his head about as big as a dollar, where the redskins had taken his scalp," while on the frightful scene "the red sunlight seemed to paint everything all over."

But if he never killed an Indian, Lincoln saved the life of one. It was an old man who wandered into camp one day, harmless and bearing a military pass, which meant nothing to the soldiers. They were ready to kill him simply because he was an Indian. Lincoln moved quickly to the old man's side. "Men, this must not be done," he said; "he must not be shot and killed by us."

"You're a coward!" one of the soldiers called out.

"If any man thinks I am a coward, let him test it," Lincoln answered quietly.

"You're bigger and heavier than we are," someone else said.

"You can guard against that—choose your weapons!" Lincoln said. There was no further argument.

In another part of the forest, Lieutenant Jefferson Davis marched with his commander, Colonel Taylor. Soon he would return to the colonel's lonely outpost at Fort Crawford, Wisconsin, where 199 he would meet and fall in love with Taylor's lovely daughter, Sarah, and marry her in two more years without her father's permission.

Meanwhile, the Black Hawk War went on, a fearful thing to read about in the nation's newspapers, where the Sauk leader was pictured as the Devil in disguise. In reality the war was a wasted effort, pathetic in its futility and the loss of good men. Slowly, through the hot suns of June and July, Black Hawk conducted a masterly retreat away from Illinois, across the swamps, forests, prairies, and rivers of southern Wisconsin. The government poured more troops into what it meant to be a war of extermination: nine companies of artillery under General Winfield Scott; another nine from the forts on the Lakes; two more from Baton Rouge. Black Hawk's only ally was the cholera epidemic that summer, which killed many more of the enemy than he could hope to. In one corps of 208 regulars, only nine were left alive.

Eventually, Black Hawk realized, he would have to turn and fight a full-scale battle. He chose to do so on July 21, at a place called Wisconsin Heights, but it was an indecisive affair, with some loss on both sides, although Black Hawk succeeded skillfully in getting the women and children safely across the Wisconsin River.

The end was in sight, however, and it came on August 1 and 2 as the fleeing Indians reached the Mississippi, near the mouth of the Bad Axe River. Black Hawk surveyed his position with growing despair. On the water stood the armed river steamer *Warrior*, barring his path to safety. Around him were suffering women and children, and warriors who were weary and starving. For the first time he understood that his struggle was hopeless. He sent 150 braves down to the edge of the water with a flag of truce. For what followed, here is the report of Captain Throckmorton, commanding the government supply steamer:

"I was dispatched with the *Warrior* alone to Wapashaw's village, 120 miles above Prairie du Chien, to inform them of the approach of the Sacs, and to order down all the friendly Indians to Prairie du Chien. On our way down we met one of the Sioux band, who informed us that the Indians (our enemies) were on Bad Axe River, to the number of 400. We stopped to cut some wood, and prepared for action.

"About four o'clock on Wednesday afternoon (August 1) we found the *gentlemen* where he stated he had left them. As we neared them, they raised a white flag and endeavored to decoy us, but we were a little too old for them; for, instead of landing, we ordered them to send a boat on board, which they declined. After some fifteen minutes' delay, giving them time to remove a few of their women and children, we let slip a six-pounder, loaded with canister, followed by a severe fire of musketry; and if ever you saw straight blankets you would have seen them there. I fought them at anchor most of the time, and we were all very much exposed. I have a ball which came in close by where I was standing, and passed through the bulkhead of the wheel-room.

"We fought them for about an hour or more, until our wood began to fail, and, night coming on, we left and went on to the Prairie. This little fight cost them twenty-three killed, and, of course, a great many wounded. We never lost a man, and had but one wounded—shot through the leg. The next morning, before we could get back again, on account of a heavy fog, they had the whole of General Atkinson's army upon them. We found them at it, walked in, and took a hand ourselves.

"The first shot from the *Warrior* laid out three. I can hardly tell you anything about it, for I am in great haste, as I am now on my way to the field again. The army lost eight or nine killed, and seventeen wounded, whom we brought down. One died on deck last night. We brought down thirty-six prisoners, women and children.

"There is no fun in fighting Indians, particularly at this season, when the grass is bright."

What had happened, as the captain's letter does not fully explain, was that Black Hawk found himself trapped between the *Warrior* on one side and General Atkinson's army on the other. Atkinson had made a forced march, leaving his baggage wagons behind, and brought his 1600 men to an exhausted halt only ten miles from the Indians on August 1. With only a few hours' rest, they attacked next day, a three-hour battle which soon turned into a massacre. Hundreds of Black Hawk's women and children, whom he had brought so far so skillfully and at such cost, were driven into the river, seeking to escape the slaughter on land, and were picked off by Atkinson's sharpshooters, who appeared to enjoy the sport. The Americans lost 27 men; the Indians lost at least 200, and very probably more.

Black Hawk himself escaped to the Winnebago village at Prairie la Cross, where White Cloud had been sending out some belated warriors and doing too little too late. There he and the Prophet decided to surrender themselves, along with Black Hawk's two sons, who had fought with him.

They went to Prairie du Chien on August 27. Black Hawk wore a dress of white deerskins the Winnebago squaws had made for him, and he was an imposing figure of a man. He and his companions surrendered to General Street, and Lieutenant Jefferson Davis took him on board the steamer *Winnebago* in chains, to be delivered to General Winfield Scott at Fort Armstrong, which stood on the island of Rock Island in the heart of Black Hawk's own country.

As he rode gloomily down the great river, Black Hawk tried to explain why he had opposed the white man so long: "We told them [the whites] to let us alone and keep away from us but they followed on and beset our paths and they coiled themselves among us like a snake. They poisoned us by their touch. . . . We were becoming like them, hypocrites and liars, adulterers and ladrones, all talkers and no workers."

But he could fight no longer. After several months of confinement at Fort Armstrong, President Jackson ordered him and his party to be brought to Washington. Sandburg describes their confrontation in the White House: "They faced each other, a white chief and red chief; both had killed men and known terrible angers, hard griefs, high dangers, and scars; each was nearly seventy years old; and Black Hawk said to Jackson, 'I—am—a man—and you—are—another.'"

Black Hawk told Jackson what he considered the cause of the war. "We did not expect to conquer the whites," he said. "They

KEOKUK
CHIEF OF THE SACS & FOXES

had too many houses, too many men. I took up the hatchet, for my part, to revenge injuries which my people could no longer endure. Had I borne them longer without striking, my people would have said, 'Black Hawk is a woman; he is too old to be a chief; he is no Sauk.' These reflections caused me to raise the war-whoop. I say no more of it; it is known to you. Keokuk once was here; you took him by the hand, and when he wished to return to his home, you were willing. Black Hawk expects that, like Keokuk, we shall be permitted to return, too."

Black Hawk may or may not have known that he was, in fact, a hostage of the United States until a satisfactory treaty had been concluded with the Winnebagoes, Sauks, and Foxes, and until Jackson decided what to do with him. The treaty came first. By it, the Winnebagoes ceded 4,600,000 acres of valuable land south of the Wisconsin and east of the Mississippi. The Sauks and Foxes gave up 6,000,000 acres. In return, the United States agreed to pay the tribes $20,000 a year for thirty years; to supply them with a blacksmith and gunsmith from among their own people, to be paid by the government; to pay the debts of the Indians; and to supply them with provisions in unspecified amounts. As a reward for the loyalty of Keokuk and the friendly Sauks who had retired from their lands peaceably, they were to be given a reservation of forty square miles on the Iowa River. It was, as the white negotiators observed, an excellent deal.

Jackson had still not decided what to do with Black Hawk and those who accompanied him, so he had them confined in Fortress Monroe, where they were treated kindly except that they had lost their liberty. But on June 4 they were released and left by steamboat for Baltimore.

Aware of the tremendous public interest in Black Hawk, the government decided to parade him through the streets of the principal cities of the East, like a captured animal. But the public, now that the danger was past, greeted him as a brave, romantic symbol of the wild frontier and treated him like a hero. Black Hawk, consequently, not only enjoyed the trip, which soon became a triumphal progress, but changed his opinion of the white man.

At a banquet given him in the Exchange Hotel, Broad Street, New York City, he replied to the principal address: "Brother: We like your talk. We will be friends. We like the white people; they are very kind to us. We shall not forget it. Your counsel is good; we shall attend to it. Your valuable present shall go to my squaw [it was a pair of topaz earrings, set in gold]; it pleases me very much. We shall always be friends."

How much the climate of the Eastern United States had changed could be judged when Black Hawk and his party called on the Seneca Indians on their reservation in upper New York State. The old Seneca chieftain, whose American name and title was Captain Pollard, urged the Sauks to go home in peace, cultivate the land, and never fight again against the white man. Black Hawk replied:

"Our aged brother of the Senecas, who has spoken to us, has spoken the words of a good and wise man. We are strangers to each other, though we have the same color, and the same Great Spirit made us all, and gave us this country together. Brothers, we have seen how great a people the whites are. They are very rich and very strong. It is folly for us to fight with them. We shall go home with much knowledge. For myself, I shall advise my people to be quiet, and live like good men. The advice which you gave us, brother, is very good, and we tell you now we mean to walk the straight path in future, and to content ourselves with what we have and with cultivating our lands."

Then the last of the great Indian leaders of the Northwest, having pronounced the obituary of his people from the Atlantic to the Mississippi, went on down the Mohawk Valley, where the war had raged for so long; on to Buffalo and the country the British, French, Americans, and Indians had contested so fiercely; to Detroit, which was only a few decades away from Pontiac and only a few years from the tomahawk. They remembered in Detroit. The whites burned Black Hawk in effigy and gave him no banquets. But there was no violence.

And so at last to Green Bay, into the country of the tribes who had recently been enemies of the Sauks and had done their best to help Atkinson. A detachment of white troops protected Black

205

Hawk's party now, accompanying them to Chicago and then down the rivers that led to Fort Armstrong once more. As they traveled through the familiar lands of his home country, Black Hawk grew ever more gloomy and taciturn. The memory of the White House, of the white leaders who had done him honor, of the Seneca chief's friendly counsel—all this was submerged in the bitter memories that overwhelmed him as he traveled through the land of his fathers and saw the smoke curling from the cabins of the conquerors.

There was one last humiliation. At a council in Fort Armstrong, the government's representative, Major Garland, announced that the condition of Black Hawk's release, by President Jackson's specific order, was that Keokuk was to be the principal chief of the Sauk nation, and the only one of the tribe entitled to that distinction. Where there had been two bands in the tribe, there would now be only one.

Crushed but still proud, Black Hawk retreated to the Iowa reservation to live out his days. In September, 1837, he made one more trip to Washington, in company with a delegation of Sauks, Foxes, Sioux, and Iowas, thirty-five in all, who had just concluded another highly satisfactory deal with the government by which the white men had acquired 26,500,000 acres for three cents an acre, in return for a variety of guarantees, most of which were subsequently disregarded.

Once more it was considered good public relations to parade the Indians before the public, and Black Hawk again made the grand tour, this time with his wife and son, climaxed by a ball at Fort Madison, Wisconsin, on Washington's Birthday, 1838. Black Hawk was invited to return on the following Fourth of July, where at a banquet his white host proposed this toast: "Our illustrious guest. May his declining years be as calm as his previous life has been boisterous from warlike events. His present friendship to the whites fully entitles him to a seat at our board."

There was infinite pathos in Black Hawk's reply: "It has pleased the Great Spirit that I am here today. The earth is our mother and we are now permitted to look upon it. A few snows ago I was fighting against the white people; perhaps I was wrong; let it be forgotten. I love my towns and corn fields on the Rock River; it was a beautiful country. I fought for it, but now it is yours. Keep it as the Sauks did. I was once a warrior, but now I am poor. Keokuk has been the cause of what I am, but I do not blame him. I love to look upon the Mississippi. I have looked upon it from a child. I love that beautiful river. My home has always been upon its banks. I thank you for your friendship. I will say no more."

Three months later, on October 3, he died in his lodge on the Des Moines River, within the reservation that Keokuk ruled in his place. According to his wishes, they buried him in the manner of the old Sauk chiefs, sitting on the ground beneath a wooden shelter made of slabs and rails, his cane between his knees, grasping it as he had in life, with all the gifts the white men had given him lying at his side.

Even in death he did not rest. The following year white vandals invaded his sepulchre, severed his head, took other parts of the skeleton, and attempted to put these grisly remains on exhibition in a tent show. Recovered again, they were placed in the custody of the Iowa Historical Society, in Burlington, where they returned at last to earth when the Society's building was burned.

12

THE SECOND SEMINOLE WAR

In the year of Black Hawk's War, an event occurred in faraway Florida which precipitated the last Indian warfare east of the Mississippi and ended the only remaining resistance to the white man in that theater.

The occasion was another of the government's treaties, inspired by President Jackson's implacable determination to remove all the Indians who could not be killed. He had dispersed the Creek nation and transported most of its surviving members into what is now Oklahoma. He meant to subject the Seminoles to a similar fate, since they were the only obstacle to total white rule. The instrument by which this was to be done came to be known as the Treaty of Payne's Landing, made on May 9, 1832.

Like most such treaties, this one which the government's negotiator, General Wiley Thompson, offered was a bland fraud. It proposed that the Seminoles give up all their possessions in Florida, and go to live on the Oklahoma reservation of the Creeks, their enemies, from whom they had seceded several years before. In return for this small accommodation, which was to be accomplished within three years, the government generously agreed to give them $15,400 when they arrived in their new home; and as a dividend, every man, woman, and child was to get one blanket and one homespun frock.

Another clause stipulated that the Seminoles were to pay for something they had not done. The government meant to investigate certain demands for "slaves and other property" allegedly stolen or destroyed by the Seminoles, and if these demands were found to be justified, it would cost the Indians $7,000.

Here was the heart of the trouble: the issue of slavery. The Creeks and Cherokees had owned slaves who sometimes escaped, as they did from the whites, and fled into the Florida swamps, where the Seminoles not only gave them sanctuary but in effect took them into the tribe through intermarriage and simple assimilation. The refugees did not have the status of native-born tribesmen, but on the other hand, their treatment was infinitely preferable to what it had been in Georgia and Alabama.

When the owners, white and red, sent slave catchers into Florida to look for the escapees, the Seminoles naturally considered them as foreign invaders and hunted them down. This had been one of the deep, underlying causes of the first Seminole War, a fact which the Spaniards seemed to understand when they sold Florida to the United States in 1819. A clause in that treaty specified that the new owner must respect Indian rights and deal with them justly.

The Seminoles soon learned how far the United States meant to honor its promise. With Florida now American property, the slave catchers roamed everywhere, protected by the government, gathering in not only Negroes but half-breeds and pure Indians as well, to be sold in the slave markets of Georgia, Alabama, and elsewhere. That compelled the Seminoles themselves to become fugitives, hiding in the swamps and defending themselves against the invaders.

The last straw was a verbal order, delivered as an afterthought to the Treaty of Payne's Landing, declaring that no one of Negro descent would be permitted to go to Oklahoma and must remain to be sold into slavery. This could only mean the disintegration of many Seminole families, since intermarriage had been prevalent for more than two decades.

One of the Indian dignitaries present at Payne's Landing was a ruggedly handsome young Indian named Osceola, scarcely more than thirty but already a leader among his people although he was

Osceola.

not a chief, either by ancestry or election. He was also known as Powell among the whites, and was said to have had a Scot father, grandfather, or stepfather, although it is probable he was actually a full-blooded Indian.

Osceola had fought against Jackson in the first Seminole War, but since then he had lived in comparative peace near Fort King, where the whites sometimes employed him to pursue deserters or capture criminals among his own people. Slowly, by virtue of his powerful personality, he rose to be an acknowledged leader of the Seminoles, although never officially a chieftain.

At the Payne's Landing council, Osceola was present but not among the seven chiefs who signed. He was openly contemptuous of the document, and affirmed his stand the following year at Fort Gibson, where a few more chiefs were tricked into apparent approval of the tribe's imminent migration. One of those who did sign at Wiley Thompson's urging was Charley Emathla, the principal chief of the tribe.

General Thompson tried once more, in April, 1835, to get unanimous approval. The chiefs who had refused to sign the treaty before stood silently and would not pick up the pen, but Osceola, in a burst of angry contempt, pulled his hunting knife and plunged it into the offensive paper. Then he began an angry quarrel with Thompson, in which he accused the general of undue coercion, bribery, and fraud, and announced that he would never agree to the treaty but would rally against it any of his people who would listen. Thompson, who suspected that a good many had already listened to him, had Osceola arrested on the spot and thrown into irons.

At this juncture the Seminole employed the simplest of strategies. He pretended that his arrest had changed his mind, agreed to sign the treaty and to do whatever he could to persuade the other holdouts, whereupon he was released. As soon as he was free, he busied himself collecting all the dissidents and organizing a campaign of harassment.

Osceola had learned the lesson of the Creek War and the first Seminole campaign. He had no intention of opposing the white men's armies in force. Instead, he conveyed the women and children to a safe place deep in the swamps and organized his warriors into small parties instructed to buzz about the whites like so many elusive bees, killing where they could and retreating into the safety of the swamps at the slightest evidence of superior force.

This campaign was so successful that the inevitable reaction occurred and regular troops were sent into the field. On Christmas Eve, 1835, Major Dade set out from Fort King with a hundred men and eight officers, confident that he would capture Osceola and end the war. On the morning of the 28th, Osceola and a strong band of followers attacked this force with stunning suddenness, killing every one of them but three men, badly wounded, who pretended death and escaped to Fort King.

So short had been the morning's work that Osceola, who led the assault, had time to accomplish a personal act of revenge. With a small party, he crept up to a house only 250 yards from Fort King, where Wiley Thompson and nine other men were having dinner, with the doors and windows open to the air and sun. Through these apertures Osceola and his band poured a murderous volley that killed five men, including Thompson. The others escaped into the fort. Thus deservedly, according to Osceola's viewpoint, died the instigator of the infamous Payne's Landing Treaty. The principal Seminole signer of it, Charley Emathla, had already suffered Thompson's fate.

In retaliation for the massacre and murders of the 28th, General Call marched 700 men after Osceola, and fought him in a brisk battle at a ford over the Ouithlacoochee River. The Indians fell back, with heavy losses and Osceola wounded, but they left 63 Americans killed and wounded. It was the only time Osceola risked such open conflict.

More troops were poured into the field. General Gaines arrived in Tampa on February 9, 1836, with a large force and sailed up the Alafia River in three steamboats, finally marching overland to the base at Fort King. He, too, sought a battle with Osceola but achieved only a series of skirmishes. The fighting dragged on through the summer. General Scott came to replace Gaines, but he could accomplish no more, and by the time autumn came, it was obvious that the American government had made no progress whatever against the Seminoles. Scott's single achievement had been the shipping to Oklahoma of some 400 Seminoles, mostly women and children, who belonged to the friendly portions of the tribe already committed to migration.

General after general came South to "wind up the war," and the collapse of Indian resistance was announced as imminent so often that it became an embarrassing joke in Washington. Every officer who failed did so at the cost of his military career, until it became difficult to find a general with any enthusiasm for the job.

In this crisis of command, President Jackson assigned the army's able quartermaster general, Thomas Sidney Jesup, who had once served Henry Clay as a second in the bloodless duel with John Randolph, to go into Florida, take command of the army, and do what all the other generals had failed to accomplish.

Arriving in January, 1837, Jesup went through the same futile motions as his predecessors for a time, pursuing and skirmishing with the Indians but never able to bring them to a decisive battle. Faced with ominous murmurs from Washington, he decided to try his hand as peacemaker, and in May he succeeded in gathering some 3000 men, women, and children at Fort Mellon, on Lake Monroe, for a council. Osceola and various Seminole chiefs attended, and the parley began.

By the middle of the month Jesup was so certain of his success that he had twenty-four transports lying off Tampa, ready to take the Indians on the first leg of their trip westward. But Osceola, observing what the proposed peace was leading up to, circulated among his people, and the whole encampment melted overnight into the morasses and swamps, leaving the unfortunate Jesup with his empty transports and an army plagued by sickness and desertions.

Jesup wrote to the Secretary of War, asking to be relieved of his command, but all he got was abuse from Congress and a promise from the Secretary that 400 Shawnees, 200 Delawares, and 100 Kickapoos were to be dragooned into fighting the Seminoles. In

September, more than a thousand of these Western and Southern Indians arrived to give extremely reluctant help in conquering the Seminoles.

But Jessup was, by this time, in a highly irritable frame of mind. He was exasperated and humiliated by his failure, and convinced that if he spent the rest of his career in Florida he could never hope to defeat the Seminoles. But if he could only capture Osceola, Jesup was convinced, the fight would go out of his elusive enemy.

The general succeeded in this objective by the most transparent of maneuvers. On October 21, 1837, he ordered Osceola and seventy-five of his warriors seized while they were meeting with the whites in council under a flag of truce. Jesup must have been utterly exasperated by what followed. Where before he had been charged with failure to capture Osceola, now he was denounced for doing it. Even those who had no love whatever for the Indians could not help being horrified by the outrageous flouting of the laws of nations, not to mention the flagrant treachery Jesup had employed.

Nevertheless, Jessup had Osceola and he did not mean to let him go. He sent the Seminoles' leader first to Fort Marion, at St. Augustine, then to Fort Moultrie, near Charleston. Osceola could not stand imprisonment. Crushed by his misfortune and consumed with bitterness at the white man's perfidy, he wasted away rapidly and died only three months after his capture, on January 30, 1838, a little more than eight months before Black Hawk lay down to die on the plains of Iowa. Osceola was brave, skillful, and intelligent, but he was not of Tecumseh's or Black Hawk's stature. If he had lived, however, he might have been a splendid leader of his people in a happier time; he was still a young man.

Jesup's fond hope that the capture of Osceola and the other chiefs would end the war proved to be an idle one. The fighting went on as before, and Jesup was removed from his command. Back in Washington, he faced a hostile Congress, bent on an investigation, but he was defended by Senator Thomas Hart Benton, who succeeded in returning him to his old job.

His successor was a figure familiar to those who followed the fortunes of the Indian wars. Zachary Taylor, the colonel who had pursued Black Hawk to his destruction, was now a general, and to him fell the task no one else had been able to do. On December 19, 1837, he marched at the head of 600 men to a point on Okeechobee Lake, where he learned that the main body of the Seminoles was on Lake Kissimmee, only twenty-five miles away.

Taylor reached the hostile camp on Christmas morning and found the Seminoles well entrenched in a dense hummock, from which they poured a destructive fire on the volunteers. For more than an hour the whites charged and charged again, until their persistence was rewarded and the Seminoles retreated, but in good order. It was the most severe battle that had yet taken place in Florida. Taylor could claim a victory, but a costly one—28 killed, 111 wounded.

Nevertheless, he was prepared to pursue his momentary advantage, and by late winter, after several other skirmishes, had laid some elaborate plans which were completely disrupted when Jackson's impatience led him to make still another change in the Florida command. Taylor was recalled and General McComb took his place.

The commanders who preceded him, even Taylor, had concluded that defeating the Seminoles was impossible. Before he departed Jesup had even resorted to importing thirty-three bloodhounds from Cuba, at the cost of several thousand dollars, and set them to tracking down the Indians. Again an outcry of indignation assailed his ears. Americans had heard grim stories of what bloodhounds did to runaway slaves. It was said by those who sympathized with the Indians and had no love for the President that, having failed to drive the rightful owners of Florida from their lands, it had been decided to tear them to pieces and let them rot on it.

No one need have worried. The hounds had been trained to follow the scent of Negroes; Indians smelled differently to them, and nothing could persuade them to chase a Seminole. Indeed, the dogs who did enter the swamps made friends with the Indians, who trained them to attack white men.

McComb had no intention of sending large armies of men or bloodhounds into the field. His instructions were to make the best possible peace, and for two years he worked hard at it, while the

HUNTING INDIANS IN FLORIDA WITH BLOOD HOUNDS.

Seminoles continued to harass him at every possible point. Once a band of red marauders encountered the wagons of an audacious theatrical troupe jogging along near St. Augustine. They poured a volley into the two vehicles, killing four men, while the women and the ambitious manager escaped into the brush. The Indians ransacked the wagon, found the troupe's costumes, and began to try them on. They were enchanted beyond words with the spangled, bright clothes, and, decking themselves out in grotesque finery, they surrounded nearby Fort Searle and dared the openmouthed garrison to come out and fight. The soldiers were too bemused by the spectacle to accept the challenge.

By the autumn of 1840, General McComb had not succeeded in either pacifying the Seminoles or signing a treaty with them, and General W. R. Armistead succeeded him, with instructions to pursue a still more conciliatory policy.

Armistead had devised what he thought was a truly brilliant plan. He brought fourteen Seminole chiefs from the new lands beyond the Mississippi to go among the resisters and try to persuade them to give up and move West. All of these chiefs had been opposed to emigrating before they gave in, and Armistead reasoned that their influence would be strong. The returnees met their brothers at a

217

council in the swamps. No white man could learn for certain what was said, but in any case the Seminoles went back to fighting and the fourteen converts went home.

"Thus have ended all our well-grounded hopes of bringing the war to a close by pacific measures," Armistead wrote back regretfully to the Secretary of War. "Confident in the resources of the country, the enemy will hold out to the last, and can never be induced to come in again. Immediately upon the withdrawal of the Indians, orders were transmitted to commanders of regiments to put their troops in motion, and before this reaches you there will be scouting in every direction."

The Secretary was not convinced, nor was the President. They believed, stubbornly, that the only reason the Seminoles had not been conquered was that the right man had not yet been sent to Florida. In the spring of 1841 they found him; he had been in Florida since 1838. William J. Worth, a Hudson, New York, boy, born of Quaker parents, had served with Morgan Lewis and Winfield Scott in the War of 1812, where he had earned distinction enough to make him commandant of cadets at West Point from 1820 to 1828.

Worth conceived an absurdly simple master stroke. He had already defeated the Seminoles in the field, and although that victory had made him a general, he was convinced, like all the others, that military means could never end the resistance.

To implement his idea, he spent the summer of 1841 penetrating the swamps to the islands where the Indians lived, and although they always fled, his soldiers methodically destroyed their shelters and their crops on which they depended to see them through the winter. In the process he contrived to capture the leading chief and five other stalwarts of the resistance, whereupon he sent word to the hostile camps that all these captives would be hanged, and any others who were apprehended would meet the same fate.

Somehow this declaration sent a shudder of fear through the hostiles. The captives could only be saved, Worth had said, if the Seminoles surrendered, and in the early fall they began to come out

of the swamps into the general's camp—perhaps not so much because of the threat but because their crops were gone and their villages burned, and they had fought to the limit of brave men.

When the Seminoles emerged, it was difficult to understand why the best talent of the Regular Army had been unable to demolish this tatterdemalion force in six years of warfare. They were emaciated, cadaverous, barefoot, and in rags. Their women and children were in wretched condition, starved and nearly naked. Their flintlocks were in lamentable shape, and their best weapons were knives and clubs.

These were the Indians who had cost the United States of America 1500 men and $20,000,000!

The final treaty was signed in 1842, and the Seminoles began to follow the westward footsteps of their brothers. But not all. There were some who refused to give up, although their numbers were too small to bother about. Time passed over them, and everyone knows them today as the picturesque natives who sell souvenirs of the Everglades to the picturesque tourists, and who, along with the flamingoes, are part of the spectacle at Hialeah.

In the Second World War most of them refused to register for the draft. They were not, they explained, citizens of the United States. They were members of the Seminole nation, an independent state.

It appears that the second Seminole War will never end.

13

"THE TRAIL
WHERE THEY CRIED"

"At first the earth was flat and very soft and wet," so the Cherokee myth begins. "The animals were anxious to get down (from above in Galunlati, beyond the arch) and sent out different birds to see if it was yet dry, but they found no place to alight and came back again to Galunlati. At last, it seemed to be time, and they sent out the Buzzard and told him to go and make ready for them. This was the Great Buzzard, the father of all the buzzards we see now. He flew all over the earth, low down near the ground, and it was still soft. When he reached the Cherokee country, he was very tired, and his wings began to flap and strike the ground, and wherever they struck the earth there was a valley, and where they turned up again there was a mountain. When the animals above saw this, they were afraid that the whole world would be mountains, so they called him back, but the Cherokee country remains full of mountains to this day."

Thus the Cherokees described the origin of their homeplace in the Valley of the Tennessee, approximately 40,000 square miles, extending from the headwaters of the Kanawha and Tennessee rivers southward to the Appalachian foothills and westward to the Tennessee, where the river runs like a vertical boundary from the

Ohio on the north to the eastern piedmont of the Carolinas on the south.

The Cherokees were an intelligent, handsome, industrious, and peaceful people who loved their mountains and rivers and wanted nothing more than to make a pleasant, prosperous world for themselves. Next to the Iroquois they were probably the most highly civilized of all the Indian tribes in America, and in many respects they made a greater effort to adapt themselves to the white man's coming.

Yet, from the beginning, they were victimized outrageously by the whites, and were divided among themselves about what they ought to do to resist being engulfed. In the end they were totally destroyed as a nation. The manner and method of their destruction wrote the last and saddest chapter of Indian life east of the Mississippi. For they were not destroyed by war; the white man simply removed them from the land, as the English had moved the Acadians. There was no Evangeline to immortalize their tragedy, but their story remains one of the best known in American history, perhaps because it epitomizes everything that happened to the red man in his long battle against white supremacy.

Here none of the usual justifications could be claimed. The Cherokees were not, at the time of their removal, a savage, warlike people who had inflicted a long series of brutalities on the white man. They were not unwilling to live in peace with the encroaching settlers, but they had one grievous fault as far as the American government was concerned: They wanted to live in the country they loved, on the lands they had always possessed.

Of course the Cherokees had gone through the customary cycle of resistance in the early days of the American nation. They had been pushed this way and that by the French and the British, and then by the English settlers. They had ceded vast territories of their original domain, and the young chiefs had fought against the onrush of white settlers who cared nothing for treaty boundaries. One of them, Dragging Canoe, had been a thorn in the side of the Americans during the Revolution and afterward. He even essayed the Indian dream of confederacy, conspiring with Alexander McGillivray to unite the Creeks with the Cherokees (an unlikely alliance, at best) in an all-out war against the white invasion.

But when Dragging Canoe died in 1792, the life went out of Cherokee resistance, and by the end of 1794, a general peace prevailed. In the War of 1812, the whole nation was united behind Andrew Jackson, and their warriors were among the friendly Indians who helped Jackson defeat the Creeks at Horseshoe Bend.

As modern historians have pointed out, the Cherokees were almost like a foreign country within the United States; their nation lay as a barrier between Eastern commerce and the Western consumer. It was early recognized in Washington that agents must negotiate with the Cherokees continuously and maintain good relations with them. They gave the Indians farm tools and a good deal of other agricultural assistance, so that the Cherokees began to develop their lands and prosper. As early as 1801 that astute agent, Colonel Benjamin Hawkins, the friend of the Creeks, observed: "In the Cherokee agency, the wheel, the loom, and the plough is in pretty general use, farming, manufacture, and stock raising the topic of conversation among the men and women."

By 1826 the Cherokee nation had developed at such an astonishing pace that they could boast 22,000 cattle, 7,600 horses, 46,000 swine, 2,500 sheep, 762 looms, 2,488 spinning wheels, 172 wagons, 2,942 plows, 10 sawmills, 31 grist mills, 62 blacksmith shops, 8 cotton machines, 18 schools, 18 ferries, and many public roads. Evidences of white culture were everywhere. While the elders still clung to Indian ways and costumes, the younger men dressed like the whites, for the most part. Gone were the wigwams of the old days. The poorer people lived in log cabins; the principal men lived in handsome houses, like Chief Joseph Vann's $10,000 two-story brick house near Spring Place, Georgia, which had been designed by a Philadelphia architect and was the center of a plantation with 800 cultivated acres. Joseph's poorer brother had a fine house, painted inside and out, and his wife entertained visitors by playing on the piano.

These were no rude tribesmen, then. They read books and had them in their homes, and perused American and English newspapers.

223

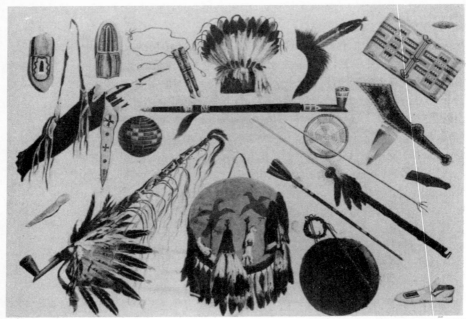

Indian Utensils and Arms. *From paintings by Carl Bodmer.*

Their daughters went off to boarding schools. An unschooled member of the tribe named Sequoyah—George Gist, or Guess, the whites called him—devised a syllabary for the Cherokee language, a brilliant achievement that revolutionized education among the tribesmen. In a year, thousands of adult Cherokees learned to write their own tongue. In 1828, another leader of the nation, Elias Boudinot, began to edit a newspaper, the Cherokee *Phoenix*, which was printed in both English and the Indian tongue.

The first issue of the *Phoenix* declared: "We would now commit our feeble efforts to the good will and indulgence of the public, praying that God will attend them with his blessings, and hoping for the happy period when all Indian tribes shall arise, Phoenix-like, from the ashes and when the terms, 'Indian depredation,' 'war-whoop,' 'scalping-knife,' and the like, shall become obsolete, and forever be buried deep underground."

In 1826, the Cherokees did what no other Indian nation had ever done. They held a convention and drafted a written constitu-

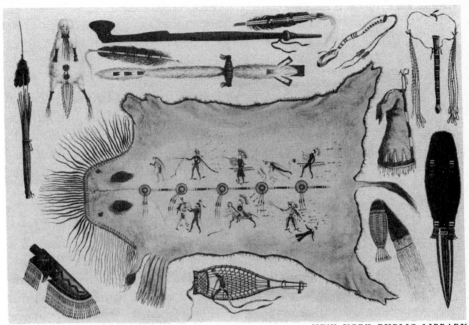

Indian Utensils and Arms. *From paintings by Carl Bodmer.*

tion, much like that of the United States. It was adopted the following year and contained a provision that the nation honestly believed
would guarantee its existence:

*The sovereignty and jurisdiction of this Government shall extend
over the country within the boundaries [as stated in the Treaty of
1819] . . . and the lands therein are, and shall remain, the common
property of the Nation; but the improvements made thereon, and
in the possession of the citizens of the Nation, are the exclusive and
indefeasible property of the citizens, respectively, who made, or may
rightfully be in the possession of them; Provided that the citizens of
the Nation possessing exclusive and indefeasible rights to their
respective improvements, as expressed in this article, shall possess
no right nor power to dispose of their improvements in any manner
whatsoever to the United States, individual states, nor citizens
thereof; and that whenever such citizen or citizens shall remove
with their effects out of the limits of this Nation and become citizens*

*of any other Government, all their rights and privileges as citizens
of this Nation shall cease. . . .*

With equally impressive sincerity, the first elected Principal
Chief under the new constitution, John Ross, raised his hand before
the General Council in October, 1828, and pledged: "I do solemnly
swear that I will faithfully execute the office of Principal Chief
of the Cherokee Nation, and will, to the best of my ability, preserve, protect and defend the Constitution of the Cherokee Nation."

Ross was no more than one-eighth Cherokee, but he had been
brought up as an Indian by his Scottish father, and had married a
Cherokee girl who was three-quarters white. There were able full-
blooded Indians on the Council—men like Major Ridge, a commanding personality who was a statesman by any measurement; and the
venerable Pathkiller, who had led his people from their more
primitive days into the new climate of enlightenment.

Yet all of their admirable effort to make the Indian nation a
model of assimilation in the white man's world, while retaining its
own integrity, was in vain. For the destiny of the Cherokees had
been decided as long ago as 1802, when the Federal government in
an agreement with Georgia had promised to move the Indians from
their own lands, which Georgia claimed, as soon as it could be done
peaceably. The government had obtained some land by cession
in 1817, but in 1822 the House of Representatives concluded that
the agreement with Georgia had not been carried out, and the
statesmen voted $30,000 to extinguish the Cherokees' land titles.

The Cherokee Council responded promptly by voting to make
no more land treaties with the government, whereupon Washington
sent a pair of commissioners. These emissaries tried both cajolery
and threats without success, and then they resorted to bribery,
offering John Ross and two other councilors two thousand dollars
each if they would sign a secret treaty.

When the Council met next day, Ross announced: "It has now
become my duty to inform you that a gross contempt is offered my
character, as well as that of the General Council," and he gave the

226

letter containing the bribe offer to the clerk to read. The meeting broke up in an outburst of angry confusion, after which the commissioners returned to Washington and reported their total failure.

But Georgia continued to maintain that the Indians were only tenants on state land, and its legislature coolly told the Federal government that if Washington did not deal with the Cherokees, the Georgians would do it themselves. The climax of this effrontery came on January 26, 1828, when Governor John Forsyth of Georgia sent a copy of the Cherokee constitution to President John Quincy Adams, asking what he proposed to do about the "erection of a separate government within the limits of a sovereign state." Forsyth called the Indian constitution "presumptuous."

Adams might have been able to use his diplomatic skill to avoid the imminent tragedy, but unfortunately, John Ross and Andrew Jackson came into office at the same moment, and there could be no hope of just treatment from a President who had never shown the slightest understanding of the Indian problem.

At once, in 1829, a removal bill was introduced in Congress, and Georgia began a drum fire of pressure to grab the Cherokee lands, whose mineral wealth and potential real estate values were not lost upon the avaricious businessmen and politicians. A popular song of the day declaimed:

> *All I want in this cre-a-tion*
> *Is a pretty little girl*
> *And a big plan-ta-tion*
> *'Way up yonder in the Cherokee nation.*

The pattern of the grab, as delineated by the Georgia legislature, was a classic of its kind. Successive laws, beginning in 1830, first officially seized the lands by extending the jurisdiction of Georgia laws to the territory. Then the Cherokees' property was divided up into so-called "land lots" of 160 acres each, and "gold lots" of 40 acres, all of these later to be acquired by lottery. As a sop to the Indians, 160 acres were to be given to Cherokee heads of families, but the Georgians thoughtfully decreed at the same time that no deeds were to be given out with these parcels.

227

The Georgians, who traditionally have professed themselves to be profoundly concerned with rights, then proceeded to deprive the Indians of those basic to free governments. The Cherokees were henceforth forbidden to testify in court against white men; their contracts with whites were declared invalid, thus canceling all outstanding white debts; they could not peacefully assemble in public for any purpose whatsoever; and they were denied the right to dig for gold. As a final fillip to this exercise in state government, Georgia required every white man who lived in the limits of the Cherokee nation to take an oath of allegiance to the State, and at the same time he was denied the right, in effect, to own land because he was barred from the lottery that was to dispose of it. That was how the State proposed to deal with the missionaries and teachers, who had denounced the whole plan for the vicious fraud it was.

Unwilling to wait for these laws to take effect, Georgians began to behave like the Indians of earlier days, firing cabins, stealing horses, and committing all kinds of atrocities on the defenseless Cherokees.

Meanwhile, the removal bill had come up in Congress, and the whole nation's interest was suddenly focused on the plight of the Cherokees. They found a few distinguished defenders. Edward Everett, of Massachusetts, rose in the House to denounce the marauding Georgians: "They have but to cross the Cherokee line; they have but to choose the time and the place where the eye of no white man can rest upon them, and they may burn the dwelling, waste the farm, plunder the property, assault the person, murder the children of the Cherokee subject of Georgia, and though hundreds of the tribe may be looking on, there is not one of them that can be permitted to bear witness against the spoiler."

John Ross took his nation's case to the Supreme Court, asking for an injunction against the Georgia laws, but Chief Justice John Marshall and the Court ruled against the Indians on the ground that the Cherokee nation could not bring an action in the courts of the United States, since it was not a foreign country. But a year later, in 1832, the Court reversed itself, in effect, in the case of two missionaries who had refused to take the oath and had been sent to prison. Declaring that the State's act in extending its jurisdiction was unconstitutional, the Court ruled: "The Cherokee Nation, then, is a distinct community, occupying its own territory, with boundaries accurately described, in which the laws of Georgia can have no force, and which the citizens of Georgia have no right to enter, but with the assent of the Cherokees, themselves, or in conformity with treaties, and with the acts of Congress. The whole intercourse of the United States and this Nation, is, by our Constitution and laws, vested in the government of the United States."

"John Marshall has made his decision," the President of the United States said, "now let him enforce it." Georgia took Jackson's hint and continued on its unconstitutional way.

The end approached rapidly. John Ross's house was confiscated, as was that of the rich Joseph Vann and other dwellings belonging to the Cherokee leaders. Ross himself was arrested in 1835, while he was entertaining John Howard Payne, who was far from his Long Island "Home, Sweet Home," on Tennessee territory. Both were soon released, but Payne wrote a blistering account of what the Georgia militia were doing to the Cherokees, and Tennessee was outraged that the arrest had taken place within its sacred borders. Soon the Cherokee *Phoenix* was suppressed, and the Indians no longer had a central source of information about their affairs.

At this juncture it was logical that the government should move to make another treaty, this one a removal treaty, and it was signed on December 29, 1835, in the presence of no more than 500 of the 17,000 Cherokees. The government pretended it was a treaty with "chiefs, head men and people of the Cherokee tribe of Indians," but not a single official of the nation's government signed this document, which was, of course, another outright fraud. Only Major Ridge, his son John, and Elias Boudinot agreed to it, among the leaders, and they were not then holders of office.

Supplementary articles added to the treaty by March 1, 1836, completed a transaction by which the Cherokees ceded everything they owned east of the Mississippi for $5,000,000. They were to be given 7,000,000 acres in the West, and for $500,000 they could

Interior of the Hut of a Mandan Chief. *From a painting by Carl Bodmer.*

purchase another 8,000,000. They were to remove themselves to this new homeland within two years.

The Cherokees were badly split by the treaty. Chief Ross declared it invalid. A petition signed by 16,000 Cherokees was sent to Washington, in which it was declared that the United States negotiator had deceived the nation, but Jackson paid no attention to it. However, when it came time for the Senate to approve the treaty, there arose a noisy debate which was due less to the Senators' sense of decency than to the determination of the Whigs to make some political capital out of what they considered a possibly unpopular move by the President. In any case, resistance was useless. Jackson organized his powerful Senatorial machine to push approval, but at that the treaty was finally ratified by only one vote.

Having approved its own perfidy, the government was immediately fearful that the Cherokees might resist with something more than words, and ordered troops into the territory to disarm the Indians. General R. G. Dunlap, one of the commanders, observed after he had begun to carry out his orders that the Indians were the ones who needed protection. For a time, too, there was considerable agitation everywhere in the country to help the Indians, but much of this was politically inspired.

The Cherokees began their removal. More than 2000 of them went west between 1836 and 1838. The other 15,000 made no move to go, apparently hoping and believing that Ross's fight to get the treaty nullified would be successful. But nothing of the kind occurred, and time began to run out; the two-year period of grace was nearly at an end. It was obvious to the government that the Cherokees would have to be removed forcibly, and in May, 1838, General Winfield Scott was sent with 7000 men to do the job.

A contemporary account describes the state of the Cherokee nation in that beautiful spring when a proclamation was posted calling on them to assemble to be removed: "There was no cold weather after the first of March. Vegetation advanced without any backsets from cold. The buds burst into leaves and blossoms; the woods were green and gay and merry with the singing birds. The Indians started to work in their fields earlier than ever before. . . . Fence corners and hedgerows were cleaned out. The ground was well plowed and the corn planted better than ever before. . . . Soon it was knee-high and growing nicely. They cultivated only the richest bottoms. An Indian never worked an acre of poor land."

Into this peaceful scene General Scott's soldiers came with their wagons to carry the Indians to the stockades where they would be held until they could be removed. One of the wagon drivers, prodding on his deliberate oxen, was a boy named William Cotter who wrote down later a heartbreaking picture of the day's events:

"After all the warning and with soldiers in their midst, the inevitable day appointed found the Indians at work in their houses and in their fields. It is remembered as well as if it had been seen yesterday, that two or three dropped their hoes and ran as fast as they could when they saw the soldiers coming into the fields. After that, they made no effort to get out of the way. The men handled them gently, but picked them up in the road, in the field, anywhere they found them, part of a family at a time, and carried them to the post. Everything in their homes was left alone for a

231

day or two and then hauled to the post. When a hundred or more families had been collected, they were marched to Ross' Landing. It was a mournful sight to all who witnessed it—old men and women with gray hairs, walking with the sad company. Provisions were made for those to ride who could not walk. . . .

"In hauling the stuff from the cabins a file of six or more men went with me as a guard. They forced open the doors and put the poor, meager household effects into the wagons, sometimes the stuff of two or three families at one load. After following me a mile or two the guards galloped away, leaving me in worse danger than anyone else; for if there had been an Indian hiding out, I would have been the one to suffer.

"But few of the Indians even went back to their homes. We turned the cows and calves together, as they had been apart for a day or two. Chickens, cats and dogs all ran away when they saw us. Ponies under the shade trees fighting the flies with the noise of their bells; the cows and calves lowing to each other; the poor dogs howling for their owners; the open doors of the cabins as we left them—to have seen it all would have melted to tenderness a heart of stone. And in contrast there was a beautiful growing crop of corn and beans."

Not all of Scott's soldiers were as humane as those Cotter describes. Some were brutal and cruel. And behind them came the frontier rabble, bent on pillage and destruction wherever they could. There was little resistance from the Cherokees during the whole process; they had become too civilized.

In the stockades the Cherokees were herded together, suffering from dysentery and fevers, besieged by white jackals who tried to get what little money they possessed in return for bad liquor. Early in June, the miserable Indians were herded onto flatboats and headed down the Tennessee River toward that fearful West, from which blew, according to their mythology, the sere wind of death. They feared the dark country ahead of them far more than the journey itself.

Yet it was the journey that proved to be the real horror. Many of the first to go succumbed to the summer's intense heat and the sickness it generated. General Scott agreed, humanely, to postpone further removals until September 1, and held to his promise although Jackson and the new landowners objected to it. A drought further delayed the final removal, but more than 13,000 Cherokees, in thirteen separate caravans, were moved to the West between October 1 and November 4. Sickness still plagued the unhappy people, who were despondent and fearful in the bargain. More than 4000 of them died on the way and never reached the new country. Ross's wife was among them; the heartbroken leader buried her in Little Rock. Small wonder that the route to the West came to be known in the Cherokee tongue as Nuna-da-ut-sun'y, "The Trail Where They Cried." We know it today as The Trail of Tears.

Such were the majestic workings of Manifest Destiny. In their new home, said the United States government, the Cherokees could remain "while the grass grows and the rivers run." It was a promise as worthless as the others.

14

THE CIVIL WAR IN THE WEST

"We are hemmed in on all sides by the unrelenting Apache," the *Arizonian* reported from that territory on August 10, 1861. "Since the withdrawal of the Overland Mail and the garrison troops the chances against life have reached the maximum height. Within but six months nine-tenths of the whole male population have been killed off, and every ranch, farm and mine in the country have been abandoned in consequence. . . ."

That was the state of affairs nearly everywhere west of the Mississippi as the call to arms in both North and South depleted the forts of their best soldiers. Some outposts were abandoned entirely; others were garrisoned by soldiers too old, too sick, or too raw to fight in the regular armies. The Indians of the Plains took such widespread and effective advantage of their new situation that Rebel prisoners, known contemptuously as "galvanized Yankees," were pressed into service to garrison the endangered territories.

With these disturbances the struggle for the western half of the continent began, at first no more than a sideshow to the grand and tragic spectacle of the Civil War itself. Unlike the long battle for eastern America, the conflict between white men and red in the West could boast of no potentially decisive conflicts, where the course of history might have been diverted if not entirely altered 235 by the outcome of a single engagement or campaign. Nor did it have the grandeur of background the earlier period possessed, when the contest was between great nations, old and new, with the Indians the unwilling balance of power.

It had taken the white man three hundred years to subdue completely the Indians of eastern America. It took the United States government only thirty years to break the resistance of the Western tribes, kill them in large numbers, seize their lands by the customary fraudulent treaties, and pen them up in reservations, where their treatment ever since has been an open shame and scandal. In that scant thirty years lived the leaders, white and red, who fought the wars that made a kind of national literature in themselves, that have been perpetuated in motion pictures and television, and that have created the only image by which Americans and a great many others of the world's people know the Old West. It is a popular saga of heroes. The reality is something less than heroic.

Between the mournful passage of the Cherokees and the outbreak of the Civil War, the new era in the West was heralded by the surge of emigration following the gold rush of 1849. As the wagon trains snaked their perilous way across the Western plains, they were beset by hostile tribes who resisted the invasion as had every tribe from the days of Opechancanough and King Philip. By this time, however, there was an American government with enough experience in handling Indians to know how to open up broad trails, liberate territories, and in general make it possible for everyone who wanted money or land to have it without the inconvenience of dealing directly with those who owned it.

In 1851 the government sent negotiators to a conference at Fort Laramie, attended by the Cheyennes, Arapahos, Crows, Assiniboins, Hidatsas, Mandans, and Arikaras. These tribes agreed to be divided by the government and each was assigned to what was ostensibly his own territory. The Cheyennes and Arapahos, to cite an example that caused later trouble, were given most of present Colorado and western Kansas.

For the privilege of building roads and military posts in the ancient lands of these Indians, which it fully meant to do in any

The Spirit of Progress.

case, the government agreed to pay $50,000 a year for fifty years. When this treaty went to the Senate, the phrase "ten years" was substituted for "fifty years"; the Indians, of course, were never told.

How much the treaty meant in other respects was soon disclosed. When the new gold rush of 1859 brought a swarm of settlers into Colorado, they simply drove out the Cheyennes and Arapahoes. The treaty guaranteed the whites only the right of transit on these lands, but instead they built cities and tilled farms and took possession of anything they desired.

Seven years later, a government commission investigating the Indian war that followed this illegal seizure made a penetrating comment that summarized the red man's plight and placed the moral question involved in a proper perspective:

237

"Before 1861 the Cheyennes and Arapahos had been driven from the mountain regions down upon the waters of the Arkansas and were becoming sullen and discontented because of this violation of their rights. . . . If the lands of the white man are taken, civilization justifies him in resisting the invader. Civilization does more than this: it brands him as a coward and a slave if he submits to the wrong. Here civilization made its contract and guaranteed the rights of the weaker party. It did not stand by the guarantee. The treaty was broken, but not by the savage. If the savage resists, civilization, with the Ten Commandments in one hand and the sword in the other, demands his immediate extermination. . . . These Indians saw their former homes and hunting grounds over-run by a greedy population, thirsting for gold. They saw their game driven east to the plains, and soon found themselves the object of jealousy and hatred. They must go."

Meanwhile, in neighboring Arizona and New Mexico, the Apaches, who were a much more fierce people, were resisting the inevitable advance under the leadership of two chiefs, Cochise and Mangas Colorado. War had broken out there in 1861 when the Indians were accused of stealing a cow and a child from the Mexican mistress of an American. Cochise and five other chiefs came to talk over this matter with a detachment of men from the Seventh Cavalry, stationed at Fort Buchanan. They met in the commander's tent, over which flew a white truce flag, an emblem that was disregarded when the soldiers could not obtain a confession. They tried to seize the chiefs, but Cochise hacked his way out with a knife. Another chief tried to follow him but was knocked down and spitted on a bayonet. The others were bound.

An exchange of prisoners was contemplated, Cochise having seized some settlers as hostages. Before it could take place, the chief's young men killed the prisoners, and a few hours later the Apache captives were hanged by the soldiers.

War raged up and down the territory with a peculiar ferocity. The Apaches were known traditionally as "wild Indians," and Cochise was one of the wildest of them. The tales of the frightful tortures he visited upon his white captives made his name a synonym for cruelty in the Southwest, although today a county in Arizona commemorates it. When Mangas Colorado was killed in 1863 "while attempting to escape" after capture, as the army put it, Cochise became the principal chief. The story that Mangas Colorado had been prodded by a sentinel's hot bayonet and murdered while he was trying to escape the torture did not improve his successor's disposition.

In September, 1862, General Carleton had arrived at the Rio Grande settlements and sent three detachments into the field, all with the same orders: "The men are to be slain whenever and wherever they can be found. The women and children may be taken prisoners, but, of course, they are not to be killed." It was to be, in brief, a war of extermination. Like most such wars, it was a failure. The Apaches were only driven into the mountains and from there conducted a guerilla warfare for years, until the white men tried negotiation again.

The effect of the Civil War on the West reached a peak in 1864, almost simultaneously with the climax of the war itself. By that time three years of unchecked Indian resistance had summoned more and better troops from the Eastern battlefronts, and military expeditions were launched in every direction. In Colorado Territory, there was particular activity because the Arapahos were increasingly desperate over the loss of their hunting grounds, which had brought them to the edge of starvation.

It was a curious situation. The Indians did not really want war, yet their plight drove them to marauding and pillage, which were answered in the most pitiless manner by the white military. James D. Horan tells us, in *The Great American West:* "By 1864 nearly every rancher had been burned out or killed along the South Platte. One valley of hay was completely burned. Freighters refused to make the hazardous trips and Denver was cut off from provisions. In 1863 flour was so scarce it sold for $45 a sack. Conditions became so bad the mail was stopped."

Both sides had cause to complain, but one reads with horror the report of a Major Downing, in command of a punitive expedition against the Indians in the spring of 1864: "We started about eleven 239 o'clock in the day, traveled all day and all that night; about daylight I succeeded in surprising the Cheyenne village of Cedar Bluffs, a small cañon about sixty miles north of the South Platte River. We commenced shooting. I ordered the men to commence killing them. They lost, as I am informed, some twenty-six killed and sixty wounded. My own loss was one killed and one wounded. I burnt up their lodges and everything I could get hold of. I took no prisoners. We got out of ammunition and could not pursue them."

The give-and-take of atrocities touched off what was to become one of the most controversial incidents in the long war between white and red men, an episode known to history as the Sand Creek Massacre. It began with an Indian atrocity, the murder of the Hungate family, who lived thirty miles east of Denver. Hungate himself was found mutilated, with eighty bullet holes in his body. His wife and children had been tortured and killed; their bodies were discovered in a well, tied together.

The whole territory was shocked and deeply angered by the fate of the Hungates, although it was worse only in degree from dozens of other similar incidents. But Governor Evans at once began to take action, appealing first to Washington for help against the Arapahos and Cheyennes, which was answered belatedly by permission from the War Department to enlist a volunteer battalion for a hundred days. This command was raised and stationed at Fort Weld in the summer of 1864, and the two principal actors of the coming tragedy now stepped on the stage.

The undeserved villain of the piece was Colonel John Milton Chivington. In fairness to this excellent officer, who was compelled to resign his commission, it must be said that he had performed a service to his country of the first magnitude. Chivington may have been a proud and unbending man, but he was also a military genius and fearless in the bargain. It was Chivington who fashioned the victory in the Battle of Santa Fe, on March 27, 1862, which has been called "The Gettysburg of the Southwest." By destroying the Confederate supply base there, Chivington prevented the South from acquiring the gold fields of Colorado, Arizona, California, and Nevada, a victory that may well have decided, in a large sense,

Attack on the Wagon Train. *From a painting by H. H. Cross.*

the outcome of the Civil War. After his feat at Santa Fe, Chivington's command was converted to cavalry, and he spent his time
hunting down Cheyennes, Arapahos, and Sioux.

The hero of the Sand Creek affair—an Indian, for a change—was
Black Kettle, chief of the Cheyennes. He was not a bloodthirsty
leader bent on vengeance, like Cochise, but he and his warriors had
collected a good many scalps, including those of women, whose
long hair was later found in his camp. He too had been guilty of
atrocities, but his great virtue in this instance was that he wanted
peace. The Cheyennes had been dazed and shaken by the relentless
aggression of expeditions like Major Downing's; although they had
fought back, they could see how useless it was, and in the summer
of 1864, they desired peace. Accordingly, Black Kettle sent word to
Major Wyncoop, in command at Fort Lyon, that he wished to
have a council of negotiation, and he proposed an exchange of
prisoners.

What happened afterward is still the subject of much dispute,
which subsequent investigation has not done a great deal to clarify.
Yet certain facts seem to survive the controversy. It appears that   241

Major Wyncoop, who knew he had no authority to conduct any kind of negotiations, went out and persuaded the Cheyenne and Arapaho leaders to come with him to Denver for a talk with Governor Evans. The delegation included Black Kettle, his brother White Antelope, and Bull Bear, all Cheyennes; and several Arapahos representing their principal chief, Left Hand.

It was a most unsuccessful conference, according to the record of the conversation. The governor's part of it consisted almost entirely of such questions as, "Who committed the murder of the Hungate family on Running Creek?" "Who killed the man and the boy at the head of Cherry Creek?" and "Who stole Charley Autobee's horses?" To which the replies were always: "The Northern Arapahos"; "Kiowas and Comanches"; or "Raven's son"—in any case, none of those present or their bands.

Evans pointed out to the chiefs that he could not make peace with them because he had no authority to do so. Peace must be made with the military, he said, in this case Colonel Chivington, who was commander of the district. But Chivington was already under orders. That very day he had received a telegram from his superior, General S. R. Curtis, Commander of the Department of Kansas, saying: "I fear agent of the Interior Department will be ready to make presents too soon. It is better to chastise before giving anything but a little tobacco to talk over." That was the official government line—chastisement before peace. The Indians must be punished first.

Black Kettle's final words were peaceful enough. "We will return with Major Wyncoop to Fort Lyon," he said. "We will then proceed to our village and take back word to my young men, every word you say. I cannot answer for all of them, but think there will be but little difficulty in getting them to assent to help the soldiers"—meaning that he thought his braves would cooperate with the military in maintaining peace. So reads the transcript, which was certainly a white man's version of Black Kettle's actual words.

Wyncoop was relieved of his command soon after the conference in Denver. Chivington's enemies later asserted it was because the major had been too friendly with the Indians. In any event, he was replaced by Major Scott Anthony, a conscientious officer, who took command of Fort Lyon on November 2.

There began a game of cat-and-mouse, or more properly, officer-and-Indian. On his arrival, Anthony found 652 Southern Arapahos under their chief, Little Raven, known to be hostile, camped two miles from the fort and ostensibly seeking peace. They came to the fort every day for provisions; Wyncoop had apparently been feeding them. Anthony told them they must give up their arms, and they turned in a sorry collection of weapons, saying it was all they had. Anthony had second thoughts about the disarming, fearing that he had exceeded his authority, and ten days later he gave back the weapons, instructing the Indians to go away, which they did except for eight lodges of them under the friendly chief, Left Hand, who chose to join the Cheyennes.

On November 6, Black Kettle's Cheyennes began to move toward the fort, supposedly to make peace. Major Anthony reported to headquarters on that day: "Nine Cheyenne Indians today sent in, wishing to see me. They state that six hundred of that tribe are now thirty-five miles north of here, coming towards the post, and two thousand about seventy-five miles away, waiting for better weather to enable them to come in. I shall not permit them to come in, even as prisoners, for the reason that if I do I shall have to subsist them upon a prisoner's rations. I shall, however, demand their arms, all stolen stock, and the perpetrators of all depredations. I am of the opinion that they will not accept this proposition, but that they will return to the Smoky Hill. They pretend that they want peace, and I think they do now, as they cannot fight during the winter, except where a small band of them can find an unprotected train or frontier settlement. I do not think it is policy to make peace with them now, until all perpetrators of depredations are surrendered up, to be dealt with as we may propose."

After a little more parleying, the 600 Cheyennes under Black Kettle, who had been thirty-five miles north, came on down, but Anthony would not let them into the fort or permit them to camp in the vicinity. He told them they might go over on Sand Creek,   243 forty miles away, and camp there. Anthony added that if he were given any authority to treat with them, he would let them know.

The Cheyennes were not pleased with this treatment, but they made their camp at Sand Creek and waited. Their mood was not exactly friendly. They sent an insulting message back to the fort declaring, "If that little ——— ——— red-eyed chief wants a fight, we will give him all he wants," meaning poor Anthony, who was suffering from sore eyes. Black Kettle felt entirely safe. There were no soldiers around except for the garrison at Fort Lyon, which was too weak to attack him.

What he did not know was that Chivington, back in Denver, had become alarmed by the whole situation. Here was Fort Lyon, with a large band of Cheyennes not more than forty miles away, and 2000 others at no great distance. No one knew where Little Raven's Arapahos might be. The colonel felt that immediate action was required, an impulse bolstered further by another telegram he had just received from General Curtis: "Pursue everywhere and punish the Cheyennes and Arapahos; pay no attention to district lines. No presents must be made and no peace concluded without my consent."

That was all the authority Chivington required. Late in November he marched out of Bijou Basin with a small force, stopping at Fort Lyon to pick up Major Anthony and his First Colorado Cavalry, along with two howitzers. On the night of November 28, they were marching eastward across the plains below Fort Lyon—about 750 men, including cavalry and artillery. They had been en route for five days, at first in snow two to three feet deep, but now the ground was clear. The night was so bitter cold that old Jim Beckwith, their trapper guide, had stiffened up and could not follow the trail, so they had to depend on a half-breed Indian. This substitute guide and two officers were about a half-mile ahead of the others.

In the pale light between daybreak and sunrise they came upon the Indian camp at Sand Creek. There were 120 Cheyenne and eight Arapaho lodges, pitched beside a shallow stream which ran sluggishly on a broad bed of sand. A herd of 1100 ponies fanned

An Engagement with the Indians. *From a painting by R. F. Zogbaum.*

out from the camp on both sides for a mile, and it was toward these animals that Chivington sent a detachment to cut off the herd from the warriors.

Only a few Indians were astir in the camp, but a squaw about her morning chores heard the pounding of the white man's horses and ran to report that a herd of buffalo was approaching. The few braves who tumbled out in answer to her calls could see, by this time, that the buffalo were a large body of troops, and they saw too what Chivington was attempting to do with their ponies. They raced to intercept him, and firing broke out between these two parties.

There has never been any agreement about the details of what followed. George Bent, a half-breed trader who was in the Indian camp, has left us this account: "When I looked toward the chief's lodge I saw that Black Kettle had a large American flag up on a long lodgepole as a signal to the troops that the camp was friendly. Part of the warriors were running out toward the pony herds and the rest of the people were rushing about the camp in great fear. All the time Black Kettle kept calling out not to be frightened; that the camp was under protection and there was no danger. Then suddenly the troops opened fire on this mass of men, women and children, and all began to scatter and run. . . . The soldiers concentrated their fire on the people in the pits [dug by the main body of Indians for protection] and we fought back as well as we could with guns and bows, but we had only a few guns. The troops did not rush in and fight hand to hand, but once or twice after they had killed many of the men in a certain pit they rushed in and finished up the work, killing the wounded and the women and children that had not been hurt. The fight here was kept up until near sundown, when at last the commanding officer called off his men. . . . As they went back, the soldiers scalped the dead lying in the bed of the stream.

"At the beginning of the attack Black Kettle, with his wife and White Antelope, took their position before Black Kettle's lodge and remained there after all others had left the camp. At last Black Kettle, seeing that it was useless to stay longer, started to run, calling out to White Antelope to follow him; but White Antelope refused and stood there ready to die, with arms folded, singing his death song: 'Nothing lives long, Except the earth and the mountains,' until he was shot down by the soldiers."

This was an eyewitness account. In the Congressional investigation of what came to be known as the Sand Creek Massacre, a whole host of other eyewitnesses filled 700 closely printed pages with infinite variations of George Bent's story. Some, for instance, said that Black Kettle ran up both an American flag and a white flag above it, understandably ignoring flag etiquette; others swore they saw no flag of any kind. Again, if Black Kettle told his people the camp was under protection, no evidence was produced to show that he had been promised anything of the kind by anyone.

But a few horrifying details did emerge from the investigation. It was generally agreed that no prisoners were taken, except two squaws and five children, and no one was allowed to escape, if possible, whether man, woman, or child. A witness told of a naked three-year-old child trying to follow his fleeing parents until a soldier fired at him and missed, whereupon another soldier jumped from his horse, shouting, "Let me try the little ———. I can hit him." He, too, missed, but a third soldier dismounted and bagged the quarry.

When the Indians could not be completely dislodged by small arms, it was testified, the howitzers were brought up about noon time and began a wholesale destruction that precipitated a running fight as the whole village retreated. This went on for five miles or so, until dusk enabled the survivors to escape.

There were widely varying estimates of the casualties. Colonel Chivington's original report declared that 600 Indians had been killed; Major Wyncoop, who was also in the action, estimated only 70. The Indians conceded 140, 60 of them warriors. Later investigation disclosed that the true total was probably 300 Indians dead, half of them warriors and the other half women and children, with 7 soldiers dead and 47 wounded, of whom 7 died later.

For once the country was stirred by the white man's treatment of the Indians. Although General Curtis's orders had been clear   247 enough, the Army threw Chivington to the wolves and put him on trial; he resigned his commission a year later, the object of vituperation and scorn from one end of the country to the other.

Was he guilty? Like so many other questions that plague the historian, the answer appears to be yes and no. That Chivington's march to Sand Creek was the act of an officer carrying out orders is unquestioned, and it was further justified from the military view by the potential danger to Fort Lyon. But the manner in which the orders were executed can hardly be justified from the standpoint of humanity; even the official policy, "pursue and punish," could not sanction the deliberate murder of women and children. Yet in the action of Chivington's soldiers, there was the powerful motivation of vengeance for the Indians' numerous outrages in Colorado, especially toward women.

It may be noted in this respect that the treatment of women captives by the Plains Indians differed markedly from those east of the Mississippi. In the East, women were almost never molested sexually, either by raiding parties or as captives; in the West, they were treated as common property, or passed from one friend to another. Nor did these Indians hesitate to torture their women captives as cruelly as they did the men. Such practices were not unknown in the East, but they were uncommon. At Sand Creek, Chivington's men were probably thinking of raped wives and daughters, as well as friends and comrades murdered. They might well, in the bargain, have had little compunction about shooting at squaws when the squaws were shooting at them.

But if there were public doubts about the treatment of the Indians at Sand Creek, there were few complaints over the course of the white and Indian war in Minnesota, where a great uprising of the Sioux, beginning in 1862, temporarily diverted attention from the Civil War itself until the final defeat of the Indians, only three months before Sand Creek.

The troubles in Minnesota began with the worst massacre by Indians the whites had ever experienced—more than three hundred settlers killed in a single week. At any other time in the nation's history it would have caused a sensation, but the late reports of the

248

Western horror had to compete with the news from the Second Battle of Bull Run, from Bragg's invasion of Kentucky, and from Antietam, where the casualties had been 23,000. To the people of Minnesota, however, the massacre and the war that followed it were a nightmare.

The Indian leader who perpetrated this outrage was Little Crow, the fifth chief of the Kapoja band of Medewkanton Sioux to bear the name. In his own tongue he was Chetan-wakan-mani, "the sacred pigeon-hawk that comes walking." Little Crow was a sharp-featured savage of dubious distinction, a lover of the bottle, burdened with no visible principles, and overbearing in manner. Born in 1820, his village eventually became the frontier town of Pig's Eye, on the site of which St. Paul stands today. Little Crow had to leave the village at the urgent request of wronged husbands. He drifted on to two other tribes, marrying and leaving two wives in one, and acquiring four others, all sisters, in the second.

The youthful Little Crow "had very little good sense," his father once remarked, but after his multiple marriages he appeared to be ready to prove his father wrong when he succeeded the older chief as head of the Kapoja band. "I was only a brave then, I am a chief now," he observed, when he was reminded of past errors. He even set himself against liquor and bad morals, and encouraged the young to be thrifty and hard-working.

The Americans certainly could find no fault with him. He appeared to be the most cooperative of the Sioux chiefs, helping them to get their treaties approved, visiting Washington in a plug hat for the purpose. He was, in fact, more popular among the whites than the Indians for a time. His fellow tribesmen, surveying his farm lands, his new wagon, and his white man's house, suspected him of having sold out to the enemy and forsaken them.

This was the kind of internal fight between the traditionalists and the partly assimilated that always seemed to occur when white and red men lived closely together. The suspicion of Little Crow was only a part of the wrangling that divided the Sioux over that fundamental question. The hunters were in sharp opposition to the farmers.

In July of 1862, however, both parties were united in a common grievance against the white man. Previous treaties had guaranteed them annuities in both cash and provisions, but in July these had become overdue, although flour, lard, pork, and sugar were in warehouses waiting to be given out. Major Galbraith, in command at Yellow Medicine, could give the hungry Indians no reason for the delay, except that the money to be given with the provisions had not arrived and nothing could be done about either until it was received, with the proper authority to begin distribution. The Indians suspected that the white man, preoccupied with his Civil War, had no money to give.

Added to this immediate grievance were the usual ones that had been rankling for a decade: cheating by traders; the inability of their chiefs to protect them from the frauds of traders and agents, who often acted in collusion; and the generally delusive character of the treaties they had signed, which became more apparent every day.

Some of the younger braves, under a firebrand named Red Middle Voice, formed what was called a soldiers' lodge, an internal organization usually devoted only to hunting and war. This time the young men meant to take over where they thought their chiefs had failed; but when they went to see Captain John Marsh, at Fort Ridgely, their minds were still on peace. They wanted to know if the fort's soldiers were going to help the traders collect their claims when the money came. "My boys are soldiers; they are not collection agents for the traders," Marsh reassured them.

When the traders heard about this meeting, they took an immediate and unfortunate action. They decided to give no more credit to the Indians until the annuities were paid and their claims collected. Signs went up at once in their stores: "No credit for Indians." An interpreter protested that if the money did not come soon and the Indians had no credit, they would starve. One of the traders, who probably had never heard of Marie Antoinette, answered: "As far as I'm concerned, if they're hungry let them eat grass."

His words became the Sioux rallying cry. "Let them eat grass" brought into hard focus all the hatreds and suspicions born of ten years of mistreatment. The soldiers' lodge met on Sunday afternoon, August 17, to discuss these matters. They did not know that during the morning four of Red Middle Voice's young braves had killed five settlers in Meeker County. The reign of terror had begun.

The dawn of Monday morning was not unlike the thousands of other early stirrings since that March day in 1622 when Opechancanough set out to right the wrongs inflicted on him by the Jamestown colonists. In 250 years, nothing had changed. The Sioux squaws busied themselves in the half-light preparing breakfast while Little Turtle's men girded themselves for the day's bloody work, just as the Virginia squaws and braves had done more than two centuries before.

At Redwood, Minnesota, as in Jamestown, the whites were up early too; and Jim Lynd, who clerked in the Myrick brothers' store, had probably eaten the breakfast cooked for him by his Indian wife, the mother of his two half-breed daughters, before he went downstairs at six o'clock and was shot dead by Plenty of Hail, one of Little Crow's braves, as he stood in his front doorway. The relentless flow of history, the endless chain that no one could stop, was still victimizing the innocents on both sides.

The houses and stores of the Lower Agency, at Redwood, one of the two Indian villages on the reservation, were first to be attacked. Captain Marsh and his men, hurrying to the rescue from Fort Ridgely, were ambushed at Redwood Ferry, and more than half of them were killed. Then the Indians spread out to the settlers' cabins. Before the bloody day ended, more than 400 civilians had been killed. By midnight the marauders had reached the Upper Agency, at Yellow Medicine, and begun looting the stores.

Tuesday was a day of confusion. Some help had arrived, a detachment of troops from Glencoe reaching Fort Ridgely after an overnight march, and more could be expected from Fort Snelling, where a private who had ridden the 165 miles from Ridgely brought the news. Everywhere settlers were trying to escape the terror, 40,000 of them streaming down the roads and across the plains. At Snelling, General Henry Hastings Sibley was instructed to put down the uprising.

Next day Little Turtle led a probing attack on Fort Ridgely, but he was repulsed and laid siege. Meanwhile, the unhappy settlers at Lake Shetek were surrounded and massacred in a piece of terrain that was thereafter grimly known as "Slaughter Slough." Obviously, General Sibley had his work cut out for him.

By Friday, 300 refugees had contrived to reach the safety of Ridgely. Little Turtle launched a major attack on the fort that day, but again he was beaten back. Something of the atmosphere in the fort can be imagined from the laconic words of an eyewitness, Major B. H. Randall, who told later how, on the previous Sunday when the trouble began, "refugees were constantly streaming in all day, many wounded and crazed with grief; some had been without food and water.

"When evening came, guards were stationed at all the doors with either axe, shovel, club or anything else that could be used as a weapon. The women worked all night making cartridges out of slugs cut by the men for the small number of guns they had been able to give the sentinels.

"Twenty old-style Dragoon carbines were found in the magazine and put into condition by Patrick Hefron, who had been for fifteen years a sergeant in the Second Infantry. The women made cartridges for these by cutting up iron rods into slugs. That night Jones sent up rockets as evidence that the fort was still there; they were seen at New Ulm, eighteen miles distant.

"There was a great fear of fire, for everything was very dry. Buckets of water were placed at one of the four scuttles that led to the barracks roof. It rained the next morning.

"On Friday near noon came an attack from three sides. By opening up the hall of the commanding officer's quarters that protected Jones' position on the south, he was able to fire the stable by sending a shell through the hall. Little Crow's charges and orders were distinctly heard but frustrated by the grape and cannister."

Meanwhile, Sibley had come as far as St. Peter, where he received frantic appeals for help from New Ulm, which he was compelled to ignore because he was convinced now that he had marched out with a force inadequate to deal with the uprising. Next day New Ulm was attacked repeatedly from morning to night; and although the Indians were repulsed, a third of the town was destroyed. On the following day, Monday, it had to be evacuated, while Sibley sat helpless at St. Peter, waiting for the troops and supplies he had summoned from Fort Snelling. They soon arrived, and three days later Sibley marched into Fort Ridgely with 1500 troops.

He found the beleagured outpost full of the wounded and ill, so that on the Tuesday following his arrival, September 2, he was compelled to send out a burial party from the fort, consisting of twenty wagons and 135 men, commanded by Captain Marsh, a young officer. At a place known as Birch Coulee, thirteen miles from the fort, the outriders sighted the army of Little Crow, Marsh ordered his wagons into the classic circle, with the horses and mules in the center, and prepared to resist certain attack.

It was not long in coming. Soon the braves were circling the wagon train in the manner immortalized by a thousand Western movies. The attack had begun at dawn, the usual time. By nightfall, only one of Marsh's 96 horses was alive and the soldiers were firing over the carcasses, which they had propped against the wheels in a barricade of horseflesh. A volunteer who tried to ride the remaining animal for help got only a few yards before the horse fell, literally shattered by bullets.

Suspecting what had happened, Sibley sent out a relief party, which reached Birch Coulee on Wednesday, thirty-one hours after the attack began. Help was too late for twenty-three of Marsh's men who lay dead or mortally wounded, but a brisk skirmish with Little Crow's warriors drove them off and saved the others.

By September 18, Sibley's command numbered 1600 men, and he had been further augmented by more munitions and supplies. Thus equipped he set out for Yellow Medicine. In four days, having marched thirty-six miles, he camped for the night near Wood Lake, only four miles from his goal. Before the sun came up he found himself engaged by about 700 Sioux warriors, the best

253

Indian army that could be raised from the Minnesota tribes. The Indians had planned their strategy well, but the battle was touched off prematurely, and it was over before all the Sioux braves could be brought into the action. Sibley's cannon proved to be the deciding factor. Howitzers frightened and dismayed the Indians, always, more than anything else the white man could produce. In this case they broke and ran, their casualties more than two-to-one compared with Sibley's.

The immediate result of the Battle of Wood Lake, as it came to be known, was that Sibley got his brigadier general's commission, and the Sioux chiefs left the field conscious that they had lost not only the battle but the war. Next morning Little Crow and hundreds of other leaders left Minnesota, bound for Canada, Devil's Lake, or the Western plains. They took scores of captives with them. Little Crow was so enraged by the loss of his eminence, his lands, and all that he had built up as a "good Indian" that he proposed to torture and kill the captives, but a rival and nobler chief, Red Iron, rose in council and declared that he would kill any warrior who laid hands on a woman or a child. Red Iron foresaw what Little Crow did not—that he might have to make peace with Sibley.

Little Turtle had the last word, however. While the wagons were being loaded to abandon the land he loved, he gathered his warriors about him and told them: "I am ashamed to call myself a Dakota. Seven hundred of our best warriors were whipped yesterday by the whites. Now we had better all run away and scatter out over the plains like buffalo and wolves. To be sure, the whites had wagon-guns and better arms than we, and there were many more of them. But that is no reason why we should not have whipped them, for we are brave Dakotas and whites are cowardly women. I cannot account for the disgraceful defeat. It must be the work of traitors in our midst."

Two Indian camps remained behind to guard the prisoners until Colonel Sibley could come up with his troops and their release could be arranged. While they waited for the colonel's unusually slow advance, occasioned by his excessive caution, the young braves

254

amused themselves by taking women captives into the woods and raping them, sometimes in gangs of ten or twelve. One girl of sixteen was raped by more than twenty Sioux.

Sibley reached the prisoners on September 26, and named the place Camp Release. He told the Indians, gathered in council, that he meant to punish the guilty, but of course all the Indian leaders present made eloquent protests that they were not the ones the colonel sought. By evening, however, the prisoners were released and an eyewitness reported: "The woe written on the faces of the half-starved and nearly naked women and children would have melted the hardest heart."

Colonel Sibley and his army stayed at Camp Release for a month, while the officer sought to find objects for punishment. But the guilty had taken Little Crow's advice and scattered. Unable to find the chiefs he sought, Sibley ordered all the Indians within reach seized, and in three weeks he declared: "I have now about four hundred Indian men in irons and between sixty and seventy under surveillance here and at Yellow Medicine." He then set up a rump court of his own devising and began dispensing justice. As many as forty men were tried in a day. By November 5, no less than 306 had been sentenced to be hanged.

Sibley sent the names of the condemned to President Abraham Lincoln and waited for permission to do the hanging. Lincoln replied on November 10: "Your dispatch giving the names of Indians condemned to death is received. Please forward as soon as possible the full and complete record of the convictions; if the record does not fully indicate the more guilty and influential of the culprits, please have a careful statement made on these points and forward to me. Send by mail." The last sentence was a reference to the telegraphic sending of the 306 names, which cost more than four hundred dollars.

As soon as he saw the records, Lincoln knew they were anything but full and complete, and he gave to two men in his administration the impossible task of sorting out the truly guilty from the less guilty. Meanwhile, all the Indian captives, including the 306, were herded into winter quarters inside a high board fence at Fort

Snelling. The condemned men were soon moved onward to a separate stockade on the Mankato River. On the way they had to pass through New Ulm, where jeering women lined the streets, threw rocks and scalding water at the prisoners, and tried to get at them with pitchforks, scissors, hoes, knives, and bricks. Fifteen of the helpless men were hurt. It was a repetition of the passage to Snelling, where children had been torn from the arms of squaws and killed.

Lincoln, as one observer wrote, "was inundated with appeals for mercy from friends of the Indian who had never seen one, from people opposed to the death penalty, and from those who regarded the convicts as prisoners of war." But there was no doubt about how the people on the frontier felt; they were for immediate execution, and no nonsense.

In December, Lincoln sent his letter to General Sibley, designating who was to die. There were thirty-nine names on the list, and the task began of finding the men who fitted the names. That was not easy, because some of the prisoners had the same name, and besides, the execution orders designated the condemned men by the numbers given to them by Lincoln's commission, and unfortunately no one could recall what number belonged to what person. Thus, as one white woman captive protested, "The Indian named Chaskadon, that the president ordered to be hanged, killed a pregnant woman and cut out her child, and they hung Chaska, who was only convicted of being present when Mr. Gleason was killed." Chaska had, in fact, protected this woman. There were other similar cases, but among the thirty-nine on the list were some whose crimes were indubitably heinous. On the other hand, most of those who had started the war and those who had perpetrated the worst of the offenses were not among the condemned. They had fled long ago and never surrendered.

The Indians were hanged on the day after Christmas. There were thirty-eight of them, since one had been reprieved, although the authorities do not agree on this matter. They protested the muslin caps pulled down over their faces, but they were herded, nevertheless, onto the huge scaffold, with its rows of loops waiting

EXECUTION OF THE THIRTY-EIGHT SIOUX INDIANS
AT MANKATO, MINNESOTA DECEMBER 26, 1862

for their necks. Swaying and stomping to the melancholy death wail of the Dakotas, "Hi-yi-yi, hi-yi-yi," repeated in monotonous cadence, they waited for death. A few screamed. Others swung about and grasped the hand of a neighbor; some shouted their names.

When the deadly rolling drum beats signaled the moment of execution, William J. Duley came forward, knife in hand, to cut the rope that would release thirty-eight platforms simultaneously. Two of Duley's children had been killed and scalped in the massacre. His knife flashed keen and sure, the traps dropped, and a low, growling roar rose from the grim lips of the soldiers and settlers who watched. The kicking, flailing bodies dangling grotesquely in the chill December air marked the end of the Sioux uprising, and darkly foreshadowed the brief and sanguinary events which would soon close forever the long war between white men and red.

There were a few footnotes to be added before the Minnesota war became history. The executed men were removed that night from their mass grave by a group of doctors who used them for

257

laboratory purposes. Little Turtle, who had fled farther west, returned in July, 1864, with his son, and was killed one evening as he prowled about a farm near Hutchinson. Sibley pursued the remnants of the Sioux into the Badlands—"Hell with the fires out," as he called it—and there on August 4, 1864, he crushed the remaining show of resistance in an all-day battle that cost the Indians more than 500 braves and chiefs.

The refugees from this catastrophe withdrew westward, always westward, but there was not much more of the continent remaining. They met the Cheyennes who had survived Sand Creek and made common cause with them, and with that meeting the stage was set for the final battles, the twilight before the night of total defeat.

15

LAST STANDS

For a year after the Minnesota war there was peace. By an ironic quirk, it was the Confederacy that achieved this respite where the Union cavalry had failed. While Sand Creek and New Ulm were distracting the North, the South moved to bring together the Western tribes in a great council that might bring peace to the frontier. What Jefferson Davis hoped to gain by this dramatic gesture is not entirely clear, but it was a noble if overly optimistic plan.

The emissary of peace chosen by the Confederate government was a brave of the Creeks named Tuk-a-Ba-Tche-Miko, who set out on a long pilgrimage through the Southwest, by horse and foot, bringing the summons to council. He talked to Osages and Pawnees, Iowas, Kickapoos, and Potawatomies, Wichitas, Kiowas, Comanches, and Apaches, Southern Cheyennes and Arapahos, Navajos, Mescalero Apaches, Northern Cheyennes, and Unkpapas, Teton and Yankton Sioux. Week after week he moved among the tribes, over a vast area, sending back after every meeting a bundle of notched sticks to indicate how many tribes he had persuaded and their population.

The Creek must have been a most persuasive messenger, for when the council finally met on May 1, 1865, on the Washita River, there were no fewer than 20,000 Indians present, perhaps the largest gathering of them ever held west of the Mississippi. The

Confederate officials present did not know of Appomattox. In good faith they secured an agreement from the tribes represented at the council—and the delegates included most of those the Creek messenger had visited—to stop the raiding that precipitated white retaliation and led to war. The Indians also promised to guarantee the peace, a promise kept in large measure throughout the Southwest for a short time.

Farther north, however, the situation was much less stable. As the restless Americans resumed their westward push, interrupted by the war, they found themselves once more in conflict with those older Americans who barred their way. The tide of emigration flowed across the western part of the continent along four main pipelines: the Santa Fe Trail in the South; the Kansas Trail to Denver; the Oregon Trail to Nebraska and Salt Lake City, thence to Oregon and California; and the Bozeman Trail, running through Wyoming to Montana.

Whereas the westward push to the Mississippi had been gradual, the post–Civil War rush beyond it was a tidal wave. Confronted with the steady onrush along the four trails, the fierce Indians of the Plains made ready to fight for survival. A few leaders sensed the futility of defending their lands, but the ablest were fanatically determined to fight as long as hope remained.

Opposing them was a tough postwar army, drawn from both the Blue and the Gray, composed primarily of men who could not readjust themselves to civilian life or who had never been any more than misfits or adventurers. James D. Horan, whose *The Great American West* depicts them in the most graphic fashion, calls them a Foreign Legion, and indeed they were—Irish, German, French, Italian, with smatterings of a half-dozen other nationalities. There were Negroes, too—the crack all-Negro Tenth Cavalry, and General Carpenter's smart infantry regiment known as "Carpenter's Brunettes." There were even Indians in the white man's army— Pawnees, Crows, Shoshones, and others who hated the Sioux, all acting as scouts.

Whatever the failings of the rank and file might be—at least they lacked nothing in courage and professional talent—their com-

260

manders were of the first order. General Grant was, of course, at the top of the military hierarchy. His chief-of-staff was William Tecumseh Sherman, and Phil Sheridan commanded the Department of the West. The roster of field commanders reads like an honor roll: Alfred H. Terry, George Armstrong Custer, George Crook, John Gibbon, Nelson A. Miles, among others.

The war these commanders fought with the Indians was not like the one which had conquered the East. There were few battles of a conventional kind, but rather a series of brief engagements, more in the nature of skirmishes and sorties. They were fought with the particular ferocity of the Plains Indians, to which could be added the savagery of desperation as the tribes saw themselves relentlessly decimated and pushed off their ancient hunting grounds. No quarter was given on either side. There was little to choose in placing the blame for atrocities. In the first stage of the postwar campaigns, from 1866 to 1875, more than 200 battles were fought, mostly with the Sioux; in the second phase, 1882 to 1887, the struggle was centered on the Apaches.

This last chapter in the history of the long war began with another peace conference, held at Fort Laramie in 1866. The truce the Confederates had purchased was nearly ended, because the Union negotiators now wanted the Sioux and the Northern Cheyennes to give emigrants the right to pass over lands ceded to the Indians only a year before, and to permit the construction of three forts designed to protect the Bozeman Trail.

General Sherman himself led the white delegation that gathered under a large tent at Fort Laramie to welcome the Indians. The hard-featured red negotiator who confronted them was Red Cloud, chief of the Oglalas and acknowledged leader of the Sioux and Cheyenne hostiles.

Red Cloud was only forty-four, and a natural commander of men. A white contemporary describes him as "a magnificent specimen of physical manhood," and "as full of action as a tiger." Dignified, and with the manners and speech of a gentleman, he came to the Laramie conference in a distrustful frame of mind because he was gifted with a keen foresight which told him accurately enough

Red Cloud and American Horse. *Photograph by Grabill.*

what would happen to his people and their lands if the forts were built along the Bozeman Trail and the path became a major highway to the Far West. There was also something of the mystic in Red Cloud; he claimed to be in direct communication with the Great Spirit, who told him what to do.

As the commissioners and the chiefs began their talks in the late spring, it was obvious to the Indians that the white men meant to have their forts and their roads no matter what occurred at the council. Even as the negotiators talked, Colonel Henry B. Carrington came up from Fort Kearney with 2000 men, and in June sent 700 of them through Laramie, under the very noses of the Indians, to effect a military occupation of the Powder River country.

At this, Red Cloud denounced Carrington and, in a rage, charged that the white men meant to seize the land by force, which in fact they were in the act of doing. He stalked out of the meeting, followed by Man Afraid of His Horses and other leaders who agreed with him. Spotted Tail, Standing Elk, and Swift Bear, all chiefs of the Brulé Sioux, decided to remain and sign the treaty, but two weeks later they were compelled to report to the white commanders that most of their young men had defected. They added the laconic warning that any parties venturing far from the fort had better "go prepared, and look out for their hair."

Thus began two years of virtual siege, during which Red Cloud and his braves maintained a constant harassing attack on Carrington's troops and anything else that moved along the Bozeman Trail. There were incidents of great courage and daring, like the ride of John Phillips, a civilian scout, through 236 miles of tempestuous blizzard and hostile Indian territory to bring relief from Fort Laramie to Carrington at Fort C. F. Smith. There was also one major encounter, in August, 1867, when Red Cloud led 3000 of his finest warriors in an assault on Fort Kearney. A heroic captain, James W. Powell, who had also done well at Chickamauga, directed his pitiful little garrison of thirty-two men so skillfully that they beat off three charges by Red Cloud's men and killed 1137 of his warriors—a nearly incredible feat.

It was matched, however, by the altogether remarkable defense

263

of Major George Alexander "Sandy" Forsyth and twenty-eight men, in the same year, when they successfully resisted a large Sioux force at Beecher's Island, in eastern Colorado. Struck by three bullets at the first charge, Forsyth calmly conducted the defense from a pool of his own blood. Then, as his wounds slowly rotted with gangrene, he held his dwindling force together through five more awful days of siege, while his starved men gnawed at the decaying flesh of their dead horses, until help came. The relief column was led by Colonel Louis H. Carpenter, who found his friend Forsyth, rifle across his knees, reading a copy of *Oliver Twist*—a magnificent gesture the gallant major later confessed he had made to avoid breaking down. He was two years recovering from his wounds.

In spite of these and other heroic actions, Red Cloud prevailed at last, by sheer dogged resolution. The government began to negotiate with him late in 1867, but the discussions broke down, were resumed in the summer of 1868, and on November 6 were finally concluded successfully—that is, for Red Cloud, who won a complete victory. The Bozeman Trail was closed; Forts Kearney and C. F. Smith were ordered abandoned.

The government was beginning to make significant changes in its Indian policy. The way to stop the Indian wars, it had been decided, was to prevent the Indians from moving about the country freely—in brief, to put them on reservations. The sop to be thrown them for the creation of these ghettos was to make them a present of the lands comprising the reservations, in many cases giving them what they already owned. The reservation idea was not new— earlier treaties had, for decades, set aside lands for the exclusive use of the Indian signatories. But the American government had learned nothing from the abuses of these treaties. The new policy contained no provision to prevent white encroachment on the reservations, nor to guarantee the permanence of the land gifts, much less of the treaties that established them.

The reservation plan began to be fully implemented in 1868, although it would take two decades to pen up all the tribes. A year later, in 1869, Sheridan persuaded President Grant to take another fateful step. No more treaties were to be made with tribes or nations, the government announced, because the Indians were thenceforth to be considered wards of the United States. Thus one of the principal causes of friction for many decades was removed, but at the same time the government assumed an obligation it had not undertaken before. As wards, unfortunately, the Indians had nothing to protect them except the presumed good will of their guardians. How much this was worth to them, history has been the sad judge.

Even as these pacific policies were being promulgated, the campaign of extermination went on. Black Kettle, having survived the Sand Creek disaster, had spent the time since that event in desultory raids here and there until 1867, when the negotiators from Washington made a new treaty with the Comanches, Kiowas, Arapahos, and Cheyennes, at Medicine Creek Lodge. Black Kettle appeared satisfied with the proceedings of this council, as did the chiefs of the other tribes represented. Handsome presents were distributed to them, and Santana (sometimes Satanta), or White Bear, a Kiowa subchief, proudly donned his gift—the uniform of the army he had been fighting until yesterday.

But the young men of the tribes were not pacified by the treaty or the presents. Their warlike temperaments had been fired up by nearly four years of constant fighting, and they were not in a mood to give up so easily. These firebrands went on as they had before, scalping and burning wherever they could; the old chiefs no longer had the power to stop them. General Sheridan, therefore, determined to enforce the peace in the customary way, and in the late autumn of 1868 began a scorched-earth campaign against the Cheyennes and any others who remained hostile.

The man he chose as field commander was an old favorite of his, George Armstrong Custer, the impulsive and dashing "Boy General" of the Civil War, just then under a year's suspension from the army after a court-martial in which he was convicted of cruelty and illegal conduct, among other counts. Sheridan succeeded in bringing him west to Fort Hays, Kansas, and put him in charge of the Seventh Cavalry.

265

As controversial in the writings of historians 'as he was in his lifetime, Custer's role in Sheridan's war against the Indians remains a matter of opinion, of which there is a great deal in print. The record of what he did is much more clear than some of his reasons for doing it.

There is no doubt whatever that on November 23, obeying Sheridan's orders, he rode out with his men toward the Washita River, where Black Kettle had settled down peacefully for the winter, surrounded by seventy-five lodges of his people, along with some Kiowas, Arapahos, and a few Apaches, far from home. Custer made a silent approach to the encampment, and on the morning of the 27th, at dawn, his troopers galloped into the village, spreading death and destruction to the music of their regimental tune, "Garry Owen":

> We'll beat the bailiffs out of fun,
> We'll make the mayor and sheriffs run;
> We are the boys no man dares dun,
> If he regards his whole skin.

Custer was obeying Sheridan's orders, but his apologists, of whom there are many, could scarcely term what happened on the Washita as anything but a massacre. It was, if anything, worse than Sand Creek. And this time Black Kettle did not survive. He died, along with an undetermined number of warriors, women, and children. By a miracle, a large part of the population escaped, fleeing at the sound of the first shots. Led by Santana and Black Kettle's subchief, Little Rock, the braves who had contrived to get away turned back and tried to exact what revenge they could. They accounted for the disappearance of Major Elliott and some fifteen men, who were missing after the battle.

Custer's friends among the historians attach no blame to him for not trying to find Elliott and his men, and it may well have been that he did not dare wait longer. Nor do they believe that the handsome commander took a pretty squaw to his bed and gave her a child, although she later swore that this was indeed a fact.

266

But there is no doubt that—again, obeying orders—he ordered

his men to burn all the tepees, destroy 1000 buffalo robes and 700 pounds of tobacco, along with the dried meat and other provisions the Indians had put by for the winter, besides seizing whatever guns, pistols, and bows and arrows had been left behind. There were also victims more helpless than the Indians. In his haste to get away before he was attacked, the cavalryman Custer ordered the captured Indian ponies—875 of them—destroyed.

Sheridan's mopping-up operations continued for some time on a smaller and less controversial scale, but there were still two large pockets of Indian resistance on the Plains. One was what remained of the Sioux Confederacy, encamped in the Valley of the Big Horn near the Powder River. The other was the "People," as the Chiricahua Apache called themselves. These were the legendary villains of the Southwest, cruel and tough, animated by a fanatic hatred of the white man. They were the "unrelenting Apache" who had terrorized Arizona Territory during the Civil War. Their faces were lean and often handsome, not like the broad-featured Sioux, and their courage was celebrated even by the white men who hated them.

Until 1871, the policy toward the Apaches had been one of simple extermination. General Ord, in command of the Department of California, reported in September, 1869: "I encouraged the troops to capture and root out the Apache by every means, and to hunt them as they would wild animals. . . ."

This policy was carried out most actively in Arizona, where the residents had a special hatred for the Apache. In April, 1871, a large party of civilian Americans, Mexicans, and Papago Indians set out from Tucson to exterminate a nearby village of the enemy. The Army post at Fort Lowell tried to intervene, but it was too late. When the post surgeon arrived at the scene, he could only report with horror: ". . . I found that I should have but little use for wagon or medicine; the work had been too thoroughly done. The camp had been fired, and the dead bodies of some twenty-one women and children were lying scattered over the ground; those who had been wounded in the first instance had their brains beaten out with stones. Two of the best-looking of the squaws were lying in such a position, and from the appearance of the genital organs

267

and of their wounds, there can be no doubt that they were first ravished and then shot dead. Nearly all of the dead were mutilated. One infant of some ten months was shot twice, and one leg nearly hacked off. While going over the ground, we came upon a squaw who was unhurt, but were unable to get her to come in and talk, she not feeling very sure of our good intentions."

Next morning, when Lieutenant Whitman came out from the post to bury the dead, he added to the story: ". . . Their camp was surrounded and attacked at daybreak. So sudden and unexpected was it, that no one was awake to give the alarm, and I found quite a number of women shot while asleep beside their bundles of hay which they had collected to bring in on that morning. The wounded who were unable to get away had their brains beaten out with clubs or stones, while some were shot full of arrows after having been mortally wounded by gunshot. The bodies were all stripped. Of the whole number buried, one was an old man and one was a well-grown boy—all the rest women and children. Of the whole number killed and missing—about one hundred and twenty-five—only eight were men. . . ."

Such was the state of white civilization in Arizona, less than ninety years ago.

The man the government sent to restore law and order and at the same time subdue the Apache was General George Crook, who took command of the Department of Arizona on June 4, 1871. Crook did not believe in extermination. He declared in a forthright statement which did not please the settlers: "I think that the Apache is painted in darker colors than he deserves, and that his villainies arise more from a misconception of facts than from his being worse than other Indians. Living in a country the natural products of which will not support him, he has either to cultivate the soil or steal, and as our vacillating policy satisfies him we are afraid of him, he chooses the latter, also as requiring less labor and being more congenial to his natural instincts. I am satisfied that a sharp, active campaign against him would not only make him one of the best Indians in the country, but it would also save millions of dollars to the Treasury, and the lives of many innocent whites and Indians."

But the President's own representative, Vincent Colyer, who came on the scene at the same time, did not favor Crook's "sharp, active campaign." He tried coercion instead, and the Apache repaid him by making fifty-four separate attacks in Arizona between September, 1881, and September, 1882, after which Crook announced his intention of punishing "the incorrigibly hostile." It took him a little more than six months to do it. On April 27, 1873, the last of the recalcitrants surrendered and peace was restored to Arizona temporarily. The government was so impressed by Crook's feat that he was made a brigadier general, a promotion unusual for the times.

Crook was a paradox. An efficient fighter of Indians, he was also their friend, believing that courage in the field ought to be matched by courage in dealing with the red men at peace. Consequently, he made proposals so far in advance of his times that he was regarded by some in the Army as an "Indian lover," and by the government as a man almost too visionary to be an officer. Not only did he stand against the Army's policy of punishment, favoring pardon instead, but he proposed that the reservations be divided into small plots so that each Indian could have his own farm and be self-supporting. He dared to believe, too, that Indians were citizens who deserved the protection of the Constitution and ought to have the rights of all other citizens, a wholly reasonable doctrine not embraced today by some state legislatures.

No one paid much attention to his recommendations; his talents in the field were too useful. After his success in Arizona, he was made commander of the Department of the Platte, where the Sioux and Cheyenne constituted the major pocket of resistance scheduled next for extermination.

While Crook had been chasing Apaches, however, a minor episode in northern California attracted public attention and made an obscure tribe, the Modocs, famous in the annals of Indian wars.

As Keith A. Murray, the latest and best historian of the Modoc affair, observes: "The Modoc Indian War was the final desperate resistance to the impact of white man's culture on the ancient Indian folkways. It marks the concluding stages of the decline in vigor

269

and numbers among a fierce people, beginning in the early years of the nineteenth century and ending when a band of beaten and spiritless prisoners were forced aboard a Central Pacific Railroad train bound for exile on a tiny reservation in Oklahoma."

The Modoc War was also a conflict of colorful personalities, perhaps more so than any of the other Western Indian wars. Where, for example, could be found a tribe whose leaders' names sounded more like a roster of twentieth-century gangland: Captain Jack, Curley Headed Doctor, Bogus Charley, Shacknasty Jim, Scarfaced Charley, Steamboat Frank, Boston Charley, Ellen's Man George, One Eyed Watchman, Hooker Jim, Old Tail, William (the Wild Gal's Man), Old Chuckle Head and One Eyed Mose, among others.

The causes of the Modoc revolt were complex, but essentially they were compounded of an old trouble, friction between the settlers and Indians, and a relatively new one, dissatisfaction with the workings of the reservation system. There were other elements in the drama. One was the rivalry between the Modoc chief Schonchin, or Sconchin, who signed the treaty creating the reservation, and his younger rival Captain Jack, who denounced it and led his band of dissidents away from the assigned lands. Another factor was the proximity of the Klamath tribe, old enemies of the Modocs, whose rights and lands were involved in the complicated reservation tangle, brought about largely by the ineptness of government administration. Intramural warfare between the two tribes was almost inevitable.

Finally there was the element of mysticism, as there had been in so many other Indian revolts. It was Curley Headed Doctor, the fanatical medicine man, who was the spiritual leader of the Modoc war and kept it alive against fantastic odds, until his medicine failed and the tribesmen lost their faith.

There were "good" Indians and "bad" Indians among the 160-odd warriors Captain Jack led away from the reservation where the white men wanted him to live in proximity with the hated Klamaths. Some were honestly persuaded, either by Jack's arguments, or by Curley Headed Doctor's exhortations to follow the old ways.

Others were murderers and thieves who would have been trouble-some on or off the reservation. But in one thing they were more or less united: They did not intend to be pushed around by the government's agents. When a force of thirty-eight soldiers came to arrest them and bring them back to the reservation on November 29, 1872, they fought off Captain David Jackson's men, killing or wounding eight of them, and with this Battle of Lost River, the war was on.

About Captain Jack's character there is still some dispute. There was a flamboyance about him reflected in his name, which the whites had given him because of his passion for dressing like one of their officers, replete with brass buttons and similar adornments. A short, round-faced, squat man with somewhat shifty manners, he was probably no adornment to the Indian nations; he may even have been involved in an Indian prostitution racket. But there could be no doubt about his military ability, for he led his dissidents away from the Battle of Lost River into an ancient retreat of caves and crevasses known to the army as "the Stronghold," actually a terrain of lava beds south of Tule Lake near the Oregon border. There, for six desperate months, he held at bay a force of more than a thousand soldiers and settlers.

He fought five major battles and several skirmishes with his pursuers, suffering only minor losses to his own meager forces and inflicting more casualties than the total number of his warriors. In one of the first battles, on January 17, 1874, his men held off 400 troops who attempted to storm his stronghold in an all-day struggle, killing nine and wounding thirty others without suffering (so it was reported) a single casualty.

Captain Jack's opponent in the field was, like General Crook, a true friend of the Indians. General E. R. S. Canby, commanding the Department of the Columbia, was a Civil War veteran who, again like Crook, had a reputation both for military successes against the Indians and fairness and honesty in dealing with them. He had been with Jackson in the Seminole War, and had played an unwilling part in the removal of the Cherokees. Since then he had served in the Mexican War, been engaged in the bloodless "Mormon War" of 1858, seen service in New Mexico, fought in the only Western battles of the Civil War, captured Mobile in 1865, been on occupation duty in the South, and functioned as military governor in four Southern states. He had come to Washington Territory directly from Virginia.

Canby wanted to prevent further hostilities against the Modocs, after it was plain that the Indians were impregnably entrenched in the lava beds. He would have favored negotiation in any case; he had justly earned his title of "the Indian's friend," as one tribe called him. The Modocs had nothing to lose by negotiation. They were masters of diplomacy, and very likely could have made wholly satisfactory terms with a man like Canby. But for reasons which now seem inexplicable, they lost their opportunity and the war by a single, mad, irresponsible act.

On April 11, Canby's commissioners rode out for a council with the Modoc leaders, to be held in a peace tent at the foot of a high bluff. The general brought with him the Reverend Eleazer Thomas; A. B. Meacham; L. S. Dyer, an agent from the Klamath Reservation; and, to interpret for the commission, a man named Frank Riddle and his Modoc wife Toby. They found eight Modocs waiting for them: Bogus Charley, Boston Charley, Captain Jack, Schonchin John (the chief's son), Ellen's Man, Black Jim, Hooker Jim, and Shacknasty Jim. They were all armed.

After a good deal of talk, most of it conciliatory on the part of the commissioners, matters reached an impasse over what parcel of land was to be given to the Modocs for their reservation, which of course had always been the crux of the problem. One of the Indians jumped up, and there was a moment of confusion during which four more Indians, carrying guns, appeared from behind some nearby rocks.

"What does this mean, Captain Jack?" one white man cried out.

"*Atwe*," Jack responded, meaning "all ready," whereupon he drew his revolver and fired at Canby, no more than three feet away. The gun missed fire but Jack recocked it and fired again. Canby fell, with a wound under the eye. Then, apparently by plan, the Indians fell upon their appointed victims. Thomas was shot and killed. Meacham engaged in a running gun duel, trying to reach his horse, but he too was killed. Canby, who was only wounded, got up and ran a little way before Ellen's Man brought him down again with a rifle shot and Captain Jack finished him with a stab in the neck. Only Dyer, Riddle, and Toby escaped.

Few events in any of the Indian wars stirred up such hot indignation as these murders. It was not simply the atrocity itself, shameful as it was, but the fact that it was perpetrated on such highly esteemed men as Canby and Thomas, who had done so much to help the Modocs and so plainly had their interest at heart. Negotiation was abandoned, and extermination became the policy once more.

Colonel Jefferson C. Davis took the field with more than a thousand soldiers, volunteer civilians, and some disaffected Modocs who acted as scouts. The pressure soon became too great, and the Modocs retreated slowly toward the hills. They might have successfully resisted even then, however, if dissension had not broken out among them, and if they had not lost their faith in Curley Headed Doctor's influence with the Great Spirit. Sixty-five surrendered on May 22. Jack held out with two other warriors and their women and children until June 1. Hopeless and desperate, he glared at the scouts who came to meet him and remarked only, "My legs have given out," as he extended his hands.

Six Modocs, including Captain Jack, were tried for the murder of the commissioners. The trial was actually a court-martial for violating the rules of war. All were convicted and sentenced to be hanged, but President Grant commuted the sentences of two men to life. On October 3, 1873, the four others were hanged from a single long scaffold at Fort Klamath. Unrepentant, Captain Jack had only one thing to say before the drop fell: "I am ready to go to the Great Father."

Thus ended the Modoc War, the most expensive in relative terms that the government had ever fought with the Indians. Its monetary cost was a half-million dollars, or more. The white men lost 8 officers, 39 enlisted men, 16 civilians, and 2 scouts killed, with 67 others wounded, besides 18 settlers killed and as many others wounded. The Modocs lost only 5 warriors, besides several women and children.

If the government had given the Modocs what they wanted, it would have cost 2000 acres of land, or less, worth about $10,000, and the establishment of an agency, which might have cost as much as $20,000 more.

Soon after the subduing of the Modocs, events began to take place in the Black Hills of the Dakotas which would bring about the final great battle on the Plains. The Black Hills were already important to the Sioux, who considered this territory as sacred ground. In 1873 and 1874, they suddenly became important to the white men, who found gold there. Both Custers were on the scene. George Custer had gone out with the first expedition to explore the Black Hills, in 1873, and his brother, Captain Tom, went the following year. Tom distinguished himself by capturing the Sioux chief, Rain-in-the-Face, who promptly escaped and vowed he would one day eat Tom's heart.

The Custers found gold in the Black Hills, and although wiser heads in the Army tried to hold back the inevitable rush until proper treaties could be made with the Sioux, there was no restraining gold-mad men. In a year, Deadwood had been founded, other towns had mushroomed, and the Indians saw their sacred land profaned in every direction. For the Sioux and Cheyenne, it was the last straw. Now there would be work for General Crook to do.

This time he faced the most formidable adversaries of his career in Crazy Horse and Sitting Bull. Crazy Horse was the military genius of the Sioux Confederacy, and Sitting Bull was a medicine man who possessed an extraordinary ability to plan and organize.

Crazy Horse was a young man, not much more than twenty-five. A Sioux of the Oglala tribe, his name (Tashunca-uitco in his own tongue) probably derived from an incident at the time of his birth, when a wild pony ran through the village. While there is no certainty about it, he most likely fought with Red Cloud in the Wyoming campaigns. Crazy Horse was a bold and independent man who had no intention of being penned up in a reservation. From the beginning he adopted an implacable attitude toward the white man's government and all its works. He was a strong leader among the Sioux, and when he married a Cheyenne woman, he became a principal figure among those people too.

Sitting Bull was cut from a different cloth. Older than Crazy Horse—he was past forty at the time of the war—he was also wiser. Indeed, he was the very model of a politician. After establishing himself as a war leader when he was a young man, he heard a call to higher, safer, and more lucrative realms, and set himself up as a medicine man and elder statesman. Fortunately, he was talented in both respects. Soon he had accumulated what amounted to a fortune, for an Indian, and began to preside in his lodge like the powerful and influential man he was, entertaining the Sioux, Cheyenne, and Arapaho leaders who hated the white man as much as he did. His hatred was not inspired by any specific incident of his life; it was simply traditional. To solidify his position, he used his wealth to distribute presents where they would do the most good.

Thus this broad, short, and heavy man, who looked like an Indian alderman or ward boss, by 1875 found himself the head of the war council, even though he was not himself a war chief. By the spring of 1876, when it appeared that war was imminent, he had accumulated in his camp on the Rosebud River, in the Valley of the Little Big Horn, from 2500 to 4000 well-armed men and boys. More were coming every day because the gold rush of 1875 had proved to be the catalyst Sitting Bull required to bring about the war both he and Crazy Horse wanted. The Sioux who had listened to Red Cloud and followed him into peacemaking with the whites were disillusioned by the invasion of the sacred Black Hills.

The unwise act that precipitated the war occurred in December, 1885, when the Indian Commissioner in Washington, alarmed by what he heard about the free-roaming activities of the Sioux, decreed that all the roving bands must return to their reservation by January 31, 1876. It was unrealistic as well as unwise. For one thing, the messengers sent out by the Indian agents to relay the message had to fight their way through the severe winter weather of the Plains; it took one man more than a month. Because the winter had been so hard, many of the tribes were far afield, seeking game, and it would have been impossible for them to return.

When the deadline passed, largely ignored, the Commissioner turned the execution of his orders over to the War Department, and it fell to General Crook to carry out orders and attack the winter villages of the Sioux. He felt reasonably confident of success because his command included ten troops of cavalry and two infantry companies, one of the strongest forces the army had sent against the Indians in the West. When two Indian hunters appeared, sighted this formidable expedition, and fled in haste, Crook sent Colonel J. J. Reynolds after them with 450 men.

At daybreak Reynolds' scouts came upon a large Indian encampment. Although they did not know it, they had discovered the headquarters of the Sioux war leader, Crazy Horse himself. Reynolds took the village by surprise, but most of the warriors had enough warning to leave precipitately and find shelter in a nearby stand of timber. Reynolds promptly burned the camp and the watching Indians saw their homes, their blankets, their food, everything they possessed, consumed in the flames. Reynolds had even captured their ponies.

Any other chief might have surrendered or dispersed his warriors in fear of their lives, but Crazy Horse demonstrated why he was the most renowned of the Sioux chiefs and their war leader. He rallied the braves, inspired them by his own example, organized a counterattack, and set upon Reynolds' men with such fury that the astute colonel was compelled to fall back with heavy losses, a retrograde that turned into a precipitate retreat. Crazy Horse took advantage of the white force's disorganization to get back his warriors' ponies.

Reynolds was able to reach Crook's main force, but the audacious Sioux leader was not through with his adversary. Mounted again, his men swept around the army and cut off most of the cattle, driving them away before Crook realized his loss. Without his meat supply, far from base on the bleak plains, the general had little choice but to march back in somber defeat to Fort Fetterman. Crazy

Horse had lost his village, but he had defeated the white man and replenished his store of provisions at the same time.

As for Crook, he saw that bringing the Sioux to heel was a far larger job than the War Department had contemplated. New strategy was devised as spring came on, and by June he was ready to start over again. The plan was for Crook to march northward into the valley of the Rosebud, while Colonel John Gibbon moved eastward from the Montana mountains until he reached the command of General Alfred H. Terry, who would then proceed from Fort Abraham Lincoln, in Dakota, up the Missouri River. The object of these advances was to close in on the Sioux from every side and deal with their scattered positions piecemeal but simultaneously, so that they could not help each other.

The various expeditions began to move in May. Crook, this time with fifteen troops of cavalry and five companies of infantry, traveled up the Bozeman Trail, passed the haunted ruin of Fort Kearney, and came at last to the Tongue River, where he got a message from Crazy Horse advising him not to cross it. This was not the kind of message to send to a veteran like Crook. Sympathetic as he was to the red men, he replied tartly that all the Indians in the nation would not prevent him from crossing that river, which he did at once.

At eight o'clock in the morning on June 17, his army of 1300 men ran headlong into the 1200 Oglalas and Cheyennes of Crazy Horse. It was an explosive battle that swayed back and forth through a long, hot day, and as night fell, it was Crook who withdrew once more, with heavy losses, leaving the banks of the Rosebud in the hands of the Sioux. Crook was deeply chagrined by his second defeat at the hands of the Indian leader, but he had to admit that Crazy Horse was a superb tactician.

While Crook waited at his base for more men and supplies to try again, General Terry, supplemented by Gibbons' force, was nearing the mouth of the Rosebud, which he reached on June 22. He did not know it, but Crazy Horse had hurried north immediately after defeating Crook and had joined Sitting Bull, with the main body

277

of Sioux and Cheyennes, in the Valley of the Little Big Horn. Crook knew the camp was there, but he made the fundamental strategic mistake of not ascertaining the strength of his enemy, and he made the further mistake, which had unhorsed so many other white commanders, of underestimating the fighting capacity of the Indians. His only fear was that Sitting Bull's forces might run and escape before he could pin them down.

Sitting Bull, on the other hand, remained in his lodge and knew exactly what he meant to do. He proposed, first of all, to sit in camp and make strong medicine while his braves did the fighting under Crazy Horse and another chief named Gall. His scouts, furthermore, were watching the white advance closely and informed him on June 22 that Terry had sent the famous Seventh Cavalry, under Custer, up the Rosebud with the obvious intention of seeking out the Indian encampment.

In fact, the plan had been for Custer to proceed as far as the headwaters of the Little Big Horn and sweep down the valley while Terry approached from the other way, catching the Indians in a vise. With this plan began one of the most controversial episodes in American history, about which dispute still rages. Was Custer a brash fool who disobeyed orders, or did he simply attempt a brilliant tactical maneuver which failed to come off? The student or the casual reader may choose his authority, but certain facts remain clear. We do know what Custer actually did.

Before he reached the river's headwaters, he turned overland toward the Indian camp, a route which would inevitably bring him into contact with the enemy before Terry could get there. His motives for this action, and whether he failed to take the proper precautions on his approach, are in question. But there is no doubt that on the fateful morning of June 25 he stood at the divide, with the Valley of the Little Big Horn on one side and that of the Rosebud on the other—a commander who did not know exactly where the enemy lay waiting, or in what numbers.

He moved into the valley during the morning and split his men into three battalions. He sent Captain Frederick Benteen with one battalion toward the south, to search for the Indian village. Mean-

Custer's Last Stand. *Lithograph.*

while, with his own battalion and one commanded by Major Marcus A. Reno, he proceeded into the valley and in the afternoon sighted his goal. He ordered Reno to the attack at once, holding his battalion in reserve as support, but after the major had gone, he apparently changed his mind and began to maneuver his force around for an attack on the rear of the camp.

Whatever Custer's motives or plans may have been, the result was disastrous. Reno's battalion, as it approached the village, was charged by an overwhelming Indian force under Gall, while Crazy Horse, commanding a predominantly Cheyenne army, swept down on Custer and surrounded him. Gall quickly drove back Reno, with heavy losses, across the river and up the high bluffs on the other side, where the survivors dug in and fought back. Leaving part of his men to carry on the siege, Gall turned northward to aid Crazy Horse, who had already encircled poor Custer. The famous last stand had begun. It did not last long. Before nightfall Custer and his entire command of 212 men had been annihilated.

Meanwhile Benteen, having found no Indians at all, turned back to the north and arrived just in time to save Reno from destruction. Their combined forces held off the Indians until the afternoon of the next day, when the besiegers abruptly lifted the siege and departed westward. Their scouts had spotted the approach of General Terry.

The Indians had won the victory, but once again they had lost the war. Of course, they would have lost it in any case, because the news of Custer's disaster aroused Washington, and more troops began pouring into the West within days. But it remains one of those inexplicable mysteries of Indian character, encountered so often in this history, as to why Crazy Horse and Sitting Bull, whose medicine must have worked powerfully on that afternoon of June 25, did not take advantage of their decisive victory, pull all their forces together and take the offensive. Instead, they broke up into several bands and went off in every direction, as though they had been defeated and expected the enemy to be in hot pursuit.

General Sheridan's report of October 25, 1877, tells what happened: ". . . During the months of December and January the hostile Indians were constantly harassed by the troops under Colonel Nelson A. Miles, Fifth Infantry, whose headquarters were at the mouth of the Tongue River, and who had two sharp engagements with them, one at Red Water and the other near Hanging Woman's Fort, inflicting heavy losses in men, supplies and animals. . . . This constant pounding and ceaseless activity upon the part of our troops (Colonel Miles in particular) in midwinter began to tell, and early in February, 1877, information was communicated which led me to believe that the Indians in general were tired of the war, and that the large bodies heretofore in the field were beginning to break up.

"On the 25th of that month 229 lodges of Minneconjoux and San Arcs came and surrendered to the troops of Cheyenne Agency, Dakota. They were completely disarmed, their horses taken from them and they were put under guard. This system was also carried out with all who came in afterward to surrender within the departments of Dakota and the Platte. From the 1st of March to the 21st of the same month over 2200 Indians, in detachments of from 30 to 900, came in and surrendered at Camps Sheridan and Robinson, in the department of the Platte, and on the 22nd of April, 303 Cheyennes came in and surrendered to Colonel Miles at the cantonment on the Tongue River, in the department of the Dakota, and more were reported on the way to give themselves up. Finally, on the 6th of May, Crazy Horse, with 889 of his people and 2000 ponies, came into Camp Robinson and surrendered to General Crook in person. . . ."

The plain military words fail to convey the melancholy downfall of Crazy Horse. Not long after the Battle of the Little Big Horn, he and 800 of his warriors had come back from the west toward the agencies, apparently hoping to seize ammunition and supplies, but General Crook, who had been following him, drove him off as he and his braves came to the aid of American Horse, a chief whose village Crook had just destroyed. Crazy Horse intended to spend the winter in the Wolf Mountains, not far from the Rosebud, but Miles trailed him there, and on January 8 destroyed his winter village with the aid of two howitzers, although again the chief and his followers escaped.

But he knew that he could do no more. Foiled in his projected attack on the agencies, he had nowhere to turn for ammunition or supplies. His Cheyennes and even his own tribesmen were beginning to leave him for various reasons. His friends begged him to surrender, and after four more months of indecision, he did so.

When he realized the white men intended to lock him up, a fit of desperation seized Crazy Horse. Drawing his knife, he tried to cut his way to freedom. Little Big Man, a friend who was with him, sought to hold his wrists and save him from further trouble, and in the confused scuffling that followed, he was mortally wounded in the stomach.

Some said a nearby soldier thrust a bayonet in him. Little Big Man, perhaps trying to save his own skin, said Crazy Horse had accidentally stabbed himself. In any event, he was dead by midnight, and his father and mother buried him secretly in the hills. Thus he saved himself from the fate the white man had planned for him: exile in the Dry Tortugas.

A captain at Camp Robinson who saw Crazy Horse on the day he died described him as looking "quite young, not over thirty years old . . . five feet eight inches high, lithe and sinewy, with a scar in the face. The expression of his countenance was one of quiet dignity, but morose, dogged, tenacious and melancholy. . . . All Indians gave him a high reputation for courage and generosity. . . . He was one of the great soldiers of his day and generation."

As for Sitting Bull, his reputation as a medicine man, which had never been higher than it was on the day of the great victory, began to diminish in the cruel winter that followed, as those who remained faithful to him saw their friends surrender and their own lot grow progressively worse under the harassments of Crook's soldiers. They retreated across the Canadian border, where the leaders of the tribe began to defect, one by one, as the misery increased. There was no choice. It was a forlorn company of men, women, and children, only 187 of them, whom Sitting Bull brought to surrender at Fort Buford in July, 1881.

Crazy Horse had been the true genius of the Sioux, but somehow it was Sitting Bull, the politician and fake spiritualist, who had become in the public mind an Indian hero of outsize proportions. The bitter and irreconcilable old man who sat in his cabin on the Standing Rock reservation for a decade after 1881, waiting for an ironic and inglorious death, was a far cry from the image created by the overheated Eastern whites. He was described variously as really a white man; a graduate of various institutions, including West Point; a scholar and a linguist; a Mason; and a Catholic. He was even credited with writing French and Latin poems. In point of fact, however, he was no more than an extraordinarily acute scoundrel, who could not even spell his own name correctly.

While the army was mopping up after Sitting Bull and Crazy Horse, there occurred another tragic "last stand," in which Indian military talent was wasted on a truly lost cause. The story of Chief Joseph and the Nez Percés has been told almost as often as Custer's, but it can hardly be ignored in any history of the Indian wars.

The Nez Percés had been compelled by the government in 1863 to leave their traditional home in Wallowa Valley, in eastern Oregon, for a reservation in Idaho. They had no quarrel with the white man; they boasted that they had never killed one. Yet the government decreed they must be moved, and the quarrel dragged on until 1877, while ruthless settlers crowded into the valley and inevitable friction developed.

Some of the Nez Percés had signed the treaty and gone to Idaho. The leader of those who resisted was young Joseph, no more than twenty-three when the treaty was signed. Joseph, or Hinmaton-Yalaktit, meaning "thunder coming from the water up over the land," loved the valley, and after 1873, when his father was buried there and he became chief, he determined that he would never obey the treaty.

General O. O. Howard, commander of the district, was more than willing to keep trying negotiation, and so was Joseph, who did not want war. But the pressure of the white squatters led at last to open hostility in June, 1877, when the chief, with a scant 400 braves, beat off a superior force of white troops. Notwithstanding this and two subsequent victories, Joseph saw that he could not hope to defeat the American Army and resolved to retreat to Canada—a retreat that would go down as one of the most extraordinary in the nation's military history.

With only 200 warriors, and hampered by the presence of three times that number of women and children, he turned toward the east, General Howard in close pursuit. Joseph took the historic Lo-lo trail through the rugged mountain terrain of western Idaho, unaware that the white man's telegraph was carrying urgent messages ahead of him to the Seventh Infantry under John Gibbon at Fort Shaw, and to other points where he might be intercepted.

Emerging into the Bitter Root Valley, Joseph marched across it, ignoring a weak detachment of American troops, and ten days later, early in August, stopped to rest his weary people at Big Hole, not far from the Idaho-Montana line. There Gibbon surprised him completely on August 9, but Joseph and his two war leaders, Looking Glass and White Bird, rallied the braves after they had been driven from their lodges, and launched a counterattack, meanwhile sending the women and children on ahead. Gibbon, severely wounded himself, retreated a little way and dug in. Joseph set the

283

prairie grass afire and would have cremated the white troops if a vagrant wind had not saved them. Then, under cover of their smoke screen, the Indians escaped.

Meanwhile, General Howard, seldom more than two or three days behind the fleeing Indians, came to Gibbon's relief, absorbed the survivors into his own command, and set off again. On the night of August 20, as pursuer and pursued neared the Wyoming border, Chief Joseph executed a daring rear-guard maneuver and captured Howard's horses before the sleeping soldiery could recover. Temporarily immobilized, the frustrated general had to wait for new mounts, while Joseph and his people went on across a corner of Wyoming and into Montana, turning north now toward Canada.

The route lay through Yellowstone Park and along Clark's Fork to the Yellowstone River. On the north side of this river General S. D. Sturgis lay in wait. Joseph executed a brilliant feint and left the general emptyhanded. Pushing ever northward he came at last near the end of September to the Bear Paw Mountains, in northern Montana, only thirty miles away from safety. There, thinking he had outdistanced his pursuers as well as outwitted them, he rested. But General Miles, who had traveled by forced marches from Fort Keogh, suddenly confronted him on September 30.

Chief Joseph now had three choices. If he abandoned his wounded and the women and children, he and his braves could escape into Canada. He could call his long retreat a failure and surrender, within sight of victory. Or he could do battle. Characteristically, Joseph chose battle, and proceeded to entrench himself with the skill of a professional engineer.

Miles possessed a single decisive advantage: he had brought howitzers and Gatling guns with him. Nevertheless, Joseph stood off the general in a pitched battle that inflicted heavy losses on the white troops. Miles concluded it would be a better course to institute a siege, and for five days he did so while his artillery kept up a destructive shelling of Joseph's camp. The Indians responded with equally destructive marksmanship; one company lost 35 per cent of its men.

Surrender of Joseph. *From a painting by Frederic Remington.*

But it was a hopeless struggle, and Joseph knew it. On the third day, October 3, he agreed to surrender and sent this melancholy and often-quoted message: "Tell General Howard that I knew his heart. What he told me before I have in my heart. I am tired of fighting. Our chiefs are killed. Looking Glass is dead. Too-hul-sul-suit is dead. The old men are all dead. It is now the young men who say 'yes' or 'no.' He who led the young men [Joseph's brother, Ollicut] is dead. It is cold and we have no blankets. The little children are freezing to death. My people—some of them have run away to the hills, and have no blankets, no food. I want to have time to look for my children and see how many of them I can find; maybe I shall find them among the dead. Hear me, my chiefs, my heart is sick and sad. From where the sun now stands I will fight no more forever."

On October 5, Chief Joseph and five warriors rode into General Miles' camp. Horan describes the Indian leader's appearance: "His scalp lock was tied with otter fur. The rest of his hair hung in thick plaits on each side of his head. He wore buckskin leggins and a gray

285

woolen shawl through which could be seen the marks of four or five bullet-holes received in the last fight. His head and wrist were also scratched by bullets. He gave his rifle to Miles, then smiled as he shook hands with Howard."

Joseph could see what damage he had done. Twenty per cent of Miles' command were dead; only seventeen of the Nez Percés had died in the battle. Yet the general could not help but admire his adversary. "Chief Joseph," he declared, "was the highest type of the Indian I have ever known, very handsome, kind, and brave."

As professional military men, both Miles and Howard had to admire Joseph's remarkable feat. He had come more than 2000 miles, over some of the most difficult terrain in western United States. His forces, even with additions here and there, had never exceeded 300 men, yet he had successfully resisted more than 2000 white soldiers, inflicting on them casualties of 176 dead and 140 wounded, at a loss to himself of 151 killed, 89 wounded. He had won three of the five battles he fought, achieved one stalemate, and lost only the last one.

Many of Chief Joseph's followers sickened and died on the reservation to which they were taken in Indian Territory. Joseph did what he could for them as long as he lived. He was given the inestimable privilege of meeting President Roosevelt, but for all his good works, he was not accorded the greater privilege of returning to the valley he loved.

This small indignity was only one symptom of the government's barbaric reservation policy. What humanity existed in its execution derived from the pressure of Eastern humanitarians, who were labeled with the practical man's swearword, "do-gooder." The Western attitude was unashamedly cruel and vindictive, as well as stupid for the most part. As for the average American citizen, then as now he had no idea what was going on and cared less. Consequently, the reservations became breeding places of disease and ghettoes of despair, run by agents who were often ignorant and corrupt.

Not everyone was insensitive to the plight of the trapped savage, however. In 1881, Helen Hunt Jackson's book, *A Century of Dis-*

honour, subtitled, "A Sketch of the United States Government's Dealings with Some of the North American Tribes," appeared. Written with honest indignation, and no doubt with a lack of balance as well, it set forth the shameful history of the white man's Indian conquest, concluding:

"Cheating, robbing, breaking promises—these three are clearly things which must cease to be done. One more thing, also, and that is the refusal of the protection of the law to the Indian's rights of property, 'of life, liberty, and the pursuit of happiness.' When these four things have ceased to be done, time, statesmanship, philanthropy, and Christianity can slowly and surely do the rest. Till these four things have ceased to be done, statesmanship and philanthropy alike must work in vain, and even Christianity can reap but small harvest."

The last words were a melancholy prophecy of what was to happen in Indian affairs for the next eighty years.

The book's publication had a tangible result in 1882, the founding of the Indian Rights Association, which led in time to other enlightened organizational moves to aid the red man in his exile. But meanwhile, the business of crushing the last resistance went on.

The Plains tribes were in hand, and there remained only the Southwest. In the Panhandle country of Texas, an abortive revolt had been put down in 1874 when Quanah Parker, chief of the Kwahadi Comanches, led 700 Comanches, Kiowas, and Cheyennes against 30 buffalo hunters barricaded inside the trading post at Adobe Walls, and failed to take this fortress after three days of battle. The white men had powerful new long-range rifles the Indians had never even heard of.

Parker, the half-breed son of a Comanche and a white girl named Cynthia Ann Parker, had foolishly dreamed of a great alliance of Plains Indians to fight off the white invader. He saw now that he was mistaken. "I can learn the ways of the white man," he remarked after the Battle of Adobe Walls, and he did. He became a citizen, started a business, and was successful in it, like any good American.

Far more unregenerate was Geronimo, the terror of the South-   287 west, who was not a chief of his tribe, the Chiricahua Apaches, but nevertheless revived the Apache terror after Crook thought he had ended it, and became the last of the Indian holdouts. Geronimo's Indian name was Goyathlay, meaning "one who yawns"; the Mexicans called him in their own language Geronimo, or Jerome in English. Geronimo had fought with Cochise and Mangas Colorado as a young man, and came to be leader of the tribe by default when the earlier strong men died.

Geronimo was an in-and-out revolter for a time. He went on a few raiding expeditions when the Chiricahuas were moved to a new reservation in 1876, but then he seemed to settle down again to farming on the new lands. He went back on the warpath in 1880, was captured and returned, but in 1882 he proclaimed himself ready to lead a band of desperate and sullen dissidents once more. Fearing trouble, the government recalled its former successful Apache hunter, General Crook, from the wars of the Plains and assigned him anew to Arizona Territory.

Crook, following his usual course of fair dealing, determined that the Indians had a fair grievance and called for a meeting, at which he must have winced to hear the old question: "Why do the white men break their promises?" He learned that a ring of crooked Tucson contractors, in league with the Indian agent, had caused the trouble, and he began to set matters right. But it was too late. The Apache were on the warpath.

There began a deadly game of hide-and-seek between Crook and Geronimo. The Apache, a powerfully built man of great strength and energy, was cruel and adroit. Crook was both persuasive and persistent. He captured Geronimo in 1883, but two years later the elusive Indian was on the trail once more, this time for a last, spectacular campaign, during which he spread terror and death through the settlements, with Crook always only a step or two away. The general pursued his slippery adversary into Mexico, where Geronimo surrendered in May, 1886. Two nights later he escaped, along with some followers, but this time the pursuit was continued by General Miles, come to relieve Crook, who had resigned because of his disgust with the government's Indian policy.

Geronimo. *From a portrait by E. A. Burbank.*

Geronimo was cornered on the Bavispe River, Mexico, in August, and a lieutenant who knew him well persuaded the fugitive to give in, which he did on September 4.

Geronimo served time as a prisoner of war in Fort Pickens, Pensacola, but later he was moved to Fort Sill, Oklahoma. In time, he became a successful farmer and stock raiser.

Parker and Geronimo were heralds of the new order. They had fought the white men and lost, but they did not spend their days clinging to the past, as Sitting Bull was doing at that moment on the Standing Rock reservation. Geronimo, whose name had been a synonym for outrage, joined the Dutch Reformed Church in 1903, went to the St. Louis World's Fair, and rode in President Roosevelt's inaugural procession of 1905. He even dictated an autobiography, which had little of truth in it, and died at last of a white man's disease, pneumonia.

Geronimo was the last of the great war chiefs. Those who were not dead had adapted themselves to the white man's ways, like Geronimo. The great war between the Indians and their conquerors was over, for all practical purposes, and its epitaph had been written in the pronouncement of an old Sioux chief who had surrendered in 1877 with the remnants of Crazy Horse's splendid army. He told General Miles:

"We are poor compared to you and your force. We cannot make a rifle, ammunition or a knife. In fact, we are at the mercy of you who are taking possession of our land. Your terms are harsh and cruel, but we are going to accept them and place ourselves at your mercy."

The quality of that mercy was soon to be demonstrated, only four years after the conquest of Geronimo.

16

THE LAST UPRISING

"When the sun died I went up to Heaven and saw God and all the people who had died a long time ago. God told me to come back and tell my people they must be good and love one another, and not fight, or steal, or lie. He gave me this dance to give to my people."

With these words a young Piute named Wovoka launched in Nevada, sometime in 1888, a new religion, and from this unlikely beginning developed the last Indian uprising in America.

Wovoka, who was also known as Jack Wilson, his Christian name, had been influenced by the theology he had heard in the missions and only half understood. The doctrine he preached was a pathetic attempt—all the more poignant because it was grasped with such desperation—to convert the white man's religion into a message of hope for the Indians.

As doctrine alone, it was a philosophy of peace. Wovoka told his followers of a vision in which the Great Spirit revealed to him that he, Wovoka, was the Messiah, returned to earth as an Indian because the first Messiah had been crucified by white men, a logical view in Indian eyes. He, the Messiah, would bring vast changes to the earth, Wovoka said. The dead among the Indians would rise again and return to their lands. The slain buffalo would rise too and populate the plains once more in their dense, black flocks. Out of a blazing volcano would come pouring a flood tide of lava that would

The Ghost Dance by the Oglala Sioux. *From a drawing by Frederic Remington.*

wipe the earth clean of white men and spare the Indians, except for those among them who were unbelievers.

Any Indian could be saved, however, by dancing the sacred Ghost Dance, which Wovoka showed them. The dance was simplicity itself; the dancers joined hands in a circle and shuffled slowly to the left. They wore special shirts that Wovoka asserted would stop a white man's bullet.

The Messiah issued specific instructions to the faithful: "Do not harm anyone. Do right always. Do not tell lies. Do not fight. When your friends die you must not cry."

A religious revival swept the Indians of the Far West, much like the one that gripped the Kentucky and Tennessee frontier in 1800. This was authentic mass hysteria, still seen in the old-fashioned fundamentalist camp meetings that survive today. Visions were seen, squaws and warriors worked themselves to a pitch of ecstasy and fell into trances, and frenzy overtook the shuffling bodies of the Ghost Dancers.

The cult of the Ghost Dance might have been harmless enough, and would certainly have disappeared in time, but unfortunately it spread over the mountains to the Indians of the Plains, whose affairs were in a much worse state. Here dwelt the bitter survivors of the last great war, near starvation, mistreated by the agents, disillusioned by the white man's promises, defeated, and confined to reservations. Life for them was hopeless, and they could not see which way to turn until the ritual of the Ghost Dance and its illusory promises was brought back to them by the delegates they sent to investigate the new teaching.

In transit, however, it took on new meanings. The peaceful basis of the religion was lost. When the Plains people danced the Ghost Dance, war against the whites was in their minds and in the doctrine as their medicine men expounded it. Worse, the magic of the ritual was believed to make them proof against bullets, against death itself. These ideas were accepted whole, with pathetic eagerness, by the Sioux, Arapahos, Cheyennes, and Kiowas, the principal victims of the government. These Indians soon worked themselves into an excitable state, claiming they had seen the reborn buffalo and talked to relatives long dead who were now returning. They believed sincerely that the millennium was at hand.

There were also Ghost Dancers who professed to be caught up in the new faith who actually saw in it a means of reviving the ancient struggle. One of them may well have been Sitting Bull, a practiced manipulator of sacred medicine, who quite naturally saw in Ghost Dancing a means to the end he had almost given up hoping would ever be accomplished.

Tension began to rise on the Sioux reservations of Pine Ridge and Rosebud during the late autumn of 1890, and by December the electric crackle of danger was in the air. Indians were disappearing off the reservation to practice secretly the rites of the Ghost Dance, and it was rumored that Sitting Bull and his supporters meant to follow them.

Still the crisis might have passed if Benjamin Harrison had not been elected in 1888, and on assuming office the following year, 293 swept out the Indian agents along with the rest of Grover Cleveland's Democratic officeholders, and installed new and inexperienced men to take their place.

The new agent at Pine Ridge, a green hand named Royer, grew alarmed by the defection of the Ghost Dancers and the rumors about Sitting Bull, and notwithstanding that a great majority of the Indians on the reservation were obviously peaceful, he called on the Army for protection. John R. Brooke, the general who responded, was no more familiar with Indians than Royer. He arrived at Pine Ridge on November 19, 1890, which was the date a large company of Ghost Dancers fled to the Badlands, burning their own houses behind them.

Apparently Brooke and other army officers were afraid that if Sitting Bull joined the Dancers, they might have a war on their hands, consequently the order was sent to Standing Rock Agency to arrest the old chief. An Indian lieutenant named Bullhead led a native police force to Sitting Bull's log cabin on the morning of December 15 and pulled him out of bed.

Before they could lead him away, the chief's angry followers gathered around, and Catch-the-Bear, an old enemy of Bullhead's who was devoted to Sitting Bull, took the opportunity to shoot the Indian lieutenant. As he fell, Bullhead contrived to raise his pistol and fire a slug into the chief's body, while at the same time another policeman, Red Tomahawk, put a bullet into Sitting Bull's head, • which killed him instantly.

The whole village erupted. In a few minutes a dozen men lay dead and three others were wounded. Only the arrival of white troops prevented an intramural massacre.

Panic engulfed the Sioux as the news of Sitting Bull's death traveled across the Plains with the speed of wind. No one knew what it meant. Was it the signal for the war the Messiah had prophesied? Or did it mean that the white men had determined to exterminate the Sioux before a war could start? Families fled to their relatives; others came to the agency for protection.

294   To restore order, the army sent out detachments to bring all

Massacre at Wounded Knee Creek.

Indians back to the reservation. Although nothing was said about it, the implication was that those who remained hostile would be shown little mercy. It was denied later, but there can be no doubt that the memory of Custer burned in many of these soldiers, some of whom had served with him.

One of the vagrant chiefs the troops sought was Big Foot, whose arrest had been ordered. When he heard about it, Big Foot started toward the Pine Ridge Agency with 356 men, women, and children. Thirteen days after Sitting Bull's murder, he encountered Major S. M. Whitside, with eight troops of the Seventh Cavalry and a party of scouts, 470 men all told. Whitside demanded Big Foot's unconditional surrender. The chief complied, and the Indians were escorted to Wounded Knee Creek, twenty miles from the agency. There they camped on the evening of December 28, 295 while the jittery Whitside sent out for reinforcements, which came at once under command of Colonel Forsyth, the hardy veteran of many Sioux campaigns.

Both sides were deeply suspicious of each other. Dark rumors raced through the Sioux encampment that the white men meant to kill their horses and ship the whole tribe off to Florida in chains. Forsyth, on his part, suspected the Sioux of treachery, as he did all Indians.

Next morning, on the 29th, Forsyth set up his men in an arc around the camp, trained his battery of Hotchkiss guns on the tepees, and prepared to disarm the Indians. There are wildly conflicting reports about what followed. Some authorities say that Big Foot's warriors were, in fact, plotting a treacherous coup and had rifles concealed beneath their blankets which they whipped out when a medicine man named Yellow Bird threw a handful of dust as a signal.

There is good reason to doubt this version. Big Foot was leading his people back to the reservation; if he had been planning war, he would scarcely have gone about it in that way. Moreover, his village was completely surrounded by a superior force which possessed the decisive weapon, howitzers, and there can be little doubt that the Indians from Big Foot on down were thoroughly frightened by what might happen to them.

The more likely account of what triggered the subsequent disaster is that Forsyth's men began to search the Indians roughly for concealed weapons, always a dangerous procedure with the proud Plains Indians, and that a scuffle developed between two soldiers who were trying to take the gun away from a brave. The gun was discharged and Forsyth's men perpetrated within a few minutes what was one of the worst massacres in the whole history of the Indian wars.

A government investigator, who could certainly not be charged as a partisan of the Indians, reported later: "The terrible effect may be judged from the fact that one woman survivor, Blue Whirlwind, with whom the author conversed, received fourteen wounds, while each of her two little boys were also wounded by her side. In a few

General Miles and Buffalo Bill Cody Surveying the Largest Hostile Indian Camp in the U.S. near Pine Ridge, South Dakota, January 18, 1891. *Photograph by Grabill.*

minutes two hundred Indian men, women and children, with sixty soldiers, were lying dead and wounded on the ground, the tepees had been torn down by the shells and some of them were burning above the helpless wounded, and the surviving handful of Indians were flying in wild panic to the shelter of the ravine, pursued by hundreds of maddened soldiers and followed up by a raking fire from the Hotchkiss guns, which had been moved into position to sweep the ravine. There can be no question that the pursuit was simply a massacre, where fleeing women, with infants in their arms, were shot down after resistance had ceased and when almost every warrior was stretched dead or dying on the ground."

The Seventh Cavalry was at last revenged for Custer. But it was typical of the white man, as Oliver La Farge has pointed out, that the affair on the Little Big Horn came to be known as the Custer Massacre while the shameful slaughter by Forsyth's men was officially labeled the Battle of Wounded Knee.

In the old days, such an atrocity would have touched off a furious Indian reprisal, and Colonel Forsyth quickly learned that the old days were not quite dead. Almost frantic with rage, the Brulé

Sioux, under Two Strike, attacked the agency, while another band struck savagely at the Wounded Knee camp on the 30th. Forsyth had to call for reinforcements, which came up just in time to save him from annihilation.

The sporadic battle raged at first one place and then the other for thirty-two days, and then abruptly it ended. The Indians surrendered and the last uprising was over, burning and dying like a strayed Fourth of July rocket against the bleak winter night.

Back in Nevada, the prophet who had started the dismal chain of events was aghast and utterly dismayed at what had become of the Ghost Dance religion. The round-faced Messiah took off the large-brimmed black hat he wore habitually above his white man's suit and covered his head with a blanket, in the old way. The Sioux had "twisted things," he mourned; it was better to "drop the whole business."

A forlorn, bent figure, Wovoka walked among his people and cried out to them: "Hoo-oo! My children, my children. In days behind many times I called you to travel the hunting trail or to follow the war trail. Now those trails are choked with sand; they are covered with grass, the young men cannot find them. My children, today I call upon you to travel a new trail, the only trail now open—the White Man's Road. . . ."

EPILOGUE

They traveled the white man's road. There were a few small local acts of resistance after Wounded Knee. The last was in 1911, and it followed a familiar pattern. In Humboldt County, Nevada, a tribesman named Shoshone Mike led a small band which killed several stockmen. A sheriff's posse hunted them down, fought them until the Indians ran out of ammunition, and then decimated them as the Shoshones, armed only with bows and arrows, made a charge of sheer desperation. They were all killed. The band's only survivors were a squaw and two children.

Farther along the white man's road the Indians encountered more polite forms of extermination. Some of the Southwestern tribes were nearly starved to death. Others were depopulated by disease brought on by the abominable conditions of the reservations. Many were systematically denied their civil rights, and are at this moment in some states. Most of them saw, and are still seeing, the continuing disregard of treaties and the seizure of lands, both by illegal methods and those that have the doubtful blessing of the courts.

In 1960 the courts sanctioned another in the endless succession of land grabs, taking a large portion of Iroquois land for the benefit of a power project. For a while the newspapers were full of letters to the editor, protesting the action. None was more pointed, or more poignant, than one written by a young Indian private first class in the American Army, printed in the New York *Herald Tribune* of March 14, 1960. Private Mitchell L. Bush, Jr., wrote:

"Where will it end? Regarding the loss of land by the Seneca and the Tuscarora members of the Iroquois Confederacy, we have seen once again, as we have seen so many times since the white man arrived on this continent, an Indian nation which has been forced to part with its share of Mother Earth. In these times, however, the situation is different. The Indian is now a civilized American; therefore, there has been no bloody battle as in the days of old. Instead, the Indian has followed the white man's trail to the courts—but for what? Only for the loss of money used to hire attorneys (money which could have been spent for tribal improvement) and the heart-sickening verdict of the Supreme Court.

"That the United States could be so two-faced appalls me—we send our officials on good will trips all over the world and we aid less fortunate countries financially, but we do not intend to allow the continent's own indigenous people (we, the Amerindians) to live in a manner we might choose. The United States government is of the people, by the people, and for the people; therefore, we must conclude that the majority is against us—but why?

"We, the Amerindians, are content to be Indians and preserve our ancient ways of life while living like the average American as best we can. Why must you, the people, be so determined to end this by taking our land and forcing our inclusion in the American melting pot? As an Onondaga Indian of the Iroquois Confederacy, I speak with experience. Take a look at an aerial view of my own reservation and what do we see—a maze of power line, salt line, gas line and water line rights of way, a dam covering a couple of hundred acres, a four-lane highway bisecting the northeastern quarter, and a whole section missing for some unknown reason!

"The Iroquois has contributed much to early America. Were it not for us, the United States might not be a democracy, for democracy was unknown in the European countries from which you came, but democracy was in full flourish here on this continent.

The Iroquois Confederacy has survived for nearly 400 years through all kinds of war and strife, why must you call for its end by scattering to the four winds the land on which we live?"

How far have we come since the first white man landed? Where, indeed, will it end?

BIBLIOGRAPHICAL NOTES

The material for this book was derived from more than two hundred books, pamphlets, and original source materials. Since the volume is not intended for the special reader, to whom all of these sources are familiar, the following notes are designed to guide those who want to explore particular areas of the Indian wars. It must be noted that there are few areas in American history where more controversy exists. In many instances there is little agreement even among the most eminent authorities. These notes direct the inquirer to those sources which the authors consider most reliable.

For the beginnings of the conflict between white men and red, Francis Parkman's *France and England in North America* remains pre-eminent. There are several one-volume condensations of the original thirteen. The standard contemporary account of the New England wars is *Narratives of the Indian Wars, 1675–1699*, edited by Charles H. Lincoln, recently published in an attractive reprint by Barnes & Noble. An excellent modern study is *Flintlock and Tomahawk* by Douglas Edward Leach, assistant professor of history at Vanderbilt University (Macmillan).

George Washington's dealings with the Indians are detailed in volume six of Douglas Southall Freeman's *George Washington* (Scribner). A concise and accurate account of Indian warfare in the Revolution will be found in *The War of the Revolution* by Christopher Ward (2 vols., Macmillan) and *The Spirit of 'Seventy-Six*, edited by Henry Steele Commager and Richard B. Morris (2 vols., Bobbs-Merrill).

For the War of 1812 and Andrew Jackson's Indian campaigns, see *The Age of Jackson* by Arthur M. Schlesinger, Jr. (Little, Brown), *The Life of Andrew Jackson* by Marquis James (Bobbs-Merrill), and *The War of 1812* by Francis F. Beirne (Dutton).

The story of Pontiac's war is best told in *Pontiac and the Indian Uprising* by Howard H. Peckham.

The literature of the Indian wars west of the Mississippi is vast and   303 highly controversial. A classic in the field is *Massacres of the Mountains* by J. P. Dunn, Jr., recently reprinted by Archer House, Inc. A graphic exposition in pictures and text is to be found in *The Great American West* by James D. Horan (Crown). There is no truly impartial account of Custer and the Sioux war, but perhaps the best recent version is the fine biography of the general, *Custer* by Jay Monaghan. By far the best narration of the Modoc war is *The Modocs and Their War* by Keith A. Murray (Oklahoma). *The Great Sioux Uprising* by C. M. Oehler (Oxford) is the best and most recent account of that event. Will Henry has told the Chief Joseph story vividly in semifictional form in *From Where the Sun Now Stands* (Random House).

For general and widely admired accounts of the Indians in North America, see *The Indians of the Americas* by John Collier (Norton), *Red Man's America* by Ruth M. Underhill (Chicago), *Indians of the High Plains* by George E. Hyde (Oklahoma), and *Pictorial History of the American Indian* by Oliver Lafarge.

The *Dictionary of American Biography* has excellent standard biographical sketches of many of the leaders, white and Indian, mentioned in this volume, and volume two of *The Pageant of America* (Yale) has biographical sketches, a succinct and generally accurate narration of events, and splendid pictures.

INDEX